The Student's Guide
to Financial Literacy

The Student's Guide to Financial Literacy

Robert E. Lawless

GREENWOOD

AN IMPRINT OF ABC-CLIO, LLC
Santa Barbara, California • Denver, Colorado • Oxford, England

Copyright 2010 by Robert E. Lawless

Library of Congress Cataloging-in-Publication Data

Lawless, Robert E., 1966–
  The student's guide to financial literacy / Robert E. Lawless.
    p. cm.
  Includes bibliographical references and index.
  ISBN 978-0-313-37718-1 (hard copy : alk. paper) —
ISBN 978-0-313-37719-8 (ebook) 1. Finance, Personal.
2. Teenagers—Finance, Personal. 3. College students—Finance,
Personal. I. Title
  HG179.L3378 2010
  332.02400835—dc22   2009050449

ISBN: 978-0-313-37718-1
EISBN: 978-0-313-37719-8

14 13 12 11 10   1 2 3 4 5

This book is also available on the World Wide Web as an eBook.
Visit www.abc-clio.com for details.

Greenwood
An Imprint of ABC-CLIO, LLC

ABC-CLIO, LLC
130 Cremona Drive, P.O. Box 1911
Santa Barbara, California 93116-1911

This book is printed on acid-free paper ∞
Manufactured in the United States of America

This book is dedicated to my children, Kaymin and Robert, the two treasures within my life that serve as sources of truth recognition, joy, and inspiration. They unknowingly teach me more about myself and the value of true existence than they will ever know, for which I will remain forever grateful. Each person's path in life is not destined, nor predetermined. The triumphs, defeats, woes, and delights of being are all important steps needing to be openly experienced. I wish them well on their individual quests toward living fruitful and fulfilling lives. I hope that they achieve everything in life that they desire while serving others and making every aspect they intentionally or unintentionally touch better for those that follow.

Contents

Introduction

I never felt as though my high school and college educations properly prepared me for the complexities associated with the ever-changing realm of personal finance. Even when majoring in finance for undergraduate and MBA coursework, topics such as the importance of budgeting and saving, 401K plans and individual retirement accounts, buying a home and choosing the right mortgage, good debt versus bad debt, tax planning, and insurance needs were never covered. Rather, I learned many lessons the hard way, and most of my experience has come from doing or from study programs outside of normal high school and college curriculums. My parents did not (and still do not) have the necessary knowledge and tools needed to make sensible and rational investment and financial planning decisions. No one ever taught them.

The world has become increasingly more complicated, faster paced, and ruthless since I graduated college and entered the world on my own. To consider my children coming into adulthood two decades later as ill-qualified is a petrifying thought. By the time most people gain the knowledge needed to develop sensible financial planning, numerous errors will inevitably have resulted in irreversible adverse financial consequences. In addition, many valuable and irreplaceable years will have passed.

I felt strongly compelled to write this book. The youth of the world needs a broad arsenal to effectively survive and compete in today's environment. The world continues to get smaller due to an increasingly integrated and global economy. In many industries, you will be expected to compete against the best of the best from around the world. Knowledge is truly a valuable asset. Without all the facts, prudent decisions cannot be made and countless mistakes will result and be repeated. The willingness to learn, research and find the best solutions is a necessary mentality for those that want to succeed. These will be the people that quickly repay student loans and other financial obligations, accumulate the money needed to purchase their own homes at early ages, and enjoy many other luxuries that less motivated and financially ignorant people cannot. The financially illiterate will not save or wisely invest, or they will continue to trust the words of biased and unskilled advisors, leave money on the table, and lag in life purely due to a lack of effort.

The early years of adulthood can count the most and have a dramatic effect on a person's ultimate quality of life, level of success, and age of retirement. The world today is extremely dangerous for the financially illiterate. Without the proper knowledge, individuals will be severely disadvantaged. As I am writing these words, the United States is experiencing the worst financial crisis since the Great Depression that began in 1929. The future leaders of America will inherit an unprecedented amount of debt owed to other nations due to the trillion dollar bailouts required by the federal government in order to avoid the collapse of the entire U.S. financial system. Such devastation within such a world-leading country has resulted in chain reactions across the globe, and any corrective actions taken to date have proven to be only moderately successful.

The past two years have been troubling, uncertain, and frightening times and hundreds of thousands of people have lost their jobs and homes. Undiversified investment portfolios took huge losses, and many people were forced to leave retirement and reenter the workforce. Others had no choice but to delay planned retirements for the foreseeable future. Many people still cannot get loans for homes, cars, and other consumer products due to an ongoing credit freeze within the banking system. Companies continue to have difficulty obtaining the funds needed to buy supplies and equipment and to meet payroll and other operating expenses. Corporate and personal bankruptcies have become overwhelming within our legal system. It has been extremely difficult to find a business or individual that has not been negatively affected by the spiraling downturn of the nation's economy and many people affected will never view the world the same again.

Today's global markets are filled with intricate and high-risk financial instruments. Each of us encounters numerous types of financial products within our daily lives. Included are an overwhelming number of options for home and consumer loans, multicolored credit cards with lots of small print, various mutual funds, and countless types of insurance products. The difficulty associated with understanding and making such choices is magnified by complex tax laws that can have differing effects based upon individual circumstances. Commission-based salespeople that may not understand the complexities of particular products are the ones recommending them to their clients. Often the more complex and riskier the product, the greater the commissions earned by the people paid to sell them. You need to be skeptical and thoroughly understand each option and its implications.

The reference to the word "student" in the title of this book may be misleading. While the teachings contained within the upcoming pages will have the greatest impact on the youngest readers as they begin preparing for financial independence, this information will be beneficial to people of all ages. It is never too late to develop or improve upon one or more of the many aspects associated with sound financial planning. In fact, many of the personal catastrophes that have recently taken place could have been avoided just by implementing some of the lessons within this book.

I encourage you to read this publication. The volatility, speed, and complexity of intertwined economies and financial markets, as well as the overwhelming number of financial products, makes the information presented within the upcoming chapters more necessary than ever. I sincerely hope that my efforts can assist others in becoming better equipped to properly assess their many options and needs and to avoid the same mistakes that millions of people continue to make each day. Having such knowledge should aid individuals in achieving their desired levels of wealth, success, and overall financial and personal fulfillment.

1

The Value of an Education

TARGETING THE RIGHT CAREER

Most of us work to make money to pay bills, help provide entertainment, and for general survival. The best way to make money is to have a distinctive skill or become an expert on a particular subject. There are many ways that people can become educated and build these talents. Self-employed individuals can learn a family business or trade and continue or start their own companies. New technologies or products can be created. Books and movies can be written. Greater levels of education can be obtained, leading to careers in areas such as corporate management, financial advisory, law, health care, sales, and so forth.

We are all unique individuals with varying personalities, motivational levels, and interests. Some of us may want to raise a family and stay at home with one or more children. Others may want to climb a corporate ladder as rapidly as possible and work 60 or more hours per week. You may be passionate about healing people or animals or working for nonprofit organizations that focus on improving or solving important problems. Someone may feel imprisoned within an office environment and need to work outside or from home. A specific career choice may be perfect for one person and a complete misfit for another.

But pursuing your dream career over one having more certainty and stability can often be a scary and risky path. This is particularly true when trying to enter the more difficult industries and trades. For most people, the chances of becoming a successful artist, actor, or dancer are slim, and supporting oneself while pursuing such a career usually requires another source of income. For example, many people that pursue acting and dancing careers

---

🗣 GUESS WHAT?

A study performed by Live Science in 2007 indicated that the majority of Americans hate their jobs and that this level of dissatisfaction is the greatest it has been during the past 20 years. This is a concerning statistic considering how much time most of us spend working.

🗣 GUESS WHAT?

Consider how much of most lifetimes are spent working. If someone works 40 hours a week for 50 weeks per year with a 30-minute commute each way and sleeps eight hours per night, sleeping and working consumes approximately 62 percent of that person's entire year! With such little remaining personal time, choosing a career that you do not enjoy can have a devastating effect on your level of happiness!

---

take jobs as waiters and waitresses for steady income and flexible or nightly hours that provide time for auditions.

When targeting dream careers in difficult fields, the more time devoted to such efforts, the more time that elapses that could have been used for other career paths. People should always strive for happiness and follow their dreams, but they should also be realistic in their abilities and recognize the likelihood of becoming successful enough to support themselves in their desired lifestyles. When targeting industries that are difficult to enter, have secondary choices in life, and consider following both paths at once.

Do not just rush into a specific career because it pays the most. Chances are that if your personality and objectives are unsuited for such a job, you will not be very good at it anyway. Spend time thinking about what you really want to do. Ask questions of people that are currently working within the field. If you want to be a doctor, talk to local doctors about what their jobs are like. Ask for a tour of a hospital or private doctor's office. It takes years to gain the experience and knowledge needed to become an expert in a particular field or industry. Finding out that you do not enjoy your targeted career and starting over again can be a major financial setback.

Another consideration regarding your ultimate career choice pertains to the expected level of demand for such positions. You might want to consider jobs and industries that have great long-term prospects. High demand for people within a certain industry can lead to greater compensation, career advancement, and job stability. For example, in an increasingly regulated environment, it appears that there will continue to be high demand for accountants and attorneys. In addition, health care and technology will most likely have strong needs for years to come.

EDUCATIONAL COSTS VERSUS BENEFITS

The cost of attending college these days is overwhelming. In fact, these expenses are growing at rates substantially higher than the average price increases for

🗣 GUESS WHAT?

According to inflationdata.com, the overall inflation rate since 1986 was 92.32 percent. During the same period, college tuition costs increased a whopping 343.81 percent. Future increases in college costs are expected to approximately double the country's rate of inflation going forward.

other goods and services. As these educational expenses continue to rise and many college students are forced to assume large loans that will take many years and even decades to repay, considering whether the costs of college are worthwhile is a valid question.

But statistics show that the value of a college education is still well worth the associated costs. College graduates earn substantially more money each year than people with only high school diplomas. In addition, those having advanced educations such as master's and doctoral degrees substantially increase this gap in income.

The University of Connecticut campus at Storrs, Connecticut. While the cost of college continues to rise dramatically, the benefits of a good education can still significantly outweigh the costs. AP Photo/Bob Child.

🗣 GUESS WHAT?

According to a 2007 College Board Study, workers ages 25 and older having bachelor's degrees earned over 60 percent more than those having high school diplomas and almost 120 percent more than workers that did not graduate high school.

🗩 GUESS WHAT?

The U.S. Census Bureau showed that in the year 2007, adults 18 and older with advanced college degrees earned more than four times those having less than a high school diploma. (See Chart 1.1.) People with master's, professional, and doctoral degrees earned an average of $83,320 per year, while those with less than a high school diploma earned about $20,873. Assuming a 3.5 percent annual inflation rate over a 30-year period results in these advanced degrees generating greater earnings of over $3.2 million!

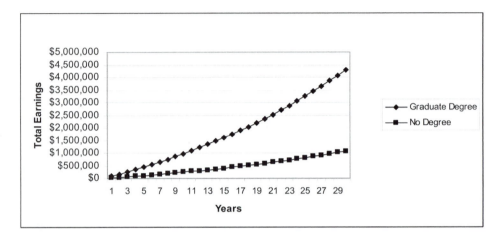

Chart 1.1
30-Year Earnings Potential

PAYING FOR COLLEGE

Some students are fortunate enough to have their parents or other generous donors pay for some or all of their college expenses. While working your way through college is a commendable act that can certainly build character, there is no doubt that life can be much easier without such financial burdens.

But many students are forced to seek other sources to cover the costs of tuition, boarding, books, and other supplies. Do not become immediately overwhelmed when you see the price tags on the universities you are targeting. Financial aid is not just limited to poor or exceptional students. In reality, about two out of every three students get at least some amount of financial aid to help make college more affordable. Students can receive a combination of scholarships, grants, loans, and work-study jobs to help reduce the costs of college.

Scholarships and Grants

Scholarships and grants are monetary awards for college that you are not expected or required to repay. Scholarships and grants are worth seeking! Scholarships are generally awarded to students based upon the student's special qualifications and are usually related to some type of merit or achievement. Grants include a broad array of gift aids to students for reasons including merit and achievement and their financial needs. Grants are also awarded to

✎ BEWARE!

There are many service providers that promise to find scholarships and grants for students for a fee. Scams seeking processing fees and other types of income are everywhere on the Internet. As with most aspects of life, when something sounds too good to be true, it often is. Be cautious of guaranteed scholarships and grants and those promised with little effort. Your school counselor is a great resource when seeking to find and pursue various types of financial awards.

minorities, to students engaged in specific fields of study, to those living in certain geographic areas, and for many other reasons.

Federal and state governments fund the larger scholarship and grant programs. In addition, almost every college and university has its own scholarship and grant program. Other providers include the military, corporations, civic groups, religious organizations, foundations, and employers. Scholarships and grants are typically awarded based upon one or more of the following:

Merit—The majority of scholarships and grants are awarded based upon a student's particular talent. An individual that excels in one or more areas, such as academics, sports, and drama or other artistic abilities, may receive a scholarship or grant.

Financial Need—The student and family financial situation is the primary determinant when granting needs-based financial awards. Usually such award recipients have proven superior skill sets in a certain area.

Athletics—Athletes that show superior performance in certain sports are offered scholarships and grants to attend specific institutions.

Ethnicity—Race, religion, or national origin are initial determining factors. Usually applicants are screened based upon such criteria, and then, those students receiving awards show promise in one or more specific areas.

Other—Additional forms of scholarships and grants may be awarded for other reasons. For example, financial awards may be available to students whose parents work for a particular company or to students who are eligible for aid based upon the objectives of the particular sponsor.

You will need to check with each college to see what scholarships and grants are being offered. You should also become familiar with any scholarships available through specific companies, organizations, and communities.

One source for information is http://studentaid.ed.gov, where you can find a copy of *Funding Education Beyond High School: The Guide to Federal Student Aid*. It may also be in your library. Or you can call 1-800-433-3243.

Student Loans

Most financial aid comes in the form of student loans, which require repayment at some time in the future. Student loans can be both subsidized and unsubsidized by the federal government. The loans that are subsidized do not require the student to pay interest. Rather, interest on these loans is paid on the student's behalf by the federal government. So if $10,000 is borrowed, $10,000 is repaid in payments starting after the time of graduation. Subsidized student loans are awarded based upon financial needs.

Unsubsidized student loans require repayment of principal plus accrued interest. If you borrow $10,000, you will owe $10,000 plus accrued interest after graduation. These loans are available for most students regardless of family income, tend to carry low interest rates, and do not start accruing interest until after you graduate.

Sometimes student loans are partially supplemented by grants that are not required to be repaid. Government-sponsored student loans have certain dollar limitations and require students to attend classes on at least a half-time basis.

Federal loans can also be provided to parents. In such cases, these loans can often be for larger dollar amounts, but interest accrual and payments begin immediately rather than after the time of the student's graduation.

In addition to government subsidized programs, private student loans are also available. These loans tend to have higher dollar limits and do not require payments to begin until after graduation. However, interest begins to accrue on these loans immediately. Private student loans can be used to supplement federal student loans when federal loans are not sufficient to cover all the needed educational costs.

Private student loans usually have variable rates of interest, and federal student loans usually have fixed rates of interest. In addition, borrowers are often required to pay up-front origination fees. The actual interest rate and origination fee for a specific loan varies based upon the credit history of the applicant. Students or parents having poor credit history can expect to pay higher interest rates and higher origination fees than borrowers having better credit. Interest rates and origination fees are discussed more in Chapter 5.

Work-Study Programs

The Federal Work-Study Program is a form of financial assistance made available to qualifying students. Normally students work part time on campus or within federal, state, or local public agencies and private nonprofit organizations that benefit the public interest, particularly those of low income individuals.

Students can earn money and academic credit for time spent within the Federal Work-Study Program. Such jobs can include internships and assistantships, such as research and teaching assignments. Qualifying community service jobs can include tutoring and teaching underprivileged children and working within health care, welfare, social services, public transportation, and numerous other types of community improvement projects.

Work-study programs are great ways for students to learn more about a particular subject, gain experience and enhance résumés, and earn money and academic credit at the same time.

ENHANCING YOUR MARKETABILITY

Once you get a college education, what are you going to do with it? If you plan on getting a job like most students, you should start enhancing your marketability prior to graduating.

Building a Résumé

In today's competitive job market, employers are receiving hundreds and even thousands of résumés from people just like you. Do you think your grade point average is going to get you a job? There are countless students across the country and across the globe that have outstanding scholastic performance as well. How about the fact that you were the captain of the football team? Throwing, catching, and running are not valued skills in the corporate world. Maybe you worked at a local restaurant part time during college. Unless you plan on serving lunch to a bunch of executives or will continue to work in the food industry, this will not help your career.

I do not mean to imply that such achievements have no value. They do. They show leadership, initiative, motivation, and other great attributes. But the better students need to show more achievements and the desire to succeed. So many people begin focusing on their careers early in life because the competition for good jobs can be fierce.

My son is 13 years old. For the past 4 years he has consistently said that he wants to become a veterinarian. My wife and I believe this to be a great career choice that can provide a substantial income and allow our son to work with and help animals. This is something that he truly enjoys. If all goes well and he ultimately becomes a veterinarian, I will no longer need to support him, and he can have a well-suited and meaningful career. I am truly hoping for such a win-win outcome!

Having a specific skill set can provide financial security and many career expansion opportunities. For example, after working for someone else and fully learning the business, our son could eventually start his own veterinarian practice. Perhaps he could save enough money to buy the building that his business will occupy and become a real estate investor as well. Maybe he will partner with one or more other veterinarians with additional specialties, such as a surgeon or laboratory expert, and open multiple locations. Providing a greater number of services under one company can lead to greater customer volume and profits.

Before my son can reach his goal of becoming a veterinarian, however, he must first be accepted by a college that specializes in this field. In addition, the better the school, the better his chances of finding training opportunities and, ultimately, a job as a veterinarian. Of course, personal performance and character traits will be important attributes in determining success, but having a solid education will help substantially.

In preparation for the college applications that will need to be submitted in less than five years, my son is working on building his résumé. Not only is he working toward a strong grade point average, which will be a key entrance consideration, he also seeks opportunities to learn more about animals and for ways to enhance his résumé. For example, he volunteers part time during the summers at an animal sanctuary that nurses sick and injured animals back to health. My son also accompanies my wife to our local veterinarian's office each time our dog or cat requires a visit. He has toured the office and spent time learning about animal care practices, surgery, and other relevant tasks associated with being a vet. He hopes to volunteer in the office next year. Each of these actions are relevant to my son's career choice and can serve to enhance his résumé and to provide him knowledge and resources when interviewing, writing essays on college applications, and so forth.

My point is that being a landscaper for the summer may pay more than working as an intern in a local law office, but if you want to become a lawyer, take the internship. Not only do you learn about the field of law, but such an experience can either further peak your interest or redirect you toward considering a different career choice. In addition, internships and other forms of pregraduation employment also provide the invaluable opportunity to network with a company's key decision makers. When it comes down to hiring decisions, employers are much more likely to hire the person that was well-liked as an intern and who has proven him or herself to be a cultural fit.

When it comes to creating your actual résumé, choose a professional format. A résumé is a personal advertisement. As the use of the Internet has exploded, employers now receive numerous résumés when seeking potential applicants for almost all jobs, and they spend limited time skimming the pile. A résumé needs to catch the eye and stand out.

When applying for jobs and mailing or submitting résumés, use a one to one and a half page cover letter that is targeted toward the specific opportunity. Do not take a mass form letter mailing approach. Stress your relevant skills that are applicable to the particular position and convey a favorable generic work ethic.

Many of the Internet employment search sites provide cover letter and résumé templates for specific types of jobs, including entry level through executive. Just search the Internet for topics such as "sample résumé templates." Take a look at several choices and see what you like best. Have your parents, friends, teachers, and counselors review and comment on your cover letter and résumé format and content. Consider these documents to be an on-going work in progress that continues to get better as you move through life.

Interviewing

When I think back on my first interviews, I am embarrassed. I did not take advantage of the training and preparation opportunities that were available. I remember being asked what my strengths were when interviewing for a finance position at Sara Lee Corporation. I responded with something like "I am hard working, knowledgeable about finance, and timely." That was it! I should have taken the opportunity to provide meaningful and detailed examples of specific times in my life when I had exhibited characteristics such as leadership, creativity, and financial expertise.

During another interview, I remember fiddling with my fingers and pen and allowing my nervousness to show. My insecure body language and monotone voice were also significant weaknesses. These are not features that hiring employers want to see. It is normal to be nervous, but I needed to learn how to properly channel my fear into positive energy and avoid letting others see it. But I did not know any better, nor did many of my peers.

I clearly recall my jealousy over the elite group of students within our graduating class that were rapidly receiving multiple job offers from the better companies. These students were outgoing and projected confidence. Their clothes, hair, and résumés all looked professional. They wanted to land great jobs, and they wanted to make a lot of money. These people were serious about their careers, and they knew how to sell themselves.

Had I attended a few mock interview sessions with the college placement agents, I would have been much more prepared. If I had read articles or a book on the best practices when interviewing, I would have had a much better chance of obtaining employment. If I thought more about what the interviewer was looking for, and if I had researched more about each company and spent time crafting intelligent questions, I would have performed much better. If my résumé was concise and more targeted for each position, my odds would have increased significantly. I finally did all these things after never being called back for a second interview from several companies. It took me a while to figure out how to play the game. I am now pretty good at it, but I wish I had done the work earlier in life.

Try to put yourself in the shoes of your interviewer. Know the company's history, including its recent challenges and achievements. Study the competition and think about the pressures that management is facing. If publicly traded, how has the company's stock price performed and why? Consider barriers to entry, product differentiation, pricing power, and current economic conditions and expectations. Show a genuine interest, and try to establish a bond with your interviewer.

Below are some basic interviewing tips that can help you to avoid some common mistakes:

- Be prepared and at your best. Lay out your clothes in advance. Try them on the night before if needed. Take a practice drive the week before and know exactly how to get to the destination. Give yourself extra time to get there on the actual date. You do not want anything unexpected to increase your stress level. Eat light foods that will not drain your energy.
- Practice and write out the answers to common questions. Even if you are not asked a specific question for which you prepared, usually general questions provide the opportunity for you to respond with personalized stories and experiences. For example, being the captain of the high school cheerleading squad can demonstrate leadership, problem solving, motivation, creativity, and other skills that are desirable to employers. Answers to a variety of questions can be crafted from the same general response. When providing responses, focus on short stories using personal examples.
- Have a counselor, parent, or friend provide mock interviews by formally asking questions in a real-life setting and assessing your performance. Be open to feedback.
- Arrive early and envision success. Do not talk too quickly. Exhibit a strong handshake while looking your interviewer directly in the eye. Be polite and attentive. Breathe deeply and slowly, and naturally pause for breath often. Do not twitch or indicate any distractions or nervousness.
- Use body language and facial expressions to deepen the effectiveness of your answers. Sit up straight. Do not seem too relaxed or too serious. Be attentive and show sincere interest toward what is being

According to www.hotjobs.yahoo.com, the Ten Biggest Interview Killers are as follows:

1. Not knowing your aim
2. Being too needy
3. Lousy nonverbal communication
4. Compromising your position
5. Falling into the answers-only rut
6. Rambling
7. Being overly familiar
8. Making incorrect assumptions
9. Getting emotional
10. Not asking specific questions

said. Leave your cell phone in the car. Be courteous and professional at all times. Remember that someone is taking time out of his or her busy day to talk to you.

- Bring a pen and paper, and take notes when applicable. A professional leather binder or appointment book looks much better than a naked pad of paper.
- If your interview is telephonic, find a quiet place with no distractions. Make sure that your vocal tones are energetic.
- Be prepared. Spend time getting to know the company, its culture, and its industry. Doing so shows initiative and that you truly have a desire to work at this company. It is also an indication that you appreciate the time of the person conducting the interview.
- If you need direction, ask questions of your interviewer such as, "What skills and character traits would be optimal for the position? How do you measure success in this role? What is the corporate culture like?" Never ask about money or benefits. There will be plenty of time for such discussions if the employer wants to hire you.
- Answers should convey your skills and competencies, but also your character, motivation, and enthusiasm; how well you work with others; and how you would fit well within a specific culture.
- Have great personal references that are relevant to the position. Strong examples would be teachers, prior employers, political officials, business owners, and community leaders.
- Within a couple days of the interview, follow-up with a short letter (one page or less) reiterating your interest in the position, briefly stating why you feel well qualified and suited for the job, and thanking the interviewer for his or her time.

Finding the Right Employers

Now that you know how to build a résumé and conduct yourself during an interview, you will need to further market yourself by finding companies that are willing to meet you. Making that first initial contact and getting your foot in the door is critical when seeking employment. Following are a few suggested ways to find the right employers.

Job Fairs—Many employers gathering to the same location with the sole purpose of meeting and potentially hiring future employees presents a great opportunity for job seekers. When attending such events, target specific companies in advance based upon your career objectives. Do the research and be prepared to meet with each company representative. If the firm is scheduling interviews in advance, submit a résumé and a persuasive cover letter, and try to get an appointment. Think about how competitive these events are, and strive to differentiate yourself to peak the interests of the employing companies.

Internships—As mentioned, prior internships can provide a tremendous advantage when seeking full-time employment. Having the inside track and being well-liked within a firm can dramatically stack the odds in your favor. Do not be shy to call upon the people that you assisted or worked for as an intern, particularly the more senior ones. Ask if there is anything they or you can do to get an interview scheduled with the right people.

Job fairs present great opportunities to meet with multiple potential employers in one location. AP Photo/Frank Franklin II.

✎ BEWARE!

If you post your resume on job search Web sites so that it can be viewed by hiring companies and recruiters, there is an extremely high probability that you will be bombarded by correspondence and advertisements offering you fantastic career opportunities, prizes, and other good fortune. The true objectives behind many of these offers are identity theft, misleading advertisements, and unwarranted fees. Some career counseling companies do offer valid services, but there are enough free resources available that these offers should not be needed. Save your money, and be careful when giving personal information. Never provide anything like a social security, driver's license, bank account, or credit card number.

School Resources—Some schools are better than others at providing job-finding resources to upcoming graduating students. While you will often be competing with countless other students when going this route, student counselors and placement agents can be invaluable and should not be ignored. Be sure to use the services provided, such as mock interviews, résumé and cover letter reviews, and general career counseling. Often school employees can speak directly to hiring companies on your behalf. If nothing else, these people should offer good advice and be able to point you in beneficial directions.

Networking—You might be surprised by how many business decisions get made based upon existing relationships and friendships. Often people do not like to refuse favors from family, friends, neighbors, and business associates. Whenever possible, find a way to have a good word provided on your behalf. Doing so could make the difference when seeking an initial interview and when actual hiring decisions are being made.

The Internet—In today's world, the Internet is a key resource that cannot be ignored. Job search Web sites bring together thousands of employment opportunities in an efficient form that can easily be searched based upon your career objectives, desired locations, and other relevant factors. Well-known sites include monster.com, hotjobs.com, and careerbuilder.com. Other sites are more specifically geared toward entry-level positions for recent college graduates, such as monstertrak.com. Placing your résumé online with such service providers allows employers and recruiters to see your résumé as well.

Newspapers—Employment advertisements in local newspapers are another source for job seekers. I find this route to be less productive when compared to the Internet and other means, but it is worth looking into. Many job search Web sites will automatically search numerous newspaper ads at one time, making the task much more efficient.

Specific Companies—If there are certain companies that you would like to work for, do not hesitate to search their Web sites for open positions. In addition, send a cover letter and résumé to the company's human resources department expressing your interest. While limited opportunities may currently be available, an appropriate position may arise in the future.

Recruiters—Job recruiters represent companies and assist them in finding the right candidates. Many companies perform this role themselves, while others seek the services of a recruiter to help narrow the search and to deliver the best people. Often times when applying for positions online, your résumé will be submitted to a recruiter that will perform the initial screening process before you are introduced to the hiring company. Recruiters are paid commissions by the employing company after a perspective employee is hired, so they are very motivated to make sure positions get filled. Recruiters can provide helpful insights regarding specific employers and excellent interview feedback that companies are often unwilling to share directly.

2

The Importance of Savings

The way to a prosperous life and early retirement requires discipline. You must continually save. Almost equally important is investing your savings into assets that make sense and that will continue to grow over time without taking on unnecessary risk. Losing a substantial portion of your savings can be a tremendous setback that can take many years to recoup.

Sooner is far better than later when it comes to saving for one's future. Dollars saved in the earlier years will amount to many more dollars than those saved in the later years. Earning money on your investments and allowing these earnings to grow and multiply over time is a powerful investment tool.

THE WONDERS OF COMPOUNDING

One of the most miraculous components of investing is the compounding of money, which has often been referred to as "the eighth wonder of the world." The beauty of compounding is that once you have invested money, the money you earn continues to make more and more money. Your savings are now working for you. Let me use an example. Assume that you invest $10,000 in a mutual fund that invests in corporate bonds issued by well-known companies. Let us also assume that you invest the $10,000 for 10 years and earn 7.5 percent per year for the term of the investment. As indicated in Table 2.1, a $10,000 initial investment equates to a value of $20,610 at the end of the 10 years. All you did was put your $10,000 in the mutual fund and watch it grow.

Chart 2.1 graphically shows the information shown in Table 2.1.

🗣 GUESS WHAT?

How much of your income should you save each year? Most financial advisors state that 10 to 15 percent of your annual income should be saved every year beginning in your twenties. To understand the benefits of early savings, assume that you save $2,500 a year for 10 years from the ages of 25 to 35 ($25,000 in total savings), and then you never save another dime. If you assume an annual return of 8 percent, by the time you are 60 years old your savings will have grown to be about $250,000. Now assume that you put off saving until age 35. From the age of 35 to age 60, you would need to save about $3,400 a month for the next 25 years (about $85,000 in total savings) to have the same $250,000 at age 60. The benefits of starting to save at a young age cannot be stressed enough!

Table 2.1
Compounding of Money Example

	Beginning Balance	Annual Interest	Ending Balance
Year 1	$10,000	$ 750	$10,750
Year 2	10,750	806	11,556
Year 3	11,556	867	12,423
Year 4	12,423	932	13,355
Year 5	13,355	1,002	14,356
Year 6	14,356	1,077	15,433
Year 7	15,433	1,157	16,590
Year 8	16,590	1,244	17,835
Year 9	17,835	1,338	19,172
Year 10	19,172	1,438	20,610

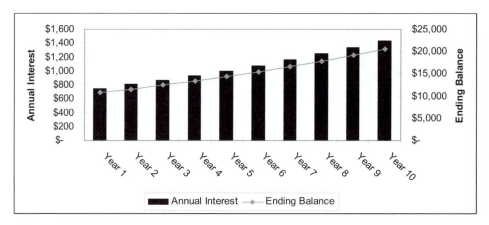

Chart 2.1
Compounding of Money Example

The advantages of compounding are magnified over time. For example, if your investment were for 30 years, a 7.5 percent annual interest rate on your initial $10,000 investment would grow to become $87,550! This is why it is so important to begin saving at an early age. The dollars saved during your younger years will be worth substantially more than the dollars saved in your later years.

As you can see from Table 2.1 and Chart 2.1, the interest income grows each year without adding any additional cash. This is because the initial $10,000 investment continues to generate earnings each year, while the interest earned on those earnings generates additional interest and so on. The higher the interest rate on the investment, the more value you will have and the greater the compounding effect. These same principals apply to most other financial instruments and investments.

The compounding of money has often been referred to as the "eighth wonder of the world." AP Photo/Frank C. Curtin.

🗣 GUESS WHAT?

Think about inflation over the long term. Let's say that you are 30 years old and that you require $50,000 a year to pay your expenses and to live a comfortable life. If you plan to retire at the age of 60, you can bet that the same expenses will no longer cost $50,000 a year. Assuming an average annual inflation rate of 3.5 percent, you will need over $140,000 a year at the time of your retirement to afford the same lifestyle!

INFLATION

Many people do not understand how inflation can negatively affect their investments. Inflation can be defined as a rise in the general prices of goods and services within a particular country. These goods and services include the costs for housing, automobiles, groceries, and so forth. The cost of a gallon of milk is now about $4.00. You can bet that milk did not cost nearly this much 20 years ago. Nor did an average car cost $20,000. The gradual increase of prices over time has been caused by inflation.

Inflation can reduce the value of an investment and adversely affect investor profitability. For example, if your investment is earning 2 percent per year and the annual inflation rate for the country is 3 percent, you are effectively losing 1 percent per year on your investment. This is because your money is growing at a lesser rate than the increase in prices for the goods and services that it can buy. Therefore, if most of your money is held in low interest bearing savings accounts, you may actually be losing money each year if the average inflation rate is greater than the rate of interest that you are earning from the bank. This is another reason why choosing higher earning investments is critical toward increasing wealth.

Chart 2.2 shows the average annual inflation rates for a 20-year period. As can be seen, the numbers can vary significantly each year based upon economic factors and cycles.

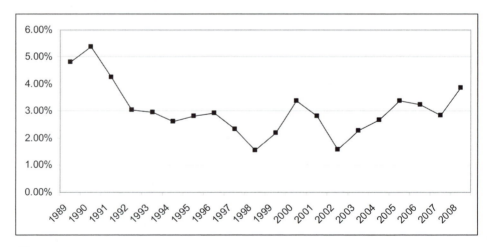

Chart 2.2
Average Annual Inflation Rates

Source: InflationData.com

Hyperinflation is defined as a period of rapid, out-of-control inflation. In Germany from 1922 to 1923, inflation surged by more than 300 percent a month. According to author Adam Smith, at one point the price of two cups of coffee in Germany rose 40 percent while customers were still drinking them!

BUDGETING

It is important for investors to have an annual budget. I did this for many years, and it really helped me to save and to manage my money. I used a basic spreadsheet to manage my budget, which really simplified the process. There are also specific software packages available for household budgets. Even a handwritten budget can be quite helpful.

At the start of every year, I would create an annual budget by month. I would include my monthly savings, rent or mortgage payments, cable, insurance and telephone bills, an allowance for groceries and entertainment, and any other specific expenses. I would even include an allowance in specific months for birthdays, holiday gifts, and so forth. There would also be costs budgeted for general repairs to cover my residence, cars, and other items, as well as a contingency allowance in case something unexpected arose. The offset was the income from my paychecks and any other sources of revenue. I never included investment income because these proceeds were always assumed to be reinvested.

Because I believe the budgeting process to be so important, enclosed in the Appendix are the instructions and a Web site address to access a House-hold Budgeting Model. The intent of this model is to assist you in identifying and tracking your personal revenues and expenses. Monthly savings should be considered one of the expense or cash outflow items within the budget. You will be amazed at how much easier it is to save and meet your invest-ment targets when you can see and track your performance each day, week, or month. Doing so causes investors to consciously and even subconsciously spend less when they are off budget, which aids in meeting monthly savings objectives.

AUTOMATIC SAVINGS PLANS

If you do not already have a steady savings plan in place, start today. Even if you begin by saving just $10 a week, getting into the habit of saving at an early

There are many misconceptions about budgeting. You don't need to be in debt to benefit from a personal budget, and budgets do not cause suffering or need to result in hours of paperwork. Rather, a budget serves to keep you out of debt and helps you to avoid suffering down the road! In addition, managing a monthly budget can take only a few minutes a week and lead to greater wealth, happiness, and free time.

age will dramatically increase your future wealth. The wonders of compounding when using a continuous savings plan over long periods of time will have astonishing effects! Stick to a minimum savings amount each week or month, and increase these dollars over time as you continue to earn more money. The younger you start, the more wealth you will accumulate, the more options you will have in your adult years, and the further ahead you will be from most of your peers.

It is important to continue saving small amounts of money over short increments of time rather than continuing to tell yourself that you will save a larger amount at some point in the future. I would much rather see you save $100 a month versus saving $1,200 at the end of the year in a lump sum. Doing so in small increments on a continuous basis makes it happen. In addition, the compounding is greater because the money is invested sooner. This can make a big difference over the years.

One way that I force myself to continue saving dollars each month rather than procrastinating and putting off this important investment commitment is to have dollars automatically deducted from my checking account each month. The funds are deducted from my local bank account on the first day of every month and electronically moved to my investment brokerage accounts with firms such as Merrill Lynch and Morgan Stanley. Brokerage firms offer this service, and the needed forms are provided on their Web sites, or they can be mailed to you.

Every month I have a certain dollar amount deducted from my bank account, which is used to purchase shares in various mutual funds or deposited into a money market account. This way, I am always saving. I just assume the scheduled monthly deductions are part of my budgeted monthly expenses, and I plan accordingly. I also benefit from what is referred to as *dollar-cost averaging*. By investing every month, I am purchasing mutual fund shares at higher and lower prices depending upon market values at the time of my purchase. This process tends to *average* or smooth the price that I am paying for my shares. Individuals investing lump sums at less frequent intervals could get caught investing their dollars at higher prices when underlying markets are up.

Table 2.2 is intended to show the benefits of dollar-cost averaging. The table assumes that $100 is invested each month and used to purchase shares of the same stock. As will later be discussed, I rarely support the purchase of individual stocks (as opposed to mutual funds) due to the limited diversification that

---

🗣 GUESS WHAT?

When comparing the benefits of saving sooner rather than later, consider someone that saves $6,000 at the end of each year for 30 years and earns a steady return each month using an annualized interest rate of 8 percent. At the end of 30 years, the investor will have $665,561. Now consider a second investor who saves the same $6,000 a year, but invests her money in $500 monthly increments. At the end of 30 years, the second investor will have $750,148! Both investors are investing the same amount of dollars each year. However, the more frequent the investment periods, the greater the effects of compounding.

Table 2.2
Dollar-Cost Averaging Example

	Invested Dollars	*Stock Price*	*Shares of Stock Purchased*
January	$100.00	$10.02	9.98
February	100.00	9.89	10.11
March	100.00	9.65	10.36
April	100.00	9.99	10.01
May	100.00	10.12	9.88
June	100.00	10.20	9.80
July	100.00	10.01	9.99
August	100.00	10.20	9.80
September	100.00	10.65	9.39
October	100.00	10.35	9.66
November	100.00	11.00	9.09
December	100.00	10.89	9.18
Average Stock Price		10.25	
Average Stock Price Paid			$10.23

single securities provide. However, the example in Table 2.2 is also applicable when buying mutual funds and other securities.

Because the shares are being purchased in fixed amounts each month at different prices, the risk of buying a large amount of stock at a single price is significantly reduced. By using such a strategy, the investor better protects herself from the market losing value shortly after her investment. A dollar-cost averaging strategy is intended to buy more shares when prices are low and less shares when prices are high. As can be seen in Table 2.2, the average price of the stock during the year was $10.25 per share. However, based on a dollar-cost averaging strategy, the investor paid an average price of only $10.23 for the shares accumulated.

BUYING YOUR FIRST HOME

Most people dream of owning their own home. Doing so is usually the largest purchase that a person will ever make. This is not surprising considering that the average home price in the United States is around $200,000. But relatively few people have anywhere near $200,000 in cash, so normally buyers finance the majority of a home purchase over many years.

Home loans are typically offered in amounts of 80 percent, 90 percent, and 95 percent of the purchase price. This means that any difference between the purchase price and the amount loaned must come from your savings. Each month, homeowners are required to make payments to their lenders. For a typical loan, part of each monthly payment is interest, and the remaining portion is principal repayment. While the monthly payment on a traditional home loan remains the same each month for the life of the loan, as each month passes, a lower portion of the payment is comprised of interest due to a declining loan balance and a greater portion consists of principal repayment. Let us look at a typical 15-year fixed rate loan in Table 2.3 as an example.

While almost all home loans require monthly payments, for simplicity, Table 2.3 assumes annual payments. As can be seen, the loan balance is gradually reduced each period. As this occurs, the composition of the payments made each year begins to shift more and more from interest to principal. At the end of 15 years, the loan is completely repaid and the homeowner owns the home debt-free.

When loan repayments can be stretched out for periods of 15 or 30 years, the payments become much more manageable. Let us look at the example shown in Table 2.4.

As you can see, the longer the term of the loan, the lower the monthly payments required by the homeowner. This is because longer loans lower the amount of principal repayment being made to the lender each month. If you borrow $160,000 over a 10-year period, you will be forced to repay the loan within 10 years, and your monthly payments will be substantially greater than when compared to a loan that allows you to repay $160,000 over 30 years.

As you might imagine, the more money you put down on a house and the less you borrow, the easier it becomes to qualify for a home loan and to receive lender approval. Most of the time, banks and other lenders willing to provide home financing are abundant. But at the time of this writing,

Table 2.3
15-Year Fixed Rate Loan Example

	Beginning Balance	Interest (7.0%)	Principal	Total Payment	Ending Balance
Year 1	$160,000	$11,200	$ 6,367	$17,567	$153,633
Year 2	153,633	10,754	6,813	17,567	146,820
Year 3	146,820	10,277	7,290	17,567	139,530
Year 4	139,530	9,767	7,800	17,567	131,730
Year 5	131,730	9,221	8,346	17,567	123,384
Year 6	123,384	8,637	8,930	17,567	114,454
Year 7	114,454	8,012	9,555	17,567	104,899
Year 8	104,899	7,343	10,224	17,567	94,674
Year 9	94,674	6,627	10,940	17,567	83,734
Year 10	83,734	5,861	11,706	17,567	72,029
Year 11	72,029	5,042	12,525	17,567	59,504
Year 12	59,504	4,165	13,402	17,567	46,102
Year 13	46,102	3,227	14,340	17,567	31,762
Year 14	31,762	2,223	15,344	17,567	16,418
Year 15	16,418	1,149	16,418	17,567	0

Table 2.4
Loan Payment Scenarios

Home Purchase Price	$200,000
Down Payment (20%)	$40,000
Bank Loan (80%)	$160,000
	Monthly Payment
10 Year Loan (7%)	$1,858
15 Year Loan (7%)	$1,438
30 Year Loan (7%)	$1,064

the U.S. housing market is in a dismal state. Aggressive and careless lending policies caused residential housing markets across the country to rise to unsustainable prices during the early to mid-2000s. Many buyers were given home loans that they could not afford. Now lenders across the country are paying for their sins. When a homeowner defaults on a loan, the lender will normally take ownership of the home and sell it in an attempt to recoup its loan amount. Defaulting borrowers have recently caused lenders to lose billions of dollars as property values rapidly declined and borrowers could no longer make their loan payments.

Because of the massive losses taken by banks and other lenders, they are being overly cautious when providing loans to home buyers and other borrowers. It is currently very difficult for many people to obtain any type of credit, but lender attitudes change over time and lending markets go through cycles. As time passes, banks will become more willing to lend and more buyers will be able to qualify for home loans.

When considering the purchase of a home, think about the following:

1. Real estate is generally considered to be an *illiquid asset,* meaning that it takes a substantial amount of time to buy and sell a property, and there are significant transaction costs associated with doing so. For example, sellers normally pay Realtors around 6 percent of the sales price to market a home. There may be up to another 1 percent of costs associated with the transfer of ownership. Title insurance must be purchased to prove that a property is owned by the seller free and clear of any obligations. Lawyers or title companies are paid to file all the needed documentation to facilitate a sale. In addition, local governments often charge fees whenever a property changes ownership. This means that if you buy a home for $200,000, it might cost you around $14,000 to sell it (7% of $200,000). In a normal market, it may take two years or more of home price appreciation just to cover these costs (i.e., you would need to own the home for at least two years before even breaking even if sold). When buying a home, realize that you are making a long-term investment in an illiquid asset. Make sure that you plan to stay in the area, that you have job stability, and so forth. Otherwise, it may be best to rent before making such a substantial purchase.

2. When buying a home, make sure that you feel comfortable that you can afford the payments. First, you need the down payment, but equally important is having the ability to make monthly payments under varying circumstances. If you stop making payments, your lender will take your home. Not only will you most likely lose your residence and any down payment that you made, but lenders will also have the right to sue you for any losses that they incur after selling the house. What if you lost your job or had unexpected expenses? Would you have enough savings or other sources of income to continue to make payments? Some loan products provide for lower payments today and higher payments down the road. Many borrowers have lost their homes due to these aggressive types of loan products. We will talk more about financing options in a later chapter.

    Not only will you have principal and interest payments each month, you will also be responsible for property insurance and property tax payments. Usually these costs are added to the monthly payment that you make to your lender. So instead of paying $1,200 a month, you might be required to pay $1,400 to cover these costs. The bank collects the money for insurance and tax payments from you and then remits the payments to the insurer and local government when due. Doing so gives lenders more confidence that these payments will be made. Home ownership also comes with repair costs. When you are a renter, your landlord is usually responsible for all repairs. As a homeowner, you are responsible. When dealing with such a high priced item like a house, the repair bills can be huge. Consider the costs of a new roof or plumbing system. Repairs costing thousands of dollars can come up unexpectedly.

3. To better qualify for a home loan, you will want to maintain low debt on other borrowings such as credit cards and consumer product loans. You will also want a strong credit score. Poor credit can result in lenders rejecting your loan application, or you may be forced to pay a higher interest rate. Higher interest rates resulting from low credit scores means greater monthly payments. A greater monthly payment means that you may need to buy a cheaper and smaller home.

4. When looking for a new home, use a realtor. As mentioned, realtor fees are paid by sellers. In addition, home prices and other terms are highly negotiated. Realtors can play a key role in helping you to negotiate the best price, and they can easily save you thousands of dollars. In addition, realtors can help to convince sellers to fix existing problems, pay a portion of your closing costs, and provide other monetary and nonmonetary benefits. A realtor can also give you good advice about a specific area, including the quality of the school district. While better schools lead to better educations for children, they can also lead to more desirable neighborhoods and help to protect and increase property values. Realtors can also provide market information, such as appreciation trends and future outlooks. If you are ever forced to sell a home, it is good to know that you are living in a desirable neighborhood.

5. Before purchasing a home, make sure that you order a home inspection. Home inspectors are trained professionals that are paid to review a property for defects prior to purchase. After a site visit, a report is prepared by the home inspector that can be shared with the seller and the seller's realtor. Often the findings from the inspection report are used by buyers to renegotiate more favorable pricing and terms, or the seller will agree to make some or all of the needed repairs. Even if you are buying a brand new house, you should still order a home inspection.

Sometimes sellers will offer home warranties to home buyers. Home warranties are insurance policies that are intended to cover home repair costs for a certain period of time. For example, a policy may state that certain repairs will be paid for by the insuring

Buying a home is usually the largest purchase a person will make within his or her lifetime. AP Photo/David Zalubowski.

🗣 GUESS WHAT?

According to the Ohio State University Extension, "Historically, retirement was a stage of life few individuals lived long enough to experience or enjoy. In the early 20th century, the average life expectancy was 47 years. As a result, most people worked until they became too sick to continue. Because the advanced medical knowledge and resources we enjoy today were not yet available, the majority of people died quickly of acute illness. Overall, time spent in retirement was only 7% of adulthood or about 3 years. In the early 21st century, 25% of one's adulthood can be spent in retirement." Many people can now expect to spend 20 years or more in retirement!

company over the next 12 months. But home warranties have countless provisions that allow insurers to avoid covering many expenses. In addition, there are deductibles that must be paid each time a repair person comes to your home. Never take a home warranty in place of a home inspection.

6. Whenever estimating costs for significant repairs always get multiple estimates. I have seen the service costs between repair people vary by huge dollar amounts. When considering the purchase of a home, make sure that you have a reasonable idea of what any needed repairs will cost. In addition, when seeking financing to buy a home, always get at least two quotes. The terms always seem to get better when a lender knows that he is bidding against someone else.

THE GOAL OF RETIREMENT

It is hard for many young people to think about their retirements. When you have recently or are about to graduate high school or college, the last thing on your mind is having ample savings for a retirement that may be decades away. But your younger years have such a meaningful effect on how much money you will have during your retirement that this topic cannot be ignored. A simple savings plan that can be maintained and increased on a continuous basis can result in millions of dollars being available in your later years.

It is unfortunate to see people working into their 70s or those who are living on overly restricted budgets during their retirement years. Many people are forced to significantly reduce their standards of living after they stop working. This seems counterintuitive. When people spend most of their lives employed, their remaining years in retirement should be viewed as a reward. This is the time when people should be enjoying the benefits from a lifetime of effort. Retirement is the time for hobbies, travel, dining out, and other forms of entertainment. To have to live less prosperously in your nonworking years than in your working years is not necessary.

As human life expectancy continues to rise with new technologies and medical treatments, an even greater portion of a person's life can be spent in retirement. In addition, the more money you save and allow to compound and accumulate, the earlier you will be able to retire, which will provide even more time to enjoy your nonworking years. While the average retirement age is in the mid-60s, there is no reason why prudent savers and investors cannot reduce the age of their retirements by many years or even decades!

Some people choose to continue working rather than retire. Many people enjoy working. People with the ability to retire may keep full-time jobs or move to a part-time basis. Others may start small businesses or take lower paying jobs that are more enjoyable. But there is a key difference between someone that works by choice and someone that works by necessity. Working because you want to work rather than because you are forced to work is a true luxury. Consider saving now so that you have the option when the time comes.

3

Investments

BENCHMARKS AND INDEXES

When borrowing money or when making investments, you should be aware of some of the more common benchmarks and indexes. Benchmarks and indexes can be used to compare investment performance among individual and groups of securities, and they serve as a starting point for banks and other lenders when determining appropriate interest rates on home and business loans and other borrowings.

There are many indexes and benchmarks that cover the investment performance of various stock, bond, real estate, and other securities markets. In addition, such measurement tools track current interest rates on key securities that are monitored by financial professionals around the globe. While there are hundreds of indexes and benchmarks that track the performance of specific financial markets and instruments in various sectors, regions, and countries, following are some well-known examples.

Prime Interest Rate—Also know as the *prime rate,* the prime interest rate is the interest rate offered by banks to their preferred or most creditworthy borrowers. The prime rate is considered a variable interest rate (as opposed to a fixed interest rate) because it adjusts from time to time based upon changes in interest rates by the Federal Reserve (to be discussed later). Many types of business and consumer loans are charged interest based upon the prime rate. For example, a borrower may obtain a loan from a bank that charges an interest rate equal to the prime rate plus a spread of 1.00 percent. If the prime rate remains at 5.00 percent, then the borrower pays an interest rate of 6.00 percent.

LIBOR—The London Interbank Offering Rate is another interest rate that is used to determine the borrowing costs on certain business and consumer loans. LIBOR refers to the interest rate used when banks borrow funds from one another. LIBOR rates are quoted for varying periods of time depending upon how long the funds are borrowed, such as 1-month LIBOR, 3-month LIBOR, 12-month LIBOR, and so forth. The interest rates on many business and adjustable rate home loans are based on LIBOR plus some type of spread. For example, a home mortgage loan may pay an interest rate of 12-month LIBOR plus a spread of 2.50 percent. Because 12-month LIBOR is being used, the interest rate on the loan will be adjusted each year. For example, if 12-month LIBOR is 4.00 percent during the first year of the loan, then the borrower will pay an annual interest rate of 6.50 percent. If at the start of the second year 12-month LIBOR is 4.75 percent, then the borrower will pay an interest rate of 7.25 percent for the next 12 months.

Treasury Securities—When the U.S. government needs to raise money, it issues bills, notes, and bonds to investors. These securities will be discussed in more depth later in the chapter. The U.S. government is viewed as being the strongest and most financially sound of all governments. Therefore, its securities are perceived as having very low risk. In addition, there are so many U.S. government securities outstanding and so many willing buyers and sellers during every second of the day, that this market is considered an accurate and reliable source of current interest rate data. Treasury securities are often used to determine the interest rates on various types of consumer and business loans.

S&P 500 Index—The Standard & Poor's 500 Index is a basket of 500 of the largest U.S. common stocks. The stocks within this index make up about 70 percent of the total U.S. stock market. The S&P 500 Index is considered to be *the market* when investors refer to the U.S. stock market. When people review the investment performance of their large company stock portfolios, they often compare them to the performance of the S&P 500 Index. For example, assume that you are paying a professional money manager to pick stocks for you. At the end of the year, you see that your portfolio earned a profit of 7 percent. If the S&P 500 Index generated a profit for the year of 10 percent,

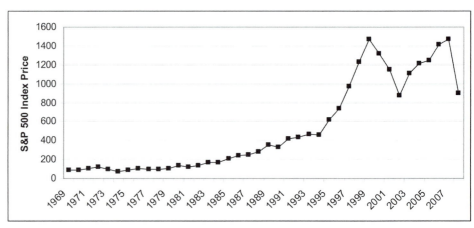

Chart 3.1
S&P 500 Stock Market Index Performance

then your money manager has some explaining to do. As will be further discussed, such a scenario would question the value that your money manger is providing and whether paying him for his services is worthwhile.

Standard & Poor's has created numerous indexes that are used daily by investment professionals to track the performance of various securities markets. Some additional examples include the S&P Smallcap 600 Index (small U.S. company stocks), the S&P Global 1200 Index (stocks trading in markets throughout the world), the S&P National Municipal Bond Index (bonds issued by individual states and local governments and agencies) and the S&P Commodity Index (tracks price changes for oil, wheat, gold, etc.).

Dow Jones Industrial Average (DJIA)—Often referred to as *the Dow,* the Dow Jones Industrial Average measures the stock market performance of 30 large stocks that trade on the New York Stock Exchange (NYSE) and the Nasdaq stock exchange. Some of the well-known Dow companies include corporations such as Exxon, General Electric, Microsoft, and Disney. The Dow is the single most watched stock market index in the world. When people refer to the market being up or down, they are usually talking about the performance of the Dow.

Nasdaq Composite Index—The Nasdaq stock exchange was first formalized in 1971 and is an electronic stock exchange. Unlike the NYSE, the Nasdaq exchange has no physical trading floor that brings buyers and sellers together. Rather, all stock trading is done through a network of computer and telephone systems. The Nasdaq Composite Index is a stock market index that tracks the performance of all the stocks that are listed on the Nasdaq stock exchange. Most of the companies within the index operate within the technology sector, so the Nasdaq Composite Index is less indicative of general stock market performance when compared to the Dow and the S&P 500 Index.

Russell Indexes—An investment firm, Russell Investments, created a stock market index that tracks the stock performance of the largest 3,000 U.S. companies called the Russell 3000 Index. The largest 1,000 companies within the Russell 3000 Index make up the Russell 1000 Index. The performance of the 2,000 smallest U.S. companies in the Russell 3000 Index makes up the Russell 2000 Index.

MSCI Indexes—A Morgan Stanley Country Index (MSCI) tracks the stock market performance of a specific country or region. For example, the MSCI Emerging Markets Index tracks the combined stock market performance for approximately two dozen countries, including Argentina, Brazil, Chile, Peru, and South Africa. The MSCI Pacific Index tracks the stock market performance of countries within the pacific regions of the world, including Japan, Hong Kong, New Zealand, and Australia. The MSCI indexes are the most widely used benchmarks for international stock markets.

Barclays Capital U.S. Aggregate Bond Index—Barclays Capital is an investment bank. The Barclays Capital U.S. Aggregate Bond Index is an index that measures the performance of a collection of bonds issued by federal and state governments, corporations, and other entities. Most bond fund managers compare the performance of their bond funds to this index.

Sophisticated investors compare their portfolio performance to the most appropriate indexes. For example, if you own a mutual fund that invests primarily in advanced European countries, you would not compare its profitability to the S&P 500 Index. Rather, it would be more appropriate to compare your fund to the MSCI Europe Index, which tracks the combined stock market performance of developed countries within Europe. If a portion of your portfolio was invested in the stocks of small U.S. companies, you would most likely compare its performance to the S&P Smallcap 600 Index or the Russell 2000 Index, both of which track the performance of small U.S. company stocks.

When borrowing money from banks and other lenders, educated investors understand how interest rates are derived. In addition, when lending money by purchasing bonds and other debt securities, they ensure that they are being adequately compensated. For example, an investor is not going to buy a 10-year bond issued by a corporation that pays an interest rate of 5 percent when a 10-year U.S. government bond is paying a similar rate. When assuming greater risk, investors should be paid higher interest rates.

BANK PRODUCTS

Checking Accounts—Most people have checking accounts with a local bank. Checks serve as currency that can be used to pay for goods and services. Some checking accounts pay a small amount of interest, and the rate of interest is often tied to the balance within the account. Such interest-bearing accounts are often referred to as negotiable order of withdrawal accounts (NOW). Most checking accounts have some type of monthly maintenance fee if the account balance falls below a certain dollar amount.

Checking accounts are used as a means to safely and efficiently transfer money from one party to another. Individuals and businesses use checks to pay bills and make purchases.

Bank Savings Accounts— A bank savings account (sometimes called a *passbook savings account*) allows the account holder to deposit money with a bank and have immediate access to the cash when needed. The bank normally pays the account holder a minimal amount of interest.

Bank checking and savings accounts invested with a Federal Deposit Insurance Company (FDIC) insured bank are insured for up to $250,000 (the current threshold in 2009) by the federal government. This means that if the bank holding your deposits goes out of business and is unable to repay you, the U.S. government will cover any shortfall up to the insured amount.

Bank savings accounts are normally used for cash that will be needed in the near future. The interest rate paid by banks on such accounts is usually lower than (or not much above) a country's rate of inflation. For example, if you are earning an annual interest rate from a bank of 2 percent, the inflation rate for the country might be 3 percent to 4 percent. This means that you are actually losing money on your investment because average prices in the country are rising by the inflation rate, while your investment dollars are growing at the lower interest rate.

When using bank savings accounts, it is worthwhile to compare interest rates and fees among banks. There can be substantial differences in the rates of interest paid by one bank versus another, and the account fees charged to holders are often set based on differing account balances and other terms. In addition, specific banks tend to offer special deals from time to time when trying to attract deposits.

Investment products such as savings and money market accounts and certificates of deposit, offered by banks such as Bank of America, can provide a conservative way to save money. AP Photo/Eric Risberg.

Money Market Accounts—A money market account is a savings account that shares some of the same characteristics of a mutual fund and a checking account. These accounts usually allow limited check writing and other types of transactions. Money market accounts are usually managed by a bank or brokerage firm and can be a convenient place to invest money for short and mid-term cash needs. Money market accounts usually offer substantially higher interest rates than bank savings accounts and are also federally insured as long as the account is held with an FDIC-insured bank or financial institution. The interest rates paid on money market accounts can vary significantly, so be sure to compare terms among account providers.

Certificates of Deposit—The most common form of certificate of deposit (CD) purchased by individual investors is a time deposit issued by a bank, thrift institution, or credit union. Most CDs have fixed maturity dates ranging from three months to five years. CDs normally accrue interest at a fixed rate and pay the investor all earned interest at the time of maturity.

Like savings accounts, CDs are federally insured for up to $250,000, which makes such an investment essentially risk free. Therefore, the interest rates paid on CDs are fairly low. Certificates of deposit can serve as a conservative option for investors to invest money for specific timeframes.

FIXED INCOME

Fixed Income refers to investment products and securities that pay a fixed or variable rate of interest. Examples of fixed income products include government bills, notes and bonds, which are issued by federal, state, and local governments to raise money for schools, roadways, welfare services, and other programs. Corporate notes and bonds allow companies to raise money to grow their businesses. Certificates of deposit and savings and money market accounts are also fixed income investments. When an employee retires, he sometimes is awarded fixed payments from an employer's pension fund, which is another source of fixed income. Annuities, which are contracts or agreements to pay investors a series of payments for their lifetimes or for a specified number of years, are also fixed income investments.

As you can imagine, there are many variations of fixed income investments that can be segregated into many subcategories, each having significantly different characteristics and risks. The following examples cover some of the most common types of fixed income investments.

Examples of Fixed Income Products

Annuities—An annuity is a fixed income investment that pays the holder a specified dollar amount each period until the annuity expires or until the time of the annuity holder's death. An investor in an annuity contract pays an insurance company a certain dollar amount either in a lump sum or by making a series of payments. In return, the insurance company promises to make certain payments over time, which includes the initial investment amount plus some amount of interest or earnings. These payments can be based upon a fixed rate of interest or a variable rate that is adjusted from period to period.

Usually an annuity contract is backed by investments in other securities. For example, a fixed rate annuity is often backed by government and high-credit corporate notes and bonds. A variable annuity is often backed by securities such as notes, bonds, and mutual funds, and periodic payments are tied to the performance of these underlying securities.

The payments to an investor from an annuity contract can be structured as being immediate or deferred. With an immediate annuity, the investor begins receiving payments immediately. With a deferred annuity, the investor begins to receive payments starting at a later date.

There are tax advantages to owning annuities. Earnings on an annuity contract are not taxed until the money is actually received by the annuity holder. This means that annuities can continue to grow in value over time and no taxes will be due until cash payments are taken by the holder.

Another reason why some investors purchase annuity contracts is to ensure the lifetime receipt of payments. While there is often a significant fee associated with this guarantee, knowing that a set amount of income will be received for the recipient's lifetime can provide peace of mind for an investor. This can be an important feature, especially nowadays as people are tending to live longer, which can increase the risk that retirees deplete their savings within their lifetimes. Some lifetime payment guarantees can be structured to include a spouse. For example, a specific annuity contract could provide for a set monthly payment for a period covering the combined lifetimes of a contract holder and his spouse.

There are many downsides to owning annuity contracts. The annual fees taken by the insurance companies are much higher than those charged on many other investment products, which means that you are most likely earning less on your investment. There are also penalties called *surrender fees* that

According to www.youngresearch.com, insurance companies charge an average fee on variable annuities of 2.4 percent per year. The average fee for a professionally managed mutual fund is less than 1.5 percent.

are often charged when an investor needs a portion of his investment back within the first few years of purchase. In addition, a penalty tax of 10 percent may be required on withdrawals made before the age of 59½. Also, the value of an annuity is only as good as the insurance company that stands behind it. If the company goes out of business, you may not get paid. This is uncommon considering the strength of the issuing companies, but it should still be a consideration when choosing providers.

Treasury Bills—A treasury bill is a short-term obligation of the U.S. government that has a maturity date of one year or less. Rather than pay a fixed interest rate, such fixed income securities are sold at a discount to the amount of principal that will be received at the time of maturity. For example, a one-year treasury bill that pays the investor $1,000 in six months might sell for $980. Treasury bills are a very conservative fixed income investment that can provide short-term investment opportunities.

Notes—A note is an obligation by the seller or *issuer* to repay a certain amount of principal and interest to the note's holder (the investor). A note may be secured or unsecured. With a secured note, if the issuer defaults and misses scheduled payments, the note holder may take possession of any securing collateral. For example, if a car dealer lends you money to purchase a new car, the note you issue is secured by your car and your promise to make the scheduled payments. If you (the issuer) default on the note, the holder (the car dealership) can repossess the car. In addition, if the value of the car does not fully repay the balance of the note, you will be obligated to pay any shortfall, which is an unsecured obligation.

Unsecured notes have no specific collateral. If the issuer of an unsecured note defaults, the note holder becomes an unsecured creditor that does not get paid until all secured creditors are paid first. In many cases under such circumstances, there may not be enough money left to repay unsecured creditors any or all of their investments after paying the secured creditors. Therefore, secured notes and bonds are usually much less risky investments when compared to unsecured notes and bonds.

The terms of a note usually require the repayment of the obligation within a 10-year period. Interest may be paid to the note holder on a periodic basis

Annuity salespeople can earn commissions of up to 15 percent on the dollar amount invested. These people are highly motivated to sell annuity products. Be skeptical, and do not be intimidated by a salesperson. Always make sure that you understand all of the applicable terms of a particular contract before committing, or consult an unbiased professional advisor.

(i.e., monthly, quarterly, semi-annually, annually, etc.) or at the time of maturity. While many principal payments are made at the time of a note's maturity, some amortizing notes require periodic principal repayments over the term of the note (i.e., monthly, semi-annually, annually, etc.). Issuers of notes can include federal and local governments, corporations, small businesses, individuals, and essentially any entity or person that can legally sign such a document.

Bonds—Bonds have the same characteristics as notes, except that they are longer-term obligations. The terms of a bond typically require the full repayment sometime after a 10-year period. As with notes, issuers of bonds can include various types of entities as well as individuals.

Municipal Notes and Bonds—These are fixed income securities issued by a state, city, or local government (*municipalities*). Municipalities issue notes and bonds to raise capital for general purposes and for specific projects like the construction of roadways, schools, and hospitals. The interest paid on municipal securities is usually exempt from federal tax, and when purchased by a resident of the state where the municipality is located, the interest payments are usually exempt from any state tax.

High-Yield Bonds—Often referred to as *junk bonds,* high-yield bonds are sold by companies having weaker credit strength than issuers of higher-credit bonds. If a company issuing high-yield bonds encounters financial difficulties and defaults on its obligations, the chances are substantially greater that holders of the company's high-yield bonds will not recover all or possibly any of their investment. To reward investors for this increased risk, they are paid a higher than normal rate of interest, or *higher yield,* than alternative securities having less risk.

Many corporations like The Boeing Company sell notes and bonds to investors to raise money to build new manufacturing facilities, start new product lines, buy other companies, and for general investment purposes. AP Photo/Ralph Radford.

🐷 GUESS WHAT?

Municipal notes and bonds can be purchased individually or by buying shares in a mutual fund that invests in municipal securities. Municipal securities are often bought by people who are in high tax brackets due to the tax exemptions provided. Because of the tax-free nature of these securities, the interest rates received are often lower than those paid by comparable corporate and federal government securities. When evaluating municipal securities and funds, a prudent investor will compare the after-tax profitability of alternative taxable investments having similar risk to the expected profitability provided by a specific municipal security or fund (we'll talk more about how to do this in the *Tax Considerations* chapter). Municipal securities are considered riskier than securities issued by the federal government, but safer than securities issued by most corporations.

The best way to purchase high-yield bonds is to invest in a mutual fund that owns a portfolio of these securities. By doing so, you are getting a broad ownership of bonds from numerous issuers operating in various industries. I would also recommend that high-yield bonds represent a fairly small portion of your total investment portfolio (i.e., usually 10% or less) as the performance of such investments can be very volatile from period to period.

Mortgage-Backed Securities (MBS)—When you buy a house and provide a mortgage to a bank in return for the bank lending you money to help with the purchase, chances are that the bank is not holding this mortgage for its entire term. If the bank were to do so, it would only have enough money to provide a limited amount of mortgage loans to its customers. Rather, the bank will often pool your loan with hundreds or thousands of other loans and then sell notes and bonds to investors secured by the pool of mortgage loans. This process, called securitization, allows the bank to recognize a profit when it sells the notes and bonds and to recycle its capital so that it can continue to make mortgage loans to its customers.

Often it is not your local bank that is completing these complicated securitizations. However, the headquarters office of the bank may be doing so, or the bank may be selling the loans directly to a company that has such capabilities, such as a Wall Street investment bank. The end result is that mortgage-backed securities that are secured by many loans are issued to various investors.

Mortgage-backed securities are notes and bonds issued by an entity owning a specific pool of mortgage loans, which serves as the collateral. Usually, when interest is paid on the loans it is passed on to the investors in the form of interest, and when principal is repaid on the loans it is passed on to the investors holding the notes and bonds as principal repayment. Therefore, when loans get paid-off ahead of schedule, the notes and bonds are paid-off ahead of schedule as well.

Mortgage-backed securities include residential mortgage-backed securities that are collateralized by home mortgage loans, but this fixed income category also includes commercial mortgage-backed securities that are collateralized by commercial loans on properties such as office buildings and retail stores. Usually each pool of mortgages collateralizes a series of notes and bonds with varying maturities to suit the needs of different investor groups.

🗣 GUESS WHAT?

An example of a mortgage-backed securities securitization would be when a bank takes a $200 million pool of mortgage loans and issues $30 million of 3-year notes, $50 million of 5-year notes, $70 million of 10-year bonds, and $50 million of 15-year bonds. All the notes and bonds would receive interest each month, but only the 3-year notes would receive any principal received from the underlying loans until these notes were fully repaid. Next the 5-year notes would receive all principal payments until they were fully repaid, and so on. This allows the bonds to remain outstanding for longer periods of time and the shorter notes to be repaid sooner. Some investors may want longer investments, while others may want shorter-term investments. Layering the maturities to correspond with the expected payments on the underlying loans allows the bank to attract a diverse group of investors to buy its securities.

Asset-Backed Securities (ABS)—Similar to mortgage-backed securities, asset-backed securities are notes and bonds backed by pools of loans and receivables. Just like a bank will issue securities backed by mortgage loans, it will do the same thing using a pool of credit card receivables, automobile loans, and many other assets. For example, if you are one of the many people that carry a monthly credit card balance (I hope not!), then there is a good chance that there are notes owned by investors that are partially backed by your credit card obligation. Asset-backed securities are usually shorter in term than mortgage-backed securities due to the shorter-term nature of the underlying assets, but the same principals apply to both types of securities.

Just like other forms of notes and bonds, mortgage-backed and asset-backed securities have different risk and reward parameters. As you can imagine, when you have hundreds or thousands of loans within a specific pool, there will ultimately be borrowers that default on their loan obligations and losses will often result. When this happens, it is usually the longer dated securities that take the losses first. This is one of the reasons that longer dated securities pay higher rates of interest to investors than shorter-term notes and bonds.

It is usually institutional investors like pension funds, insurance companies, money managers, and bond funds that purchase mortgage-backed and asset-backed securities. However, many fixed income mutual funds own some of these securities.

Yield Versus Interest Rate

When talking about fixed income securities, it is important to differentiate between the interest rate and the yield that is expected to be earned on a particular investment.

🗣 GUESS WHAT?

According to Asset-Backed Alert, approximately $145 billion of asset-backed securities were sold in 2008. Of this amount, approximately 43 percent were backed by credit card receivables, 22 percent were secured by automobile loans, and 19 percent were collateralized by student loans.

An investor's *yield* is a more important consideration than the interest rate a fixed income security is paying. This is primarily due to the fact that securities are often worth more or less than their stated principal values depending on what interest rate the security is paying versus current market interest rates for comparable securities. Based on whether a specific security is paying the same, a higher or lower interest rate than investors are currently demanding for similar securities will determine whether the security will sell at par value or a premium or discount to its par value.

A security that is worth par value means that the interest rate being paid to investors on the security is equal to the interest rate that investors are currently demanding to be paid for similar securities based on current market conditions. For example, if an outstanding bond with a principal value of $1,000 (its par value) is currently paying 8 percent interest, and similar termed bonds of similar risk are also paying 8 percent, then the bond will be worth $1,000, or par value. In this case, an investor can buy this bond for $1,000, earn an 8 percent interest rate (and 8% yield) each year, and receive $1,000 when the bond matures and is repaid by its issuer.

Now let us consider an example when a bond will sell at a premium to its par value. Assume a 10-year bond was sold 3 years ago by a corporation and today has 7 years remaining until it reaches maturity and repays its investors. Also assume that this now 7-year bond is paying an interest rate of 8 percent, and its par value (the amount of principal it repays at the time of maturity) is $1,000 per bond. If the bond is scheduled to pay interest once a year and all principal at the time of maturity, investors will be paid $80 per year in interest and $1,000 at the time of maturity. But this bond was issued 3 years ago. Market interest rates change constantly and can move dramatically over a 3-year period.

Assume that today while the bond having 7 years remaining is paying an interest rate of 8 percent, a similar 7-year bond is paying an interest rate of only 6 percent. This would mean that our bond is paying more interest to investors than current market conditions require. So why would the bond still sell for $1,000? It would not. Rather, the bond would sell for something more than $1,000, say $1,110, so that the yield investors receive is 6 percent (the current market rate). In this case, we say that our bond is selling or is valued at a premium. A premium means that a fixed income security is worth more than its par value in order to lower its yield to investors to be more comparable to current market interest rates.

A fixed income security would be valued at a discount if current interest rates were higher than the interest rate being paid by the security being evaluated. For example, if our 7-year remaining bond was paying its 8 percent interest rate, but the current market rate for a similar 7-year bond was 10 percent, then our bond is paying a lower interest rate than the interest rate that investors are currently demanding for similar securities. This means that our bond should sell for less than par in order to increase the yield to its investors. Therefore, instead of the bond being worth its par value of $1,000, it would be worth something less, like $900. A discount means a fixed income security is selling below its par value in order to raise its yield to investors to be more comparable to current market interest rates.

The Yield Curve

Knowing what a yield curve is and how it works is an important part of understanding the fundamentals of most fixed income products. Under normal market conditions, investors usually demand higher yields the longer their investment dollars are outstanding. For example, all other things being equal, a 10-year bond should pay a higher yield to investors than a 3-year note sold by the same issuer.

The standard yield curve comprises is comprised of U.S. federal government securities, and the yields paid to investors for most fixed income investments are derived from comparisons to the yields along this curve. Under normal market conditions (which is most of the time), the yields being paid to investors on government bills, notes, and bonds shown in the yield curve increase over time to reward investors for more risk. However, sometimes the yield curve can take different shapes.

An inverted yield curve is when shorter-term interest rates are higher than longer-term interest rates, which some economists view as an indication that a country is headed toward an economic slowdown and recession. An inverted yield curve is an indication that investors are expecting interest rates to decline in the future.

A flat yield curve is when short-term interest rates and longer-term interest rates are fairly equal. A flat yield curve is often seen during transitions between normal and inverted yield curves.

Chart 3.2 shows examples of normal, inverted, and flat yield curves.

The yields paid to investors on most fixed income securities when bought and sold are based on the yield curve. This is because most investors are comparing their investment choices to government securities. Why should anyone buy a 10-year bond from a corporation that pays an equal or lower yield

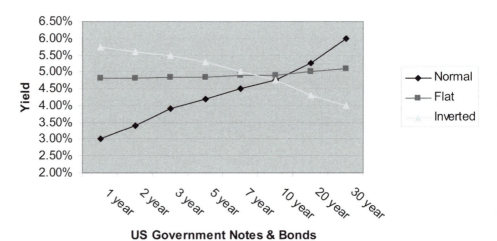

Yield Curve Examples

US Government Notes & Bonds

Chart 3.2
Yield Curve Examples

According to a report published by Pimco in December 2007, the global bond market was over $70 trillion. Of this amount, 39 percent of the total bond market consisted of U.S. bonds, 26 percent were from the Euro-zone, 12 percent were from Japan, 6 percent were from emerging markets, and 5 percent were from the United Kingdom.

than a 10-year U.S. government treasury bond? They should not. The U.S. government has a much lower chance of defaulting on its obligation than a corporation, and government securities are usually more liquid, which means that investors can buy and sell these instruments quickly and with minimal trading costs. In order to sell its bonds, a corporation is going to need to offer a higher yield than what the government is paying in order to attract investors.

Assume that a corporation wants to issue 10-year bonds to help finance the construction of a new manufacturing plant. Based on the corporation's perceived credit strength and other characteristics, investors are expecting the bonds to pay a yield that is 1.5 percent above the current yield being offered on a 10-year government bond. This means that if a 10-year U.S. government bond is paying a 6 percent yield, then the corporation will need to pay a yield of 7.5 percent for investors to purchase its bonds.

The issuers of other fixed income securities go through a similar analysis when determining proper yields to pay their investors. For example, banks look at government securities when setting yields for certificates of deposits, money market accounts, and other product offerings. In addition, the interest rates charged on home and business loans are also based on the yield curve and usually change at least daily.

EQUITIES

Equity investments are ownership interests in some type of entity. Equity investors share in some or all of the profits and losses of a particular investment. For example, a doctor, lawyer, or architect that owns his own business with other partners is an equity owner in the business entity. An entrepreneur is an equity owner in her company. Many times real estate developers will create an entity to hold one or more pieces of property and then find investors willing to finance the venture. These investors are usually given some percentage of the profits once the real estate is developed and/or sold. In these cases, the investors are equity owners as well.

Common Stock

The most common type of equity investment is the ownership of the common stock that is issued by a corporation. Companies sell common stock to investors to raise money to purchase new property and equipment, pursue new investment opportunities, and to generally grow their businesses.

Most large companies list their common stock on national and global stock exchanges so that their stock is more liquid and can be easily bought and sold by a large number of investors. This allows these companies to raise money more efficiently and more quickly than if their stock was not listed.

To have a company's stock listed on a major U.S. stock exchange, the company must be a *public* company. This means that the company's activities are governed by the Securities and Exchange Commission (SEC). To qualify to have its stock publicly traded on an exchange, a company must comply with specific exchange and SEC regulations, like making certain types of reporting available to the public on a periodic basis. Such reporting includes quarterly and annual financial statements and the disclosure of major items, assumptions, and events pertaining to the company's financial condition and operations. In addition, many of these disclosures are reviewed or audited by third-party accounting firms. Because of the significant amount of disclosure made by such companies, investors maintain a higher degree of confidence in the greater transparency of public companies and therefore are more comfortable investing in these firms versus private companies.

Private companies are entities that have chosen not to become public companies. These entities cannot list their stock on major stock exchanges, and they are not required to disclose as much information to investors, have their financial statements audited, or comply with other specific exchange and SEC regulations. Some private companies choose to be private because they do not want to bear the costs associated with being a public company. Paying audit firms, lawyers, and other third parties to meet regulatory requirements does not make sense for all companies. This is especially true for smaller entities.

The common stocks of many large public companies trade daily on the New York Stock Exchange. AP Photo/Beth A. Keiser.

🗨 GUESS WHAT?

Many entrepreneurs and other owners in private companies become very wealthy when an IPO takes place. Google, Inc. first listed its common stock on the Nasdaq stock exchange in August of 2004 at a price of $85 per share. In October of 2004, the company's stock was trading at over $190 per share. In 2008, the company's common stock was selling for over $700 per share! Larry Page and Sergey Brin cofounded Google and are both multi-billionaires!

Some companies choose to be private companies until they become large enough that becoming public and listing their stock on a major stock exchange is more cost efficient. When such a company becomes public and lists its stock for the first time, this is called an *initial public offering* or an IPO.

Other companies choose to be private entities because they were once public companies that were at some point taken private. When a privatization takes place, the stock of such companies is delisted from the major stock exchanges, and these companies no longer have to conform to the same requirements as public companies. Due to the stricter regulations (the Sarbanes-Oxley Act in particular) that were imposed on public companies after massive accounting errors and fraudulent behavior was discovered within companies such as Enron and WorldCom, many companies decided to go private and avoid significant costs and administrative burdens.

In most cases, private companies are more risky than similar public companies. This is due primarily to the greater liquidity and disclosure that public companies tend to provide. In addition, public companies can usually raise capital faster and cheaper. Public companies are usually much larger than private companies. However, there are exceptions. There are many large and stable private companies, and some private companies are substantially less risky than other public companies. There are always specific features of a particular entity that will increase or decrease its risk profile.

Small, Mid, and Large Cap Stocks

Small Cap Stocks—The term *small cap stock* usually refers to a company that has a market capitalization of under $1 billion. A company's market

🗨 GUESS WHAT?

Many companies periodically pay out a portion of profits to their owners in the form of a "dividend." A dividend is usually a cash payment paid on each share of stock. The "dividend yield" on a particular stock is computed based upon the dividends paid and the current price of the stock. For example, consider a stock that is valued at $10 per share that is paying a quarterly dividend of 10 cents per share of stock. Ten cents per quarter times four quarters in a year equals an annual dividend of 40 cents per share. Forty cents divided by a stock price of $10 per share equals a 4 percent annual dividend yield. Companies are not required to pay dividends. Normally a company's board of directors determines when and how much to pay to shareholders in dividends. Most large corporations pay quarterly dividends to shareholders.

capitalization is computed by taking its total number of shares of common stock outstanding times the current share price. For example, if a company has 100 million shares of its common stock outstanding and the company's current stock price is $8 a share, then the company has a current market capitalization of $800 million. This would be an example of a small cap stock. The term *micro cap stock* is sometimes used to refer to the smallest of these companies, usually having market capitalizations of less than $250 million.

Stock prices for small cap companies tend to be more volatile than the stock prices for larger companies due to many of the limitations of being a smaller company. Such factors include less liquidity, because many mutual funds and institutional investors do not invest in these companies, and a higher cost of capital when issuing stocks, bonds, and other securities. In addition, being a smaller and less diversified company often leads to more earnings volatility and a lesser ability to weather recessions and other adverse market conditions when compared to larger companies.

Small cap stocks can definitely be a valuable holding within a diversified portfolio and often provide higher profits to their investors when compared to larger stocks. However, because of the increased volatility, most sophisticated investors limit the amount of small cap stocks in their portfolios to 20 percent or less.

Mid Cap Stocks—The term *mid cap stock* refers to a company that has a market capitalization between $1 billion and $5 billion. Mid cap stocks tend to have less volatility than small cap stocks, but more volatility than large cap stocks. Mid cap stocks can also add substantial value to a diversified investment portfolio.

Large Cap Stocks—As you probably guessed, the definition of a *large cap stock* is a company that has a market capitalization of over $5 billion. While still having the normal risks of an equity investment, large cap stocks tend to have less volatility and lower risk than small and mid cap stocks. These companies tend to have a better chance of having broader investor bases and more diversified revenue streams. Many large cap companies derive a significant portion of their revenues from multiple product lines as well as from international sources. Most stock portfolios comprise mostly large cap stocks, while owning a lesser portion of small and mid cap stocks.

Growth Versus Value Stocks

Each of the common stock categories mentioned previously can be further divided between *growth stocks* and *value stocks*. Companies that have substantial business opportunities and the ability to significantly expand their operations are often known as growth stocks. These are the companies that tend to pay little if any profits or dividends to shareholders and, instead, reinvest most of their earnings back into company operations.

A more formal definition that determines whether a company is either a growth stock or a value stock is based on a measurement tool called the Price/Book ratio. The Price/Book ratio compares the current market price of a stock to the *book value* of the same stock. This ratio indicates how much of a premium investors are paying for a stock's future earnings potential.

Book value is determined by looking at a company's financial statements (primarily the balance sheet) and determining how much money would be left over for common stockholders if the company were to sell all of its assets and pay off all of its fixed-income investors and other creditors. Any value remaining would be paid to the common shareholders. The estimated amount of cash that each share of stock would receive after liquidating the company is referred to as the company's book value per share because the computation is performed by looking at the company's financial statements or *books*.

Why is the market price of a company's stock greater than its book value? This is because companies are valued as ongoing entities based upon their future expected earnings. By paying a price today for a company's stock, you are entitled to the earnings of that company for the rest of its existence, which is assumed to be an indefinite period of time. A company having an infinite life and the ability to continue to grow profits each year is clearly worth more than a company that ceases operations and sells all of its assets. The market value of a stock is based on future earnings potential. The book value of a stock is based upon its liquidation value.

When determining if a company should be classified as a growth stock or a value stock, many investors look at the Price/Book ratio of the company. For those stocks having a Price/Book ratio that is greater than a certain number, these stocks are classified as growth stocks. For those stocks having a Price/Book ratio that is less than a certain number, these stocks are classified as value stocks. For example, a stock analyst might evenly divide the 500 stocks in the S&P 500 Index between growth (250 companies) and value (250 companies) based upon each company's Price/Book ratio.

This same analysis can be done by looking at a company's Price/Earnings or P/E multiple as well. A common method for valuing a company's stock is to measure the relationship between its stock price and its annual earnings. For example, assume a company's common stock is currently selling for $12 per share. Also assume that the company is expected to earn $10 million next year and that the company has one million shares of common stock outstanding. This would imply earnings of $1.00 for every share of common stock ($10 million in earnings divided by one million shares of common stock). The company's P/E multiple is then 12, which is computed by taking the $12 price for each share of common stock divided by $1.00 per share of earnings.

Stocks having high Price/Earnings multiples are often classified as growth stocks, and stocks having low Price/Earnings multiples are often classified as value stocks. Using our example of a company having a P/E multiple of 12, if half the companies in the S&P 500 Index have P/E multiples of over 10 and the other half have P/E multiples less than 10, then the stock of this company would likely be considered to be a growth stock.

Essentially, whether you use the Price/Book ratio or the Price/Earnings multiple, you are concluding that companies that have higher premiums over their book values or higher multiples on their earnings are expected to earn greater profits and are thus labeled as growth stocks. Stocks are classified as value stocks (because their current price might be considered a *value*) when their stock prices reflect a lower premium over their book values and a lower multiple on their earnings.

●:   GUESS WHAT?

According to seekingalpha.com, the value of stocks worldwide peaked in October 2007 at $62.5 trillion before dropping to $36.6 trillion approximately one year later. This massive decline in the value of global stock markets of 41 percent or $25.9 trillion was attributed to a global recession.

Most studies show that value stocks have historically outperformed growth stocks. However, there are definitely substantial periods of time when growth stocks have outperformed value stocks as well. Both types of companies should be in a diversified portfolio. If you are buying mutual funds, usually you will automatically own both growth and value stocks. Some mutual funds are specifically geared more toward one strategy over the other. In fact, many funds use the words *growth* or *value* in their names and specifically target these types of companies.

Preferred Stock

Preferred stock is an additional type of stock issued by companies. Preferred stock is an unsecured ownership investment that has no stated maturity, and often times it is convertible into common stock. In addition, preferred stock receives dividends like common stock. However, unlike common stock, preferred stock usually has a specified dividend rate that is defined when the preferred stock is issued and cannot be changed as long as the preferred stock is outstanding (unless through bankruptcy or by vote of the preferred stockholders). In contrast, the dividend rate for common stock (if any) is usually set by a company's board of directors each quarter and can change at any time. For example, you might buy one share of a company's preferred stock for $25 and be promised a dividend yield of 9 percent based on the original price of $25. After all the company's operating expenses and its debt payments are made, the preferred stock gets paid its dividend. Any profits left over belong to the common stock holders.

The terms of a particular preferred stock might allow the investor to trade one share of preferred stock for some amount of common stock in the future. If the investor chooses to convert, then he will no longer be a preferred stock owner. Instead, he will become a common stock owner. When this feature exists, the security is called convertible preferred stock due to its conversion option. Preferred stock investors will sometimes convert to common stock when a profit opportunity exists. For example, if the price of a company's common stock rises to $40 per share and a preferred stock holder that paid $25 for a share of the company's preferred stock can convert one share of preferred stock for one share of common stock, a profit of $15 per share can be made.

As mentioned, most preferred stock has no stated maturity date. Such preferred stock is called perpetual preferred stock because its term is viewed as being infinite or perpetual. However, usually issuing companies have the right to repay (known as a *call option*) the preferred stock at some point in the future (i.e., after five years). This must be a consideration for investors as they may get repaid their investment unexpectedly.

When looking at the same company, preferred stock is viewed as being more risky than the company's debt obligations, but less risky than the company's common stock. If a company were to file bankruptcy, the fixed income holders would be paid before the preferred stockholders, but the preferred stockholders would be paid before the common stockholders. Therefore, the profits that investors receive from a preferred stock investment should be somewhere in between what the company's fixed income investors are earning and what the company's common stock investors are earning.

Cumulative preferred stock means that if there is not enough cash to pay the stated dividend in a given period, the amount owed to preferred stockholders will accumulate. When such payments are missed, common stockholders cannot be paid any dividends until the preferred stockholders are paid all current and past unpaid dividends in full.

Non-cumulative preferred stock is very rare and much less attractive to investors. If dividends are not paid for a given period on non-cumulative preferred stock, then the issuing company has no obligation to make up for the missed payments in the future. Once a payment is missed, it is missed forever and never repaid.

Participating preferred stock allows the preferred investor to receive a portion of a company's profits in addition to the stated preferred dividend under certain circumstances. For example, a specific participating preferred stock may provide that if the common stockholders receive a dividend in excess of a certain amount, then the preferred stockholders receive an additional dividend based upon some percentage of this amount. Most preferred stock does not provide this feature.

Stock Market Orders

When purchasing stock and many other types of securities, there are several types of market orders that investors should be familiar with. Even if you do not purchase individual securities, such information is helpful when talking to stock brokers, advisors, and other financial professionals.

Ticker Symbol—Stocks and other securities that trade on exchanges have unique symbols consisting of a series of letters that identify the security and are used for trading purposes. For example, if you want to buy the common stock of The Coca-Cola Company, you or your broker would reference the ticker symbol "KO." The ticker symbol for the common stock of the International Business Machines Corporation is "IBM." Microsoft Corporation's common stock ticker symbol is "MSFT."

Stocks that trade on the New York Stock Exchange (NYSE) have ticker symbols consisting of three characters or less. Nasdaq-listed securities have four or five characters. Mutual fund ticker symbols have five characters and end in an X.

Bid Price—The bid price is the price that a buyer is willing to pay you when you are selling a security. The bid price is always lower than the ask price for a specific security.

Ask Price—The ask price is the price that a seller is willing to accept when you are buying a security. The ask price is always higher than the bid price for a specific security.

The bid-ask spread is the difference between the price that someone is willing to pay to buy a specific security and the price at which someone is willing to sell the same security. The following reflects a bid-ask spread (the difference between the bid and ask prices) of $0.01 per share of common stock for The Coca-Cola Company:

Symbol	Bid Price	Ask Price
KO	$58.10	$58.11

If you were interested in buying or selling common stock shares of The Coca Cola Company, you could go to any broker's Web site and get the current bid and ask prices by requesting a quote using the ticker symbol "KO." If you wanted to buy shares, you would pay the ask price of $58.11 per share. If you wanted to sell shares, you would be selling at a price of $58.10 per share. This means that you are buying at the slightly higher price and selling at the slightly lower price. The bid-ask spread is the difference between these two prices and is a profit provided to the market maker. The *market maker* is a person, bank, brokerage firm, or other financial institution that is buying stock from sellers and selling stock to buyers and "making a market" in the stock.

Trading Commissions—To *trade* in the financial markets means to buy and sell securities. Brokers and other agents working for firms such as Merrill Lynch and Fidelity Investments are used to execute buy and sell orders for investors. Customers can place orders to brokers by telephone or over the Internet. Once received, the broker chooses the best market to buy or sell the security. For this service, brokers are paid a commission. The amount of each trading commission varies based upon the level of service being provided by the brokerage firm and the specific security being bought or sold.

Market Order—An order to buy or sell stocks and other securities immediately at market prices is a *market order.* This means that whenever you place an order to buy or sell a security, your order will be executed as soon as possible at prevailing market prices.

Limit Order—A buy limit order is an order to buy a security at no more than a specified price. For example, you may enter a buy limit order for KO at $57.00 per share when the stock is currently selling for $58.11 per share. Your order to purchase KO stock will not be executed unless the price drops to $57.00 or below. If KO's stock price reaches your limit order price, the order may get filled at exactly $57.00 per share or something less depending upon how quickly the price falls.

A sell limit order is an order to sell a security at no less than a specified price. If you owned KO common stock and were only willing to sell at a price of $60.00 or more, you could enter a sell limit order for $60.00 per share. Your stock would only be sold if KO's price reached $60.00. You might sell at $60.00 or something higher depending upon how quickly the stock price rose. Usually for securities that have large trading volumes, limit orders are executed at prices equal to or very close to the limit order price.

Stop Loss Order—Investors often use stop loss orders to protect their positions. A stop loss order allows you to place a trigger price on a security that you own. Once the stock price drops to or below the price specified in your stop loss order, the order immediately converts to a market order and the shares are sold at the best available price. For example, if someone owned shares of KO that were selling for $59.50 per share, he may want to limit the amount of value reduction if KO's stock price begins to rapidly decline. If the investor enters a stop loss order at $55.00 per share, if KO's stock price falls below this level, the stop loss order will be triggered and the stock will be sold at the best available price. Stop loss orders are used to protect an investor from significant drops in stock values and to lock in a portion of profits when stocks have gone up in value since the time of purchase. Stop loss orders can also be entered to buy securities at a certain price. These orders are applicable when investors borrow and sell stock that they do not own (called *short selling* and discussed later in the chapter).

Stop Limit Orders—A stop loss order and a limit order can be combined into a *stop limit order*. When placing a stop limit order to sell a stock, once the stop price is reached, the order becomes a limit order to sell at no less than the specified limit price. A stop limit order has two prices, the stop order price and the limit order price. For example, assume that an owner of KO stock places a stop limit order to sell his shares. He may enter a stop price of $55.00 per share and a limit price of $54.25 per share. If the price of KO's stock falls below $55.00 per share, the limit order will be triggered and the investor's stock will not be sold unless a price of $54.25 or better can be received. Without the limit order component, under a stop loss order the stock could fall rapidly to a price below $54.25 before being sold. Stop limit offers can also be created to buy securities when investors short sell stock.

Day Order—When entering market orders, a *day order* will remain in effect for the current day. For example, if you enter a limit order, if your limit order price is not reached during the day that the trade was entered, the order will expire.

Good 'Til Cancelled Order—A *good 'til cancelled order* remains in effect for 30 days or until you cancel it. This means that an unexecuted order will continue to carry over for additional days until execution, expiration, or cancellation.

Other Equity Investments

Warrants—Warrants might be awarded as part of a bond or preferred stock offering. A company may have trouble selling its securities, or it may want to pay a lower interest or dividend rate on its securities. Investors may be willing to purchase the company's bonds or preferred stock at more favorable pricing to the issuing company if warrants are provided to the investors as an additional incentive.

As an example, assume that a company wants to issue $100 million of bonds. It knows that it can sell the bonds to investors if it is willing to pay the investors a 9 percent annual interest rate. As an alternative, also assume that the company can issue the same bonds to its investors and only pay an interest rate of 8.5 percent if it gives five warrants with each $1,000 bond it sells. If the company's common stock is worth $15 a share, it might issue the warrants with an exercise price of $18 a share and a life span of 10 years. This means that for each $1,000 bond an investor buys, he will get five warrants that may or may not have value over the next 10 years.

If the company's stock price exceeds the $18 exercise price of the warrants over the 10-year period, the holding investor can purchase five shares of the company's common stock for each $1,000 bond owned at the exercise price of $18 per share. Warrants can also be sold separately from the bonds after they are issued, so some investors will own bonds and others will own warrants.

Most individual investors do not own warrants. However, mutual funds and money managers may buy and sell them when managing a portfolio.

Partnerships and LLCs—Often times investment opportunities are set up in separate entities created to pursue a specific purpose. For example, a real estate transaction may be set up in a limited liability company (LLC). A real estate developer might find a piece of land that he wants to build an apartment or office building on. Chances are that he will need some amount of equity before banks will provide him with any debt financing. If he does not have enough personal cash to fund the equity portion of the investment, he will look to outside investors for some or all of the needed funds. For their equity investment, investors are promised a portion of the project profits. If the project loses money, these investors can lose up to their initial investment (unless they are guaranteeing any debt, which can magnify losses). If the project makes money, then the investors and the developer will earn a profit.

Limited liability companies provide a couple advantages. First, they are not treated as regular corporations for tax purposes. The earnings and losses from an LLC flow directly to their owners, and the LLC is not treated as a separate taxable entity. Therefore, investors are not subject to the double taxation problem that many corporations are subject to (most corporations pay taxes on their earnings, and then their shareholders pay taxes on any dividends received, resulting in taxes being paid twice on the same earnings). A benefit that an LLC receives that is similar to a corporation is the limited liability protection to its owners. For most debts, lawsuits, and other liabilities, investors are shielded by limited liability status.

Partnerships can be structured in several ways. The traditional partnership is an entity formed by two or more individuals to conduct some type of business activity, and the owners are personally liable for all the debts of the business. A limited partnership is set up with one or more general partners that manage the operations of the entity and are personally liable for its debts and with one or more limited partners who are liable only to the extent of their investment.

I recommend that any considered investment in a limited liability company or a partnership be reviewed by an attorney. These are usually private equity investments, and the terms and conditions vary dramatically for each transaction. The profit and loss sharing percentages can be very unequal, and investors may have limited or no voting rights. In addition, there might be significant management fees to specific parties, and the overall risks associated with the entity may be well above normal due to excessive debt allowances and other specific features.

MUTUAL FUNDS

Mutual funds provide an efficient way to invest in numerous companies, industries, and types of investments. Purchasing individual stocks or bonds of a single company often exposes investors to an unacceptable level of risk. Mutual funds allow investors to spread this risk among hundreds and even thousands of securities.

Open-ended Mutual Fund—There are two general types of mutual funds. An open-ended mutual fund is a mutual fund that can issue new shares to buying investors. The proceeds from such sales are used to buy additional securities and to grow the fund. In addition, when investors want to sell their investments within an open-ended mutual fund, the fund will buyback or redeem existing shares. When investor shares are sold, the fund may need to sell securities to raise cash and the fund size declines. Open-ended mutual funds can be purchased from a mutual fund company or sponsor, or through a broker that sells shares on behalf of a mutual fund company and earns a sales commission.

Closed-ended Mutual Fund—A closed-ended mutual fund has a limited number of shares outstanding. Money is raised and shares are issued when the fund is started, but new shares are rarely issued after the fund is launched. In addition, the mutual fund company will not repurchase or redeem shares in a closed-ended fund until the fund is closed and liquidated. The shares of closed-ended funds are usually traded on stock exchanges, and like stocks, buying and selling takes place between parties brought together by a broker or market maker.

Choosing the Right Mutual Funds

There are literally thousands of mutual funds covering different investment strategies and types of securities. The most common mutual fund investments are cash (i.e., money market funds), stocks, and bonds, but there are subcategories within each asset class. For example, a stock fund may target a particular industry such as technology, energy, health care, or utilities. These funds are often referred to as *sector funds* because they focus on specific sectors or industries. Other stock funds may target large companies (large cap), medium sized companies (mid cap), small companies (small cap), or some combination. Others may specifically target growth-oriented companies (growth stocks), undervalued companies (value stocks), or both. Each mutual fund may target investments in one or more specific countries or regions.

Bond mutual funds can offer an array of varying risk profiles ranging from type of issuer (i.e., the federal government, state municipalities, or corporations), type of security (i.e., U.S. treasuries, mortgage-backed and asset-backed securities, or corporate junk bonds), and average maturity (short-term, mid-term, or long-term). In addition, bond funds can invest primarily in U.S. securities (a domestic fund), foreign securities (an international fund), or both.

Some mutual funds may primarily target longer-term capital appreciation versus current income, while other funds may specifically focus on generating current income. A fund might consider itself to be *balanced,* meaning that it invests in stocks and bonds and provides current income and future potential growth.

When deciding which mutual funds to purchase, start by choosing each fund one-by-one. Before researching and comparing specific funds, you should narrow the broad universe of mutual funds by selecting the fund characteristics that you would like to target. For example, do you want to purchase shares in a fund that invests primarily in fixed income securities (i.e., notes and bonds), equity securities (stocks), or a balanced fund that invests in both? Do you want this fund to invest primarily in the securities of domestic or international issuers?

After you have chosen a general type of fund, you'll need to further define the specific securities that the fund will own. For example, if you are seeking a fund that invests in fixed income securities, you will want to specify the average maturity or term of the fund's holdings. If this is a short-term investment, you will want to minimize your investment risk by purchasing shares in a fund that invests in short-term securities, such as a money market fund or a short-term bond fund.

If planning to purchase mutual fund shares in a fund that invests in equity securities, you will need to determine whether the fund will own large, mid, or small cap stocks. Will it have a value or growth focused strategy? If there will be international investing, what countries or regions will the fund target?

What tax objectives do you have? You may want to have higher tax generating investments in your tax deferred retirement accounts and lower tax generating funds in your non-retirement accounts. If you are in a high tax bracket and seeking a fairly conservative investment, you may want to consider a tax-free municipal bond fund. We'll talk more about important tax considerations in an upcoming chapter.

Net Asset Value

Before discussing the various types of mutual fund fees, let us first define the common industry term *Net Asset Value*. The Net Asset Value, or NAV, is the current value of the net assets that a mutual fund owns. NAV is most often shown as a per share amount and is usually calculated at the end of each trading day.

You may see the term *NAV* in a few circumstances. When you buy and sell shares in an open-ended mutual fund, the transaction price is equal to the end-of-day NAV per share (excluding any type of commissions) as new shares are issued or redeemed. Shares of closed-ended funds may sell at NAV or slightly above or below this amount to reflect investor demand because there is a limited supply of shares. Also, certain expenses are often shown as a percentage of NAV.

Using an example to compute the NAV of a specific fund, assume that a mutual fund owns common stock in various companies, and at the end of the

🗣 GUESS WHAT?

According to investopedia.com, there are more than 10,000 mutual funds in North America alone!

day all of the stocks the fund owns are worth $20 million. Let us also assume that the fund has two million shares outstanding. This fund would then have a NAV of $10 per share ($20 million divided by 2 million shares).

Mutual Fund Fees

There are several types of common fees associated with mutual funds. Their timing can vary by charging the investor at the time of purchase, during the ownership of the fund, and at the time of sale. These costs should be clearly disclosed to potential investors by each fund provider. It is up to you to determine whether a fund's fees are competitive and worth paying.

Share Classes—A noteworthy point regarding mutual fund fees is that funds often offer more than one class of shares within the same mutual fund. For example, you may see a fund offering "Class A," "Class B," and "Class C" shares. Each class is invested in the same fund and the same securities as the others. But each class will have a different fee structure to reflect the differing costs of servicing different types of investors. For example, one class may be sold through brokers and charge an upfront fee, but charge lower monthly fees. Another class may charge higher monthly fees and no upfront fee. A third class may require a very large minimum investment, only be available to financial institutions, and have lower overall fees.

Because of the differing characteristics of each share class, differing performance will result based on which class you own. In addition, different classes should be considered depending upon your investment horizon and objectives. When it comes to evaluating alternative mutual fund classes, just make sure you are researching the right type of share classification and are aware of the fee structure associated with each one.

Management Fees—A management fee is charged to cover a mutual fund's advisory role (the costs of paying a professional portfolio manager and his staff) and its administrative costs. Many funds combine an administrative fee and an advisory fee when quoting a management fee, but sometimes these costs can be shown separately. To ensure that you are comparing "apples-to-apples" between funds, make sure that both the advisory fees and administrative costs are included.

Usually management fees are disclosed to investors as a percentage of the fund's average assets. But other times, management fees can be structured as flat fees or fees with breakpoints, so that as the value of a fund's assets increases, the management fee percentage paid by the fund decreases.

12b-1 Fees—Named after an SEC rule, these are fees paid by a specific share class on an ongoing basis to cover the promotion, marketing, and distribution expenses of a fund. The amount of the fee is expressed as a percentage of total fund assets and is disclosed in each mutual fund prospectus. A prospectus is a document that legally must be provided to each potential mutual fund investor before purchasing shares.

Expense Ratio—A mutual fund's expense ratio measures the total fees of a particular mutual fund as a percentage of the fund's average assets. For example, if a fund had annual operating expenses of $5 million and average assets during the year of $500 million, then the fund would have an expense ratio of 1.0 percent ($5 million divided by $500 million).

Looking at a fund's expense ratio and comparing this percentage to those of other mutual funds is a helpful way to determine the reasonableness of each fund's overall costs. Remember that high expense ratios decrease investor profits. In addition, there is absolutely no reason to believe that higher expense ratios lead to better performance. Just make sure that when you compare expense ratios, you are comparing funds with similar investment strategies. For example, funds investing in small, undeveloped countries will have higher expense ratios than funds investing in large domestic companies due to the greater amount of research and other costs required. Funds that are actively buying and selling stocks and other securities also have greater expense ratios than those that are more passively buying and holding securities.

Front End Load—This is a type of sales commission charged by a mutual fund to the investor at the time of purchase. For example, a front end load of 5 percent means that if you purchase $1,000 worth of shares in a mutual fund, only $950 of your money is actually going to be invested. The other $50 is a fee to the seller of the fund. Front end loads are usually charged on Class A mutual fund shares.

The benefit of many front end loaded funds is lower ongoing 12b-1 fees. In essence, an investor pays an upfront fee (the front end load) but is charged lower monthly 12b-1 fees. In addition, most mutual funds that charge front end loads offer discounts at certain breakpoints when greater dollar amounts are invested. Table 3.1 shows an example of how front end sales commissions can decline when certain investment breakpoints are reached.

Mutual funds may offer purchasers of Class A shares breakpoint discounts based upon the size of their initial purchase as shown in Table 3.1. In addition, discounts may be provided by aggregating other mutual fund holdings with the same fund family. For example, if you are buying $20,000 worth of Class A shares in a large cap domestic stock fund, you would normally be charged a 5.75 percent front end sales commission assuming the fee schedule in Table 3.1. But if you also owned shares worth $10,000 in a bond fund with the same mutual fund provider, the commission charged on the $20,000 investment would be reduced to 5.00 percent. Sometimes mutual fund companies will allow you to aggregate the holdings of other family members when computing breakpoint discounts as well. Other times, when you commit to make additional purchases over time, lower commissions can be achieved.

Table 3.1
Mutual Fund Breakpoint Example

Class A Shares Investment Amount	*Front End Load*
Less than $25,000	5.75%
$25,000 or more, but less than $50,000	5.00%
$50,000 or more, but less than $100,000	4.00%
$100,000 or more, but less than $250,000	3.00%
$250,000 or more, but less than $500,000	2.00%
$500,000 or more, but less than $1,000,000	1.00%
$1,000,000 or more	0.00%

🗣 GUESS WHAT?

Studies have shown that funds with front end loads are more expensive than funds without them, which often results in less favorable investment performance for front end loaded funds. The primary benefit of front end loaded funds is the advice provided by the investment professionals that sell the funds. If this advice is not sound or needed, it makes more sense to purchase funds without front end loads.

Funds with front end loads should only be considered by investors that plan to invest in the same mutual fund for long periods of time because it often takes many years before lower monthly fund fees will offset the cost of any front end load. In addition, investing your money between multiple mutual fund families may reduce the opportunities to receive breakpoint discounts. Most major mutual fund companies offer hundreds of funds that provide investors with numerous investment alternatives.

Back End Load—A back end load, or a *deferred sales charge,* works in a similar fashion as a front end load except that the fee is paid when an investor sells his shares in a mutual fund. Often times, this fee is waived after the investor has owned the shares for a minimum period of time, and the fee sometimes declines the longer the investor holds the shares. Such costs are often intended to deter investors from short-term trading so that mutual funds do not have to worry about redeeming as many unexpected shares. Rather, they can keep more of the fund's money invested in securities and hold less cash. Bank end loads are frequently associated with Class B shares. Class B shares typically have higher 12b-1 fees than Class A shares. Sometimes Class B shares will automatically convert to Class A shares once the back end load is no longer applicable. When this happens, the investor begins to pay lower 12b-1 fees.

Measuring Mutual Fund Performance

When researching particular mutual funds, one must consider how specific funds have performed over time. Securities laws require that each fund disclose the average annual total returns for 1-, 5- and 10-year periods, or since inception if shorter. Many funds provide performance returns in additional increments.

You should review specific mutual fund performance in comparison to an appropriate benchmark index. For example, when looking at the specific performance of a particular large cap fund, you might see something like Table 3.2.

Table 3.2
Average Annual Total Returns as of June 30, 2009

	Fund XYZ	S&P 500 Index
Year-to-Date	4.25%	5.67%
1 Year	8.88%	9.42%
5 Year	10.56%	9.97%
10 Year	11.21%	10.47%

Fund XYZ should be disclosing its net returns after all of the fund's operating expenses and sales costs have been deducted. However, you should always check the disclosures provided to make this determination. While this fund has not outperformed its benchmark (the S&P 500 Index) during the past year, it has done so on average for the past 5- and 10-year periods. When it comes to comparing investment returns, you usually want to base your decision on consistent, long-term performance. How a fund performed compared to its benchmark for a 1-year period is a lot less important than how the fund performed during the past 10 years.

Morningstar Mutual Fund Ratings—An easier way to assess the performance of a mutual fund is to review Morningstar ratings between funds. Morningstar, Inc. is an independent investment research company that provides ratings on thousands of mutual funds, as well as on many other types of investments. Many brokerage firms and mutual fund sponsors publish Morningstar ratings for the products they sell.

A fund with a five star Morningstar rating is considered to be in the top 10 percent of the designated Morningstar category. For lesser performance, funds may receive ratings of four stars (Above Average), three stars (Average), two stars (Below Average), and one star (Lowest). The ratings are based on specific periods of time (i.e., 3, 5, or 10 years). Make sure that you read the definitions of the ratings anytime you are comparing funds, particularly if across different fund providers.

Morningstar ratings consider the performance of a particular fund, as well as the amount of risk that was assumed by the fund in order to generate such performance. For example, one stock fund may have provided an average annual return of 12 percent for the past 10 years and received a Morningstar rating of 4. However, another stock fund may have provided an average annual return of only 9 percent during the past 10-year period and still be rated a 5. This would imply that the fund earning 9 percent assumed substantially less risk than the fund earning the 12 percent return.

Lipper Ranking—Lipper Analytics, Inc. is well known for its rankings of specific mutual funds within a larger universe of funds having similar investment objectives. For example, over a 10-year period, you may see Lipper rank a specific large cap U.S. equity fund as being #56 out of 200 large cap funds. This means that during this period the fund performed better than 144 funds and worse than 55 funds having similar investment objectives.

Many brokerage firms and mutual fund sponsors will allow you to search for funds on their Web sites based on specific ratings. Of course, this should not be your only criteria, but doing so can allow you to immediately ignore funds not meeting your specific ratings threshold. Mutual fund ratings and ranking systems are another tool that investors can use to help narrow the

GUESS WHAT?

In early 2008, the worldwide value of all mutual funds totaled over $26 trillion (Wikipedia).

vast search for the right funds and also serve as a means to help solidify your views on particular funds.

EXCHANGE TRADED FUNDS

An exchange traded fund, or ETF, is a relatively new investment product that was created in the early 1990s. An ETF is an investment vehicle that holds a basket of stocks or bonds and trades on a national stock exchange. Most ETFs hold the same securities as a specific index, such as the S&P 500 Index or the Dow Jones Industrial Average. However, actively managed ETFs having professional portfolio managers employing various investment strategies are becoming more common.

When someone wants to buy shares in an open-ended mutual fund, new shares are issued to the investor by the mutual fund. The cash received from the investor is used to purchase additional securities within the fund. When an investor sells shares in an open-ended mutual fund, securities are sold, the cash generated from such sale is paid to the investor, and the number of shares in the fund is reduced.

An ETF's share purchase and redemption process differs from the redemption process of an open-ended mutual fund. More like closed-ended mutual funds, ETFs trade throughout the day on national stock exchanges. ETFs trade at or very close to their net asset values, which is indicative of the values of the portfolio of securities that they own at any given moment. When someone wants to buy shares in an ETF, the purchase is being matched with a willing seller through a broker. Therefore, new shares are not being issued or sold to accommodate the sale. Rather, just like when common stocks trade, someone is selling and someone is buying.

ETFs are very similar to mutual funds. Like closed-ended mutual funds, ETFs can be bought and sold at current market prices throughout the day on national stock exchanges. However, most mutual funds are open-ended, which means they can only be bought and sold using their end-of-day NAV prices. Being able to buy and sell in seconds at current market prices is one of the most attractive features of using ETFs.

ETFs provide great diversification benefits. Because each ETF owns a broad array of securities, which is usually matching some type of index, investors are provided with diversification across an entire index. In addition, multiple ETFs can be purchased to include investments in specific industries and sectors and individual countries and regions. ETFs own stocks, bonds, commodities, and so forth.

ETFs generally have low investor costs because they are passively holding a portfolio of securities. In addition, because ETFs do not need to buy or sell securities to meet the needs of buying and selling shareholders, there are lower trading costs when compared to most actively managed mutual funds.

ETFs are also very tax efficient. Because most are passive investments, there is very little buying and selling of securities. In addition, ETFs do not need to sell securities in order to meet redeeming shareholders. These features significantly limit any recognized profits and lead to lower investor tax obligations when compared to most mutual funds.

The process of buying ETFs is similar to buying common stocks. Just like when buying common stocks, there is a bid-ask spread associated with buying ETFs. The true market price of a stock or ETF is usually in the middle of the bid-ask spread. When you purchase an ETF, you are paying a fee equal to the difference between the ask price and the market price. When you sell an ETF, you are paying a fee equal to the difference between the market price and the bid price. The larger ETFs with greater trading volumes tend to have lower bid-ask spreads when compared to smaller, less traded ETFs. Most mutual fund shares are not bought and sold using a bid-ask spread.

A significant disadvantage of ETFs when compared to mutual funds is the commission required to buy and sell shares. This is particularly true when making small scheduled investments and less important when making much larger investments. For example, assume that an investor invests $100 a month into a mutual fund. In this case there should be no commission or fee charged to the investor, and the entire $100 is used to purchase new shares within the fund. However, if the same investor was purchasing $100 worth of shares in an ETF each month, there would be a trading commission charged by the broker selling the shares. In such cases, a commission of $10 may be charged resulting in only $90 being invested. Losing 10 percent of your money to trading commissions is not a prudent investment decision.

Commissions charged on ETF purchases do become much lower based on larger investments. For example, a $100,000 investment might result in the same $10 or $20 commission that a much lower investment might be charged. But for those investors using small scheduled investment strategies, ETFs should be avoided.

Evaluating the performance of an ETF is similar to the evaluation of a mutual fund. Historical performance and expense ratios should be considered. In addition, firms such as Morningstar, Inc. compare and rate various ETFs.

REAL ESTATE

In my last book, *How to Make Money in Any Real Estate Market,* I discussed the many reasons why real estate can serve as a great investment vehicle.

- Real estate serves as strong collateral that allows investors to borrow from banks and other lenders. By using other people's money to leverage an investment, substantially greater profits can be earned. This concept is used by most real estate investors ranging from individuals to large real estate companies.
- The interest payments on borrowed money are usually deductible for tax purposes. Any repair and maintenance, property management,

insurance, property tax and other relevant expenses can also be deducted for tax purposes. In addition, the government allows investors to take tax deductions for property depreciation. These tax deductions result in tax savings and even tax refunds for real estate investors.

- Sometimes tax credits and special tax deductions are awarded to real estate investors for developing properties that are beneficial to a community or to the environment.
- Real estate has historically proven to be a strong performing investment that has provided greater profits to investors when compared to many alternatives.
- During inflationary times when the prices of goods and services are rising quickly, real estate prices and rents have risen faster than the values of many investment alternatives leading to inflation protection and greater investor profits.
- Real estate values often move differently than the values of other investment choices such as stocks and bonds, which can help to diversity an investor's total portfolio. For example, in a given year, stocks prices may be down, but real estate values may be up.

Leverage

Being able to borrow most of the money needed to purchase real estate investments is a powerful tool that many investors use on a daily basis. Usually, banks and other lenders are willing to lend greater amounts under more attractive terms when providing real estate loans versus other types of borrowings.

Often times when investors borrow money using non–real estate collateral, such borrowings are for fairly short periods of time, they may have financial conditions and restrictions that must be maintained, and the interest rates are usually higher than when borrowing against tangible and more generic assets like real estate.

When you can borrow from someone and invest the money, you can make a profit on the borrowed money. In addition, most real estate loans are so standardized that they have minimal transaction costs, and you can borrow for long periods of time at attractive interest rates. We will talk more about the benefits of leverage in a later chapter.

Tax Benefits

Payments made for property maintenance, repair costs, interest payments and other expenses can provide significant tax benefits to an investor. Table 3.3 provides an example of how such deductions can significantly reduce an investor's income tax obligations.

Scenario 1 in Table 3.3 illustrates in a given year what the tax burden would be like for an investor if the normal income tax deductions were not available. In this case, the investor would be forced to pay taxes on the full amount of rental income produced from the property. Under Scenario 1, the investor would be required to write a check to the government for $5,500 each year.

Table 3.3
Real Estate Tax Deduction Example

	Scenario 1	Scenario 2
Rental Income	$22,000	$22,000
Property Taxes	–	(1,100)
Repair Costs	–	(2,400)
Property Management	–	(2,200)
Property Insurance	–	(1,000)
Interest Expense	–	(10,400)
Depreciation	–	(4,730)
Net Property Income	$22,000	$170
Taxes Due	$5,500	$43
(assumes 25% tax rate)		

Scenario 2 presents a more realistic example of the tax benefits provided by owning investment property. When normal property expenses are considered in Scenario 2, the investor is only required to pay the government $43 for taxes each year. Repair and maintenance costs and other expenses associated with owning and managing a property are tax deductible. In addition, so are the interest payments made to banks and other lenders.

Depreciation provides another substantial tax deduction. The general idea behind depreciation is that residential and commercial buildings, improvements, and fixtures tend to lose their values over time as a result of wear and tear, aging, and obsolescence.

Depending on the depreciation method used, the value of a house or building might be depreciated for tax purposes over a period of 20 to 30 years. For example, assume that you purchase a single-family home for $200,000 that you intend to rent to a tenant as an investment property. Also assume that when you bought the property an appraisal showed a value of $50,000 for the underlying land and $150,000 for the actual house. This means that you will be depreciating the $150,000 value of the house each year until its value for tax purposes is reduced to zero.

💬 GUESS WHAT?

Land is not depreciated because it is assumed to hold its value. But physical real estate structures are depreciated because the accountants believe that their values will decline over time and that they will ultimately become worthless. Such misconceptions prove highly beneficial for real estate owners. While investors are deducting depreciation expense on their annual tax returns, which assumes that the value of a property is steadily declining, usually the opposite is taking place. Real estate generally tends to increase in value over time. Therefore, investors are receiving tax deductions and lower tax bills each year, while their investment values are actually increasing! This is a gift provided to real estate investors by the federal government.

Tax Credits

Federal and local governments sometimes provide incentives to motivate real estate investors to develop and improve certain buildings, sites, and communities. For example, the federal government allows tax credits to be taken by investors when restoring buildings placed in service before 1936 and for certified historic structures. Generally, a percentage of the costs invested into a designated structure will qualify as a tax credit. For example, for every $100 in costs, a real estate investor may receive $20 in tax credits that can be used to help pay for project costs and to offset other taxable income.

Tax credits may also be awarded for improvements to low income areas as well. Low-income housing tax credits are awarded to real estate developers and investors by each state in an effort to provide inexpensive housing to low-income families. Tax credits are also provided by the federal government for commercial real estate projects in an effort to create jobs, improve streets, and revitalize specific areas and communities.

Tax credits and additional tax deductions are sometimes available for other real estate initiatives such as for the construction of energy-efficient homes and buildings and the installation of solar power. Rules pertaining to such tax credits and deductions can change and vary depending on particular locations and local governments. When applicable, how such potential tax benefits pertain to your specific investment and situation should be discussed with an experienced tax advisor.

Historical Performance

Real estate has historically performed well and has often been a more profitable investment choice when compared to many other investment alternatives. Chart 3.3 shows the historical performance of several stock market indexes compared to the stock performance of a group of real estate investment trusts (REITs).

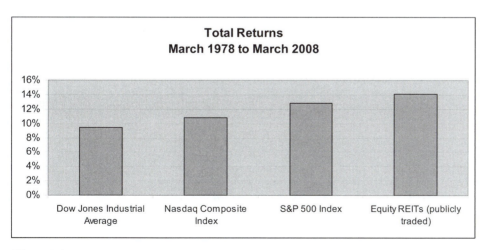

Chart 3.3
Historical Investment Performance

A REIT is a company that invests in real estate–related assets, including hotels, shopping centers, apartment buildings, warehouses, marinas, golf courses, and other property types. In addition, some REITs make loans to borrowers that are secured by real estate. An *equity REIT* owns and operates income-producing property. These companies buy real estate properties and lease them to tenants. A *mortgage REIT* lends money to real estate owners and developers. A *hybrid REIT* combines the activities of an equity REIT and a mortgage REIT by both owning and managing properties and by lending money to property owners.

Inflation Protection

Many investors like real estate because historically it has provided strong returns, and it has tended to be a good investment to protect against inflation. When inflation is high, the prices of the goods and services that consumers purchase (i.e., food and beverages, transportation, housing, etc.) rise quickly, and unless your investments are growing at an equal or greater rate, you are essentially losing money. In periods of high inflation, real estate values have tended to rise faster than in periods of lower inflation. In addition, the rents being charged to tenants can usually be increased more during periods of high inflation.

Diversification Benefits

Real estate can add diversity to an investor's portfolio. Most well-balanced and diversified portfolios should have some exposure to real estate. The performance of real estate is not highly correlated with the performance of other investment products, including many types of stocks, bonds, and alternative investments. When you own different kinds of investments, the profitability of your total portfolio can become more stable and have less risk. A major U.S. stock or bond market decline does not mean that the value of your real estate investments has decreased during the same period. In fact, they may have increased in value. Having diverse investments that perform differently over time provides diversification and can lead to greater profits while assuming less risk. We will talk more about diversification in the next chapter.

Real Estate Investments

REITs—We have talked about the strong performance that REITs have historically provided to investors. Investing in REITs is a great way to passively own real estate that is overseen by experienced management teams. REITs pool capital from many investors by selling their stock. There is no minimum dollar amount required for investors to purchase stock in a REIT. To purchase individual properties, particularly large properties like hotels, office and apartment buildings, and shopping malls, requires millions of dollars. By owning the common stock of one or more REITs, small investors are able to indirectly own portions of many large properties that they would normally be unable to afford. The stocks of many REITs are traded on major stock exchanges. Buying and selling stock on a national stock exchange is much easier, faster, and cheaper than trying to buy and sell individual properties.

REITs usually pay significantly larger dividends than most other types of companies due to a tax requirement that REITs pay out at least 90 percent of their taxable income to shareholders in order to maintain REIT qualification. Thus, REIT stocks tend to be a good source of income (like fixed income investments) that also provide the potential for stock price appreciation.

Buying REIT securities is as simple and efficient as buying any other type of security. Investors can purchase REIT stocks and bonds individually, or gain such ownership through mutual funds.

Residential Real Estate—One of the simplest and most affordable ways that investors can own individual real estate properties directly is through the purchase of single-family homes. Many investors understand how the cash inflows and outflows work from such an investment because they have had similar experiences through the ownership or renting of their own homes.

Investors can buy condominiums and houses, rent them to tenants, collect the income, and hold them indefinitely or sell them at some later date. If you are experienced in home repairs and renovations, you might want to use these skills to buy properties in need of repair at a discount. You can then sell or *flip* the properties or hold them as rentals. Many investors have made significant profits from such endeavors.

But directly owning a piece of property for investment has its headaches and risks. It is very stressful when a piece of property is not rented and you are making monthly loan and repair payments with no offsetting income. Also, selling real estate at a fair price usually takes a substantial amount of time, and there are significant transaction costs involved with buying and selling property. Often there is no income being generated during this process. To sell quickly, investors usually have to discount the price, which can result in lower profits or even losses.

Chart 3.4 shows historical annual changes in national home prices in the United States. The dramatic declines caused by the housing market bust that started in 2007 can be seen due to the substantial and abnormal appreciation that resulted during prior years. Home prices have continued to plummet during the year 2009 in many regions, and a bottom has yet to be reached.

Multifamily Residential Properties—For the average investor, owning single-family residential investment property is a significant accomplishment. For most investors, this is about as far as I recommend going in terms of directly owning real estate. Most investors can get more than enough portfolio diversification through REIT ownership, and others can enhance this exposure by owning one or more rental properties. However, some investors will become more passionate about real estate investing and will want to go to the next step.

Multifamily residential property can include something as simple as a duplex, which is essentially two homes under one roof. This would be very similar to owning single-family rental properties. The primary difference would be two rental streams and two tenants instead of one. Some of the costs will be higher due to the fact that you now have two kitchens, separate heating

🗨 GUESS WHAT?

I have included the following suggestions in prior writings that should be considered when purchasing single-family homes for investment purposes. While these suggestions may not fit all investment strategies, they should prove helpful when evaluating most single-family rental properties.

- Consider multibedroom property in good neighborhoods that will attract families who will often rent for extended periods of time. Tenant turnover costs can be expensive.
- Purchase generic properties without luxury features that can cause additional expense and liability (i.e., swimming pools, fancy equipment and fixtures, etc.).
- Avoid poor locations (like next to highways) and floor plans, garage conversions, and other features that could make a home less desirable for sale or rent.
- Have one or more professional inspections performed on the home before purchase, and obtain estimates for any significant needed repairs.
- Get at least two quotes on financing alternatives and at least two estimates on all major repair work. I have seen huge differences between service providers.
- Obtain credit reports on any prospective tenants. I recommend requiring the first and last month's rent and a security deposit equal to one month's rent to cover any potential damages to the property.
- Forecast income and expenses, and be comfortable that you can manage the payments when the property is occupied and vacant for significant periods of time.
- Do not base your total investment strategy on the expectation of abnormal, rapid price increases in home values.
- Forecast the expected profitability of owning the investment for a certain period of time using conservative assumptions. Many investment properties are purchased without rational investment strategies.

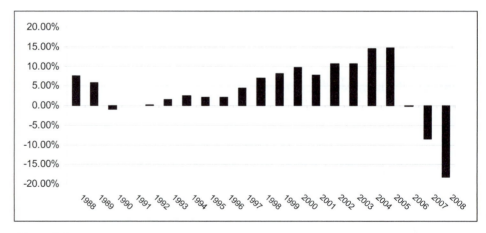

Chart 3.4
Changes in U.S. National Home Values

Source: S&P/Case-Shiller U.S. National Home Price Index

and air conditioning systems, and perhaps twice as many groups of people wearing on your property. But after owning single-family homes, a duplex should not require a significant increase in expertise.

The next step up from a duplex is a multitenant apartment building. Such properties can hold just a few apartments or thousands of units. Today, most of the large apartment complexes are often owned by REITs and other real estate funds and partnerships. These investments offer greater opportunities, but also present more problems and higher risks. Before ever considering such a purchase, you should have built a successful track record with single-family homes and established a steady source of cash flow that can be used to support larger properties when needed. In addition, potential lenders will want to see that you have a proven success record and that you are experienced enough to handle a multitenant property.

Commercial Properties—Examples of commercial properties include the real estate in which shopping centers, offices, factories, warehouses, restaurants, and retail stores are operated. Again, most of the larger properties are often owned by REITs and other real estate funds and companies. Such owners usually have the expertise and scale to manage commercial properties efficiently and effectively. Most individual investors do not have these resources.

The leases on commercial properties are more complex than those for residential properties. They are more formal legal agreements that often require the services of an attorney. Each lease with each tenant is a separately negotiated instrument and usually serves as collateral for any bank financing provided to the property owner.

The easiest commercial lease to manage from an owner's perspective is called a triple net lease. This means that the tenant is responsible for the three primary expenses associated with a property: maintenance, insurance, and taxes. Other forms of lease may require the owner to pay for virtually all expenses, while others might require the landlord and tenant to share the costs of specific items.

Real Estate Development—Often real estate investors and developers seek individuals and financial institutions to invest in and help finance their projects. For example, a real estate developer may seek funds to facilitate the purchase of land and the construction of one or more homes, an apartment or

🗨 GUESS WHAT?

Many commercial real estate markets move in cycles. For example, the demand for retail or office space can vary significantly based upon local, regional, and national variables such as the state of the economy or specific industries. Also, commercial real estate can be very difficult to sell and can require substantial amounts of cash to maintain.

One of the greatest risks associated with commercial real estate is the specificity of use for a particular property. Chances are that you will not be able to lease office space to a restaurant operator or replace a tenant in a warehouse other than with another warehouse operator. Due to the limitations of use for such properties, vacancies can last for years. Did you ever drive by an empty storefront or gas station that has shown no activity for many months at a time? Somebody owns that property and probably wishes it was occupied.

Most large commercial properties are owned by real estate investment trusts (REITs) and other types of real estate companies that have significant management expertise and access to large amounts of capital. AP Photo/Rodney White.

condominium complex, an office building, a storage facility, or any other type of residential or commercial structure.

Investing in real estate development can be very risky. There are political hurdles including different zoning and municipal codes that will dictate what can and cannot be built on a certain piece of property. There may be environmental or flood problems that must be resolved. Once building permits and financing are in place, the construction process presents a number of additional challenges and risks. Managing various tradesmen, adhering to design, and staying on a cost and timing budget requires significant skill and sometimes luck. Many real estate developers are very successful and make huge profits. Others are less successful, projects fail, and investors lose money. If you choose to invest with a particular developer, make sure that you are fully aware of his track record with prior projects and that he has proper experience and a favorable reputation.

ALTERNATIVE INVESTMENTS

Alternative investments include investment products that are outside of tradition stock, bond, and cash (i.e., money markets, CDs, etc.) investment choices.

🗣 GUESS WHAT?

Sometimes real estate developers construct buildings on a preleased or presold basis, meaning that as soon as the project is ready, a tenant will move in or a buyer will purchase the property. Other times, there remains the risk of finding a tenant or buyer. Such "speculative" development projects (those that start construction first and then worry about finding a tenant or buyer during the project or after completion) are substantially riskier than those having a buyer or tenant in place before starting construction.

A general definition of *alternative investments* includes financial derivatives, hedge funds, and private equity funds. In addition, nonfinancial products such as wine, art, and rare coins may also be considered alternative investments.

Because of the additional complexities associated with such products, alternative investments are usually used by sophisticated financial institutions and high net worth individuals. Benefits of alternative investments can include portfolio diversification by adding specialized investment products that perform differently when compared to more traditional investments. Alternative investment can also provide the opportunity to earn significant profits. However, such investments can also expose investors to high levels of risk.

Financial Derivatives

A derivative is something that derives its value from the value of something else. A financial derivative is a financial contract or instrument that moves up or down in value based upon the changes in value of an underlying asset. For example, a financial derivative contract's price may be based upon movements in an individual company's stock or bond prices, a general stock or bond market index, the price of a particular commodity like gold or oil, economic variables, or even weather conditions.

Financial derivatives have the ability to cause disastrous results. Such outcomes are usually from speculation and betting on the direction of one or more financial markets or instruments. But financial derivatives also provide investors with a means to reduce risk. While investing in financial derivatives should be left to the most sophisticated investors, following is a brief description of the most common financial derivatives: futures, options, and swaps.

Futures Contracts—When people want to ensure delivery of something in the future at a specified price today, they can purchase the product using a futures contract. A futures contract is a standardized contract that trades on an exchange and allows people to reduce the risk that an underlying asset will increase or decrease in price over time. For example, if a manufacturer needs cotton to produce its garments, it may want to ensure delivery at a fixed price at one or more points in the future. The company may enter futures contracts that allow it to purchase certain amounts of cotton in 6, 12, and 24 months.

Alternatively, assume that an orange grower wants to ensure that it can sell its oranges when harvested at a certain price. In order to reduce the risk that the prices of oranges will fall before harvest, the company may enter one or more futures contracts promising to sell oranges to one or more parties at certain prices on one or more future dates.

Option Contracts—A futures contract requires the contract holder to take delivery of the product when the contract matures. In contrast, an option contract gives its holder the right or option to act at some point in the future. Under an option contract, the buyer of the contract does not need to act. Rather, he has the option to act, or he can do nothing and let the option contract expire.

There is a seller and a buyer of each option contract. The seller of an option contract receives money from the buyer of the contract. The buyer is paying for the option he is receiving under the contract, which may be the right to buy or sell a specified amount of a certain asset on a certain date. The seller is obligated to perform under the option contract if the buyer chooses to act.

A *call option contract* gives the buyer of the contract the option to buy a certain asset at a certain time at a specific price. A *put option contract* gives the buyer of the contract the option to sell a certain asset at a certain time at a specified price. Let us use a couple examples to further explain call and put options.

Assume that Bank of America's common stock is selling for $10 per share, and you believe that the stock price is going to increase significantly over the next two months. You see that two-month call options to purchase Bank of America's stock at $10 per share are selling for $0.50 per share. This means that for every 50 cents you pay the seller of the call option, you will have the right to purchase one share of Bank of America's stock from the call option seller at $10 per share anytime during the next two months.

Now let us assume that you purchase a call option that gives you the right to buy 100 shares of Bank of America common stock at $10 per share for the next two months. For this right, you pay the seller (known as the *writer* of the option) $50 (50 cents per share for the right to purchase 100 shares). If during the two-month period Bank of America's stock price remains below $10 per share, you will not exercise your call option because it has no value (it is *out-of-the-money*). Therefore, you will have let the call option expire worthless, you will have lost $50, and the seller of the call option would have earned $50 for writing the call option.

But what happens if Bank of America's stock price reaches $15 a share during the two months that you own the call option? Now your option has value (it is *in-the-money*). If you choose to exercise the call option, you can buy 100 shares of Bank of America stock for $10 per share when the market price is $15 per share. You just made $5 per share on 100 shares, or $500. This means that when you subtract the $50 paid for the option, you have a profit of $450 on your original investment of $50.

Now let us consider a put option example assuming that Bank of America's stock is still selling for $10 per share and you own 100 shares. You are concerned that the price of the stock is going to go down, but you do not want to sell the stock in case it rises. Also assume that someone is willing to sell a put option on the stock for $0.25 per share that will allow you to sell the stock for $9 per share anytime during the next three months. If you exercise the put option, you will be selling 100 shares of Bank of America stock for $9 per share and the seller of the put option will be required to buy the shares from you for $900.

If at the end of the three-month option period, Bank of America's stock is selling for $18 per share, you would not exercise your put option (it is out-of-the-money). Rather, the value of your 100 shares of stock would have increased in value by $800 since you purchased the put option. Therefore, you would let the put option expire worthless and you would have a profit of $775 ($800 in stock price appreciation less the $25 paid for the put option). Under this scenario, the seller of the put option would earn a $25 profit on the expired option.

However, if at the end of three months Bank of America's stock is selling for $7 per share, you would exercise your rights under the put option and sell your 100 shares of stock to the seller of the put option for $900 (the option is in-the-money). In this case, you would have earned $2 per share on the put option to offset the reduction in value of your stock. So while the 100 shares of Bank of America stock that you had owned are now only worth $700, you were able to sell them for $900. This allowed you to avoid a loss of $175 (the $200 profit earned from the put option contract less the $25 paid to the seller of the put option contract). The seller of the put option contract would have lost $175 (the $200 decline in stock price less the $25 received for writing the option).

These option examples are very simplistic. Much larger contracts trade throughout the world on exchanges such as the Chicago Board Options Exchange (CBOE) and the Pacific Stock Exchange (PCX). Like futures contracts, option contracts can be written and purchased on an array of financial products.

Swap Agreements—Simply put, and as the name implies, a swap agreement allows two parties to exchange or *swap* their positions under a financial contract. For example, assume that Company A has borrowed $5 million from a bank for 10 years at an adjustable interest rate equal to 12-month LIBOR plus 2 percent. Also assume that the interest rate is adjusted annually based upon where 12-month LIBOR is at the beginning of each year.

12-month LIBOR can go up and down dramatically each year. If this interest rate benchmark goes down, then Company A benefits and pays less interest expense on the loan. For example, if, when Company A enters the loan, 12-month LIBOR is 5 percent, then the company is paying an interest rate of 7 percent for the first year. If 12-month LIBOR drops to 3 percent at the time the loan's interest rate is reset at the beginning of the second year, then Company A will pay 5 percent for the following year.

But Company A is also exposed to the risk that interest rates will rise over time and that the loan will become more and more expensive. For example, assume that 12-month LIBOR rises to 8 percent. Company A's interest rate would then jump to 10 percent. To eliminate the risk of rising interest rates, Company A may choose to enter an interest rate swap.

Company A could enter an interest rate swap agreement whereby it agrees to pay Company B a fixed rate of interest, say 6.5 percent, on a balance of $5 million for 10 years (the life of the loan). In return, Company B agrees to pay Company A an adjustable interest rate equal to 12-month LIBOR on the same balance of $5 million for the same period of time. The result is that Company A has converted an adjustable interest rate to a fixed interest rate. Company A now has a fixed interest rate of 8.5 percent (the 6.5% fixed rate paid to Company B plus the 2% spread over 12-month LIBOR owed to the bank) on its loan for 10 years through the swap agreement.

Chart 3.5 illustrates the results of the interest rate swap between Company A and Company B. Normally, a bank or other financial institution will serve

🗣 GUESS WHAT?

According to the Chicago Mercantile Exchange, 76.5 percent of all option contracts held at the date of contract expiration at the exchange expired worthless over a three-year study period.

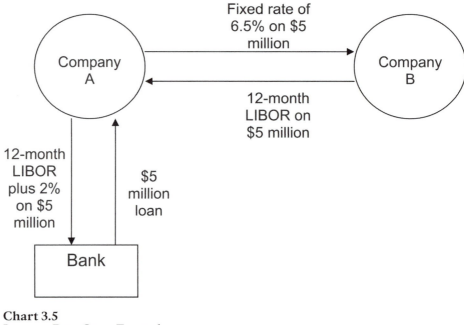

Chart 3.5
Interest Rate Swap Example

as an intermediary between the two parties for a small fee, and all payments will go through these entities. Such financial institutions bring parties together with different needs. For example, Company A wanted to convert an adjustable rate of interest to a fixed rate of interest. Company B wanted to convert a fixed rate of interest to an adjustable rate of interest.

Most swap agreements are entered by companies and sophisticated individual investors to exchange interest rates and foreign currencies. For example, an American company scheduled to receive payments in British pounds for the next two years may want to convert these payments into U.S. dollars through a currency swap agreement. By paying someone a certain amount of British pounds that it receives each month in exchange for fixed payments in U.S. dollars, the company can reduce the risk that British pounds will decline in value and be worth fewer U.S. dollars.

More complex swap agreements can allow parties to exchange the risks that a specific company will default on its securities. For example, a *credit default swap* allows one party to pay another party a payment each month as insurance in case a specific company defaults on its securities. For example, if Company X owns the bonds of Company Y, it may enter a credit default swap with Bank Z to guarantee payment on Company Y's bonds. Company X will

👤 GUESS WHAT?

In 2007, the credit default swap market was valued at $62 trillion (www.moneyhowstuff works.com). The massive size of this unregulated market has caused concern for many industry and economic professionals.

make periodic payments to Bank Z. In return, if Company Y defaults on its bonds, Bank Z will pay Company X for its loss.

Financial derivatives can have devastating effects, and billions of dollars have been lost from such instruments. While derivatives can be used to reduce risk, they can also be used for speculative purposes. Many investors will create extremely complicated positions by buying and selling various financial derivatives at one time. When people gamble and bet on the direction of certain markets or securities using financial derivatives, they can make or lose tremendous sums of money.

While few individual investors will enter swap, option, or futures contracts, some of the investment companies and funds that you purchase may use such instruments. When assessing a particular investment, investors should consider the complexities and risks associated with the strategies being employed.

Hedge Funds

Hedge funds are private investment vehicles that are normally open to a limited number of wealthy individuals and financial institutions. Most hedge funds are unregulated because they cater to sophisticated investors that must meet minimum income or net worth thresholds. Hedge funds employ more aggressive investment strategies when compared to many other types of funds.

Hedge funds are exempt from many of the rules and regulations governing many other types of investments, so they often provide very limited information to their investors. Most hedge funds set extremely high minimum investment amounts ranging anywhere from $250,000 to more than $1 million. Managers of hedge funds usually receive an ongoing management fee ranging from 1 to 3 percent of a fund's net asset value and a percentage of the fund's profits (i.e., 20%).

Hedge funds employ investment strategies that may include the use of large amounts of debt and financial derivatives. Each hedge fund will typically focus on a particular investment strategy, which will be described within the offering documents used to sell shares to investors. For example, a fund may focus on buying and selling distressed notes and bonds at substantial discounts in hopes of earning abnormally high profits. Others may create complex strategies using numerous financial derivative contracts to bet on market movements.

Many funds focus on *short selling,* which consists of selling securities that they do not own. Rather, they borrow the securities from brokerage firms and other financial institutions. They then sell the securities with the obligation to purchase and replace them at some point in time. People will short sell a

🗣 GUESS WHAT?

Nick Leeson was an employee of Barings Bank. He lost well over $1 billion by making unauthorized trades using financial derivatives. Barings was founded in 1762 and for centuries was considered one of the most stable banks in the world. Based upon Mr. Leeson's actions, Barings became insolvent and was forced to declare bankruptcy.

During the 2008 financial crisis that threatened the stability of the entire U.S. financial system, the SEC took what it called "emergency action" and temporarily banned investors from short selling the stocks of about 800 financial companies. So many investors were short selling these stocks that prices were rapidly declining. In addition, critics accused some investors of spreading false rumors about certain financial companies in order to push their stock prices lower and make money on short sale positions.

security when they believe that the price is going to decline and that it can be purchased at a later date for a lower price. For example, assume that Company F's common stock is selling for $25 a share today, and you think its price will significantly decline over the next few months. You then borrow 100 shares of Company F's stock from a brokerage firm for a small fee and sell the stock for $2,500 (100 shares at $25 per share). Two months later, Company F's stock price has declined dramatically, and you are able to buy 100 shares for $10 per share or $1,000. You then return the shares borrowed from the brokerage firm. You just made a profit of $1,500 (less the cost to the brokerage firm for borrowing the shares). Of course, if Company F's stock price had risen to over $25 per share, you could have lost a large amount of money.

Hedge funds do engage in very risky investment strategies. However, most hedge funds enter many offsetting positions to protect or *hedge* their investment holdings. This concept is based on taking investment positions that are expected to perform differently from one another so that if one position loses money, another is making money and offsetting the loss.

Private Equity Funds

Private equity funds are another investment vehicle used by wealthy individuals and financial institutions to diversify their portfolios and to provide opportunities to earn significant profits. Like hedge funds and as required by law, individual investors usually need to meet minimum income or net worth thresholds prior to investing in private equity funds.

Private equity firms raise money from investors for specific funds. These funds are not publicly traded on a stock ex change, and your invested dollars can be tied up for several years or longer. Each fund usually has a primary and specialized investment strategy. Following are some of the general strategies employed by private equity funds.

Venture Capital—As will be discussed in a later chapter , venture capital firms often make investments in startup and immature businesses. In return

While difficult to estimate due to the limited reporting provided by hedge funds, according to the *AIMA Roadmap to Hedge Funds*, during the summer of 2008, hedge funds may have been managing around $2.5 trillion in various types of assets.

for their investment, venture capital firms are usually given an ownership position in these companies. Such ownership gives venture capitalist firms varying levels of control over the direction of a business and can provide huge profits if the business is successful.

Traditional venture capital financing has been associated with the technology industries. Venture capital firms have been known for making substantial investments in Internet-based, medical and data processing companies. But venture capital firms will consider investing in most industries where the potential for rapid growth exists. These firms provide early financing for businesses that are usually unable to obtain bank loans or issue securities. Venture capital firms seek to reap profits in a target company either through the sale of stock when listed on a public stock exchange or through the sale of all or a portion of the company.

Buyout Strategies—Private equity funds will buy companies from their existing shareholders often by borrowing a substantial amount of the money and increasing the amount of debt owed by the company upon purchase. For example, if the common stock of a particular company is selling at a historically low price, a private equity firm may see an opportunity and attempt to buy the company. It may do so by borrowing money from banks and by selling bonds and other types of securities to raise money to buy all or a controlling amount of the common stock from existing shareholders. Because these types of buyouts often require a substantial amount of debt, or *financial leverage,* they are referred to as *leveraged buyouts* (LBOs).

Companies may sell themselves to private equity firms voluntarily or involuntarily. The management of a company may believe that selling to a private equity firm is in the best interest of its shareholders. In this case, management works to negotiate the best price and terms before having shareholders approve the transaction. If management is unwilling to negotiate with a private equity firm, a *hostile takeover* may be pursued. In this case, a private equity firm will bypass a company's management team and offer to buy the common stock from shareholders directly. If a private equity firm can buy the majority of a company's stock, it can then take control of the company.

Once in control of a company, private equity firms may layoff employees and cut other costs, replace management teams and board of directors, sell assets, and make other dramatic changes to increase the profitability of the company. Buyout strategies focus on inefficient and undervalued companies. Private equity firms target opportunities often ignored by prior management teams to increase the value of a company. Usually a plan is put in place prior

🗨 GUESS WHAT?

Federated Department Stores became the target of a hostile leveraged buyout by Robert Campeau, a Canadian financier who paid a huge premium and a total price tag for the company of about $6.5 billion. Approximately 97 percent of the purchase price was raised by having the company issue various forms of debt. The transaction closed in 1988, and the company filed bankruptcy in 1989 due to its inability to make interest payments to its lenders.

to purchase that will improve the company's operations and profitability so that all or portions of the company can be sold for a large profit. A private equity firm hopes to exit its position by selling stock, specific assets, or the entire company at a significantly higher price than its original investment.

Distressed Lending and Investment—When businesses are struggling, raising money can be a problem. Some private equity funds take advantage of such situations by lending money to distressed companies at very high rates of interest. As an additional incentive, private equity funds may receive warrants or other types of equity ownership in return for lending money. Such rights may allow private equity funds to buy common stock or to convert their debt into common stock at later dates at discounted prices. If the distressed companies can use the money received to turn around their operations, the private equity funds are well compensated. If a borrower ultimately fails, private equity funds are often willing to invest more money and take control of the company under favorable terms.

Private equity funds may also purchase an ownership position in a troubled company. Many companies in need of cash are forced to sell stock and other forms of ownership at very low prices or risk having to file bankruptcy. In return for such investments, private equity funds may receive seats on a company's board of directors, voting rights, and the ability to buy an additional portion of the company at a discounted price in the future.

Real Estate Strategies—The real estate investments targeted by private equity firms are usually more complicated and riskier than traditional real estate investments. Most of the properties acquired by private equity funds require some form of development or improvement. Private equity firms will usually borrow as much money as possible to finance their property purchases. In addition, because private equity funds have so much money to invest, they usually focus on larger property acquisitions.

Properties that are subperforming due to slow sales, high vacancies, and low lease rates, or that need major renovations and overhauls, can provide significant upside potential. Many private equity funds purchase such properties, lend to real estate operators and investors, or buy existing loans or securities that are collateralized by real estate at discounted prices.

Commodities

Materials that are sold in bulk in the financial markets are called commodities. Examples include gold, silver, copper and other precious metals, oil, natural gas, oranges, pork bellies, wheat, corn, and cocoa. Commodities are generally raw materials that are used to produce other products. Manufacturers buy commodities as needed for production. Investors also buy commodities as investments.

🗣 GUESS WHAT?

According to the Private Equity Council, there are 2,150 private equity firms worldwide. These firms made investments of $234 billion in the year 2007 and raised $341 billion in 2008.

Commodities such as gold are bought and sold daily on large financial exchanges around the world. AP Photo/Seth Wenig.

Commodities trade in financial markets just like stocks trade on a stock exchange. For example, the Chicago Board of Trade (CBOT) focuses on trading grains such as corn, wheat, oats, and rice. The New York Mercantile Exchange (NYMEX) is best known for trading energy and metals such as crude oil, natural gas, silver, and platinum. Commodities can be purchased and sold at current prices in what is referred to as the *spot market,* or they can be bought and sold using financial derivatives to guarantee a certain price at some point in the future.

Investors buy commodities for several reasons. When high inflation causes the prices of goods and services to rise quickly, many commodity prices also rise. During periods of high inflation, many stocks and bonds perform poorly. Therefore, owning commodities can lead to enhanced investment profitability during inflationary periods. Because factors that affect commodity prices tend to be unrelated to factors affecting the values of most stocks and bonds, owning commodities can increase portfolio diversification.

Some investors speculate with commodity investing and try to buy low and sell high. When an economy is strong and growing, commodity prices can soar as consumer and business demand for production increases. When an economy is slowing, commodity prices tend to decline because there will be less demand for the ultimate products that use the commodities. Betting on commodity markets using financial derivatives can expose an investor to tremendous risks.

Commodity values can change quickly and significantly based upon specific demand and economic cycles. Chart 3.6 shows the profits and losses investors would have earned in prior years from owning a commodities index that includes an assortment of various commodities.

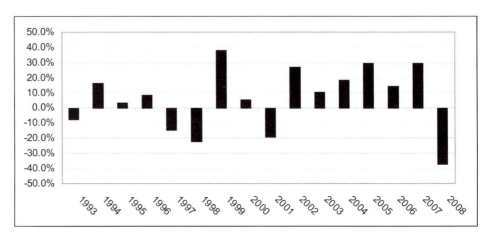

Chart 3.6
Historical Commodity Prices

Source: Indexmundi.com

AVOIDING INVESTMENT SCAMS

Unethical people make a living from stealing money from others. Investment scams come in all shapes and sizes, but their underlying objective is to take or *scam* money from you. The people selling them look and sound educated and professional and are often very friendly and have great interpersonal skills. Scam artists are also very sneaky in how they reach and convince you to act.

You can lose all of your savings to a financial scam, but most con artists focus on smaller dollar amounts from each member of a much larger targeted audience. Scams can include fake magazine subscriptions, fees related to scholarships and grants, phony lottery winnings, and nonexistent investment opportunities offering unrealistic profits. Con artists have no morals and often try to hide behind religious and other reputable community organizations.

Sweetheart swindles are examples of investment scams whereby con artists nurture relationships with people, usually through Internet chat rooms and dating sites, so that they can convince the victim to send them money one or more times. Another form of fraud is when a con artist sends a victim a fake check in return for wiring him money. The con artist receives the stolen money before the victim receives the returned check from the bank and realizes that it was fraudulent.

The terms *spoofing* or *phishing* refer to fishing for confidential information so that identity theft and credit card and bank fraud can be committed. Usually an e-mail is sent to a person from a phony government agency, financial

GUESS WHAT?

Amaranth Advisors was a U.S. hedge fund that was managing approximately $9 billion in assets. In 2006, the company collapsed after losing roughly $6 billion in a single week betting on natural gas futures contracts. This failure was the largest in hedge fund history.

institution, or other reputable organization requesting that confidential information be verified or corrected. Once this information is obtained, the crook can assume the victim's identity or access his or her accounts.

The growth of the Internet has helped to increase the number of scams and allowed con artists to reach a much broader group of people very quickly at little cost. Building Web sites, creating pop-up messages, sending mass e-mails, and entering chat rooms are ways to reach huge audiences. The Internet has also allowed crooks to become more creative with the ways that they approach and convince unsuspecting victims. Many messages look credible, and it is difficult for readers to determine what is real and what is not.

The National Consumer League released its list of Top-10 Internet Frauds for the year 2007 as follows:

1. Fake Check Scams
2. General Merchandise
3. Auctions
4. Nigerian Money Offers
5. Lotteries
6. Advance Fee Loans/Credit Arrangers
7. Prizes/Sweepstakes/Free Gifts
8. Phishing/Spoofing
9. Sweetheart Swindles
10. Internet Access Services

The National Consumer League released its list of Top-10 Telemarketing Frauds for the year 2007 as follows:

1. Fake Check Scams
2. Prizes/Sweepstakes/Free Gifts
3. Advance Fee Loans/Credit Arrangers
4. Lotteries/Lottery Ticket Buying Clubs
5. Phishing/Spoofing
6. Magazines
7. Credit Card Issuing
8. Scholarships/Educational Grants
9. Buyers Clubs
10. Nigerian Money Offers

For more information on these scams and how they work, visit the National Consumer League's Web site at www.natlconsumersleague.org.

↗ BEWARE!

Federal statistics show that Americans reported losing almost $200 million from Internet fraud in the year 2006. For more tips about how to avoid online fraud, read Internet Fraud: *How to Avoid Internet Scams* by visiting the Securities and Exchange Commission (SEC) at www.sec.gov/investor/pubs/cyberfraud.htm or by calling (800) SEC-0330.

⚡ BEWARE!

Even the wealthiest and most sophisticated investors can fall subject to an investment scam. In 2008, Bernard Madoff, the owner of a highly regarded New York investment firm and a former chairman of the Nasdaq stock exchange, admitted to defrauding investors of approximately $50 billion. Madoff's victims included charities, celebrity actors and athletes, money mangers, hedge funds, and some of the largest financial institutions in the world.

Following are some suggested actions when considering an investment that will help avoid investment scams:

1. Always recognize that any deal that looks too good to be true most likely is too good to be true. Realize that most unsolicited e-mails offering investments, lottery winnings, and so forth are fraudulent.
2. All investments have risk. Any investment using terms such as *no risk* or *guaranteed return* are fraudulent. Avoid or heavily scrutinize investments that offer spectacular profits in short periods of time.
3. Never make immediate on-the-spot decisions.
4. Always check the licenses and reputations of any company or individual offering investment products.
5. Anything you consider should be in written format. Never give anyone money based upon a verbal promise or commitment. Ask any telemarketers to follow-up with something in writing by mail. If invited to any sales seminars, social events, or to invest by phone, always ask for the details in writing.

The story of Bernard Madoff shows that even sophisticated investors can be swindled by crooks with a good story. AP Photo/Louis Lanzano.

6. Always research the specific investment by reading offering memorandums and prospectuses, company financial statements, and other relevant information. If you do not feel qualified to review such materials, ask someone that you trust to do so for you (i.e., a CPA or financial advisor).
7. Never respond to any unsolicited inquiries requesting personal information regardless of how credible the source appears. In particular, never provide your social security, passport, or driver's license numbers, or any online passwords or other personal information that can be used for identity theft. Forward any such e-mail solicitations to the SEC at enforcement@sec.gov.
8. Never make any payments payable to a salesperson. Always make your payment to the investment company.
9. Check your account statements carefully, and make sure that you are receiving them at least quarterly. Ask questions when needed, and ensure that an official company address is included on each statement.
10. Be knowledgeable and understand how various types of investments work. Most victims of fraud are financially illiterate.

The Better Business Bureau offers an extensive list of financial resources to aid investors in locating reputable financial advisors, researching investments, reporting complaints, and for general investing information. You can visit its Web site at www.bbb.org.

4

Principals of Investing

While it is important to save, it is equally important to make wise investment decisions. Keeping all of your money in bank products such as savings accounts and certificates of deposit will most likely lead to substantially lower compounding and a significantly smaller amount of total savings down the road. Having a diverse portfolio of stocks, bonds, real estate, and other securities can significantly increase investor profits and actually lower risk.

But the higher earning investments such as stocks, bonds, and real estate tend to encompass greater levels of risk, which can lead to lower investment profitability and increase the chances of loss. So why would you even consider such investments? The key is to pursue higher profits while mitigating risk.

RISK VERSUS RETURN

One of the underlying principles of investing is based upon the relationship between risk and return. The *risk* associated with an investment can be defined as the probability of earning an expected profit. For example, if you deposit $1,000 into a savings account at your local bank, you would expect this to be a low-risk investment. Banks are generally conservative, and savings accounts are guaranteed by the federal government up to a certain dollar amount. If the bank promises to pay you a 2 percent annual interest rate, the chances are great that at the end of one year you will have $1,020. Thus, there is a high probability that you will earn a 2 percent annual profit, and this would be considered a low-risk investment.

🗩 GUESS WHAT?

If someone saved $500 a month for 30 years and earned an average annual return of 8 percent, at the end of this period he would have $745,180. If the same $500 a month was invested for 30 years and earned only 3 percent, the investor would have only $291,368. Choosing the right investments will have a huge effect on your total net worth and your quality of life!

Now let us consider a riskier investment. Assume that you purchase 40 shares of Microsoft Corporation common stock for $25 a share or $1,000. On average and over the long term, Microsoft's stock price may be expected to increase by 10 percent per year. However, this is a much riskier investment than a bank savings account. While Microsoft's stock price may rise at an average rate of 10 percent per year when measured using a 10-year period, the stock price may be very volatile when measured in shorter-term increments. For example, in one year the stock price may fall by 15 percent. In another year, it may rise by 25 percent. To assume an average price increase of 10 percent, investors need to consider longer time periods. For this investment, there is much less probability that the investor will earn 10 percent during a one-year period and a much greater chance that the investor could lose a portion of his investment. Therefore, because Microsoft stock is a much higher risk investment when compared to a bank savings account, investors should be rewarded with higher expected profits when buying Microsoft stock.

The *return* provided from an investment can be defined as the total profitability earned by an investor. This can include appreciation in value and any current payments received in the form of dividends and interest. For example, assume that you purchase shares in a mutual fund for $1,000 at the beginning of the year. Also assume that during the year, you receive checks totaling $30 in dividends that are paid by the fund. If at the end of the year you sell your investment for $1,060, you have earned an annual return of 9 percent. This total annual return is computed by taking the $30 in cash dividends received plus the $60 in appreciation earned when the investment was sold, divided by your $1,000 initial investment ($90 divided by $1,000 = 9%).

When comparing two investments, if one has more risk than the other, the more risky investment should be expected to generate a greater return to the investor. Risk can come from several sources. The longer the term or length of an investment, the greater the risk. For example, a bond issued by a corporation that requires repayment in 1 year has substantially less risk than a bond issued by the same corporation that requires repayment in 10 years. There is more uncertainty over the 10-year period. The company has more time to default on its obligations, there could be management fraud, intense competition could cause the company's prospects to deteriorate, and so forth. In addition, the interest rate being paid to the investor during the 10-year period may become too low over time when compared to other investment alternatives.

Credit Strength

Due to the many types of issuers of securities, there are different levels of risk associated with each one. When the U.S. federal government issues securities,

🔊 GUESS WHAT?

The credit rating of the United States is "AAA" (referred to as "triple-A"), which is the highest rating awarded. Most credit rating scales go from AAA (being excellent) and move downward in increments to something substantially lower like "C" or "D" (which means that whatever is being rated is currently in or about to default). An investment-grade rating is considered to be BBB− ("triple-B minus") or above. Anything below this rating (i.e., BB+, BB, BB−, B+, and below) is considered to be noninvestment grade. Some institutional investors have guidelines that allow them to purchase only investment-grade securities.

The General Electric Company was ranked by *Forbes* **in 2009 as the world's largest company.** During the same year, the company's credit rating was cut one notch from "AAA" to "AA+" because of concerns of losses within its finance unit. The lower credit rating makes it more expensive for the company to borrow money. AP Photo/Paul Sakuma.

such as bills, notes, and bonds, they are viewed as being backed by the highest credit strength available. This is because the U.S. government is considered the strongest issuing entity in existence. Other countries and governments sell securities to investors, but those issued by the United States make up the largest and most credit-worthy markets.

One way of receiving an unbiased, third-party assessment of an issuer's credit worthiness is to look at the issuer's credit rating (although some issuers are not rated). There are three primary credit rating agencies located in the United States that issue ratings on securities, companies, and countries around the globe. Standard & Poor's (often just referred to as S&P), Moody's Investors Service, and Fitch Ratings are the three most popular rating agencies.

There are additional ratings sources for other investment products as well. For example, A. M. Best Company is a great provider of ratings for insurance companies, and this resource should be used when purchasing various types of insurance and annuity contracts. Morningstar is a great ratings provider when looking to purchase stocks, mutual funds, annuities, and even college savings plans. Each rating agency maintains its own ratings symbols and methodologies. I encourage you to visit the Web sites of each rating agency to get a better idea of the actual ratings and how the ratings process works.

Liquidity

The *liquidity* of an investment can also lead to more or less risk. Investments that cannot be sold quickly result in more risk to their investors. Those that require substantial discounts in price in order to be sold or that result in large transaction costs are also considered to be illiquid. As previously mentioned, real estate is usually considered to be an illiquid asset. It takes time to buy and sell real estate, and there is substantial expense associated with realtor commissions and closing costs. In addition, if someone wants to sell a building or piece of land quickly, the price will normally need to be discounted in order to attract a buyer. Some investments, such as private equity and hedge funds, do not permit investors to sell or liquidate their investments for a specified period of time.

Type of Security

Different types of investments being offered by the same company will have more risk than others. For example, a company's bonds have less risk than its preferred stock, and its preferred stock has less risk than its common stock. This is because when a company experiences financial difficulties, the first people to be paid are the bondholders. If any money is left over, the preferred stockholders are paid next. If any funds remain after the preferred stockholders are repaid, they are distributed to the common stockholders. When there is a shortfall, the common stockholders lose some or all of their investment before anyone else. Therefore, investors will expect higher returns from preferred stock when compared to bonds and from common stock when compared to preferred stock. Chart 4.1 illustrates this relationship.

As indicated in Chart 4.1, different types of securities have differing levels of risk, and the greater the expected risk, the higher the returns that should be expected by investors.

DIVERSIFICATION

While it is important to understand the dynamics of each specific investment instrument, it is even more important to see the forest from the trees and understand how all of your individual investment components interact with one

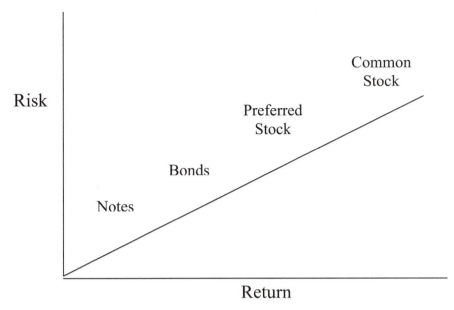

Chart 4.1
Security Risk Versus Return

another under changing economic and market conditions. For example, just because your stock mutual fund is down for the year, it does not mean that your total portfolio or net worth has declined. Often times when stocks are performing poorly, other investments are performing more favorably. Declining U.S. stock markets may become the focal point of most investors, but your bond, real estate, and international stock portfolios may be up for the year. One of the key aspects of any investment strategy is diversification.

Asset Class Diversification

When selecting investments, you will want to diversify by asset class. An *asset class* can be generally defined as a broad group of assets, such as equity (stocks and other forms of ownership interests), fixed income (bills, notes, bonds, annuities, etc.), real estate (such as office and apartment buildings), and commodities (like gold and oil), that share one or more common characteristic.

🗨 GUESS WHAT?

The main concept surrounding the benefits of diversification is based upon spreading the wealth and not putting too many eggs into one basket. When one investment is down, another two investments might be up and vice versa. For example, U.S. bonds and foreign stocks might be performing exceptionally well in a given period, while U.S. stocks and real estate may have declined in value. Over the long run, these differences tend to meld together as some investments perform better or worse in certain years. The end result should be an upward sloping trend that shows your profits and net worth continuing to increase.

If a person's total portfolio is narrowly invested within only one asset class, such as owning just the common stocks of large U.S. companies, then the individual is betting that large U.S. companies will consistently perform better than small- and medium-sized companies and all other broad domestic and foreign asset classes such as fixed income, real estate, commodities, and so forth. A portfolio owning U.S. and international large, mid and small cap stocks, bonds, and real estate would have much better asset class diversification.

However, an asset class can be broken down more granularly to include individual investment instruments. For example, the definition of a fixed income asset class can include all types of bonds among other investments. However, as discussed, there are numerous types of bonds, and not all bonds perform the same under different economic and market conditions. For example, bonds issued by the U.S. government are perceived as being virtually *risk free* due to the stability and financial strength of the United States. High-yield bonds are considered to be much riskier, and the companies that sell such bonds have a much higher chance of defaulting than would the U.S. government.

Often when the economy is under duress and uncertainty, many investors will purchase U.S. government securities due to their perceived safety (sometimes referred to as a *flight to quality*). This increased demand will cause the prices of the government securities to rise, and they will increase in value. Under similar economic circumstances, investors become concerned about the quality of corporate high-yield bonds, and demand for these securities begins to lessen, thus causing their values to decline. This example illustrates the fact that the various investments defined under a broad asset class can lead to significantly different performance results. During the same investment period, an investor may make money from owning government bonds, while at the same time he may lose money from his investment in high-yield bonds.

Geographic Diversification

History has proven over and over that a region or entire country can experience hardships due to poor economic variables, abnormal geographic weather conditions and natural disasters, political decisions, and tragedies such as terrorist attacks. By limiting the investments within a portfolio to local, regional,

Global investing is an important aspect of portfolio diversification. By investing only within your home country, you are essentially ignoring the rest of the world. Just as there are countless investment opportunities within your own country, there are limitless opportunities in countries abroad. The economy in the U.S. might be in recession, while many European or Asian economies are thriving. Having a portion of your portfolio invested in companies operating in other countries can provide enhanced diversification and potentially higher returns and lower risk.

Investing in different regions of the world can provide significant geographic diversification and attractive investment returns. This is an aerial photo of the city of Hong Kong. AP Photo/Anat Givon.

or even country-specific areas, an investor is taking on an unnecessary amount of risk, while at the same time, missing many suitable investment opportunities that could generate additional profits.

Industry Diversification

On a more micro-basis, crafting a portfolio to have sufficient industry diversification is crucial. Some industries move in cycles, which mean that they naturally move up and down depending upon demand for their products. For example, when residential real estate values are high, the stocks of home building companies do very well. When uncertainty and an excess inventory of homes exist, the stocks of these companies tend to perform poorly.

Some industries are more dependent upon other industries and economic variables than others. The demand for appliances is often tied to the amount of new construction taking place. If builders are building fewer homes, they will need less refrigerators, dishwashers, and ovens. The demand for luxury items like jewelry and high-end automobiles is directly tied to the strength of the economy and consumer confidence.

⚡ BEWARE!

The Nasdaq Composite stock market index tracks companies that operate primarily within the technology industry. Throughout the mid and late 1990s, investors became crazed over the Internet and the prospects for new technology growth. The stocks of companies that were expecting to lose money for years to come were being bought at ridiculous prices. Countless people moved money from other investments into the technology sector in fear of missing a fast ride to riches. But as people began to think more rationally, many poorly run companies with unrealistic business plans began souring, and technology stocks plummeted. From peak to trough during the years 2000 through 2002, the Nasdaq stock market lost about 78 percent of its value. Over six years later, the Nasdaq was still over 65 percent lower than its peak value reached in March of 2000. The bursting of the "dot-com" bubble is a perfect example that stresses the need for investors to diversify among industries.

Term Diversification

Remember to also diversify your portfolio by maturity or term. As mentioned, longer-term investments usually have greater risk when compared to comparable shorter-term investments. When cash is being saved for short-term needs, emergencies, and unexpected events, this money should be invested in short-term investments such as money market and short-term bond funds.

Some term diversification will be achieved in part when diversifying by asset class. Each asset class or subcategory of an asset class will be a longer- or shorter-term investment. For example, stocks and stock funds have no maturity dates and are usually considered to be long-term investments. On the other hand, bonds and bond funds have specified maturity dates or average maturity dates. By diversifying between stocks and bonds, you have already achieved a level of term diversification.

When looking at individual investments, do not tie up too much of your money in securities or investments that are difficult to sell (illiquid). For example, you would not want the majority of your investments to be in private, long-term real estate transactions when you have a pending college tuition payment. You will need to allocate your investment choices between those that can meet expected and unexpected cash needs and those that can provide long-term profit and growth opportunities.

Issuer Diversification

Investing a significant amount of your portfolio into a single company or issuer is not a prudent decision. Sure, you could hit a home run and make a fantastic return by buying the stock of that one company that takes off. However, the odds are against you, and there is usually a much higher probability that you can create a more balanced portfolio that has significantly less risk and a far better chance of earning higher profits.

Chart 4.2 illustrates one of the fundamental principals of investing. Owning the securities of only a few issuers, whether it be stocks, bonds, or other investment instruments, exposes an investor's portfolio to an unacceptable level of risk.

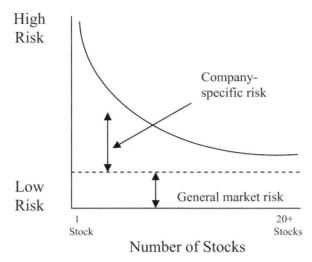

High
Risk

Company-
specific risk

Low
Risk

General market risk

1
Stock

20+
Stocks

Number of Stocks

Chart 4.2
Company-specific Versus General Market Risk

To truly understand and appreciate the message being displayed in Chart 4.2, we first need to talk more about risk. When buying the securities of individual companies, there are two primary sources of risk. The first is *company-specific risk,* which applies to any type of security being issued by a particular company. This is the risk that an investor assumes when buying the securities of an individual issuer.

By owning the securities of multiple companies, you can diversify away the company-specific risk. As shown in Chart 4.2, when an investor owns just one stock, her risk is very high. This is because of all of the company-specific risk factors. However, as the stocks of additional companies are added to her portfolio, the company-specific risk gets lower and lower. If one company is performing poorly, there are many other companies that can offset this weakness. Some companies will do better, and some companies will do worse during specific periods. In general, stocks tend to increase in value over time. The diversification provided from owning multiple stocks allows an investor to average the total returns from the various companies, significantly lower investment risk, and take advantage of long-term increases in stock prices.

After enough companies are added to a portfolio, the company-specific risk becomes minimal, and what remains is primarily *general market risk.* This is the second type of risk highlighted in Chart 4.2.

🗣 GUESS WHAT?

Examples of company-specific risk include events that can affect an individual company such as management fraud, labor strikes, and missed earnings projections. Companies are also subject to risks such as bad weather, regional slow downs, and currency and political risk from foreign operations. When you buy the securities of one company, you are exposed to all of these company-specific risks.

🗩 GUESS WHAT?

General market risk is a risk that cannot be diversified away by adding additional securities. This is the risk of one or more global events affecting the securities of most companies (i.e., significantly moving an entire stock or bond market). For example, a recession, depression, or major terrorist attack will cause the vast majority of an entire stock market to decline. There is no way to avoid this risk if you are invested solely in stocks. However, you can reduce the general market risk associated with a particular asset class by diversifying among additional asset classes.

Diversification Examples

When comparing investment alternatives, it may be difficult to imagine a portfolio that can achieve higher returns and at the same time have lower risk, but I will illustrate this relationship using a couple tables from my first book.

Look at Tables 4.1 and 4.2 to better understand how portfolio diversification works. Table 4.1 shows four hypothetical portfolios. Each portfolio is invested solely in one asset class. Company-specific risk can be virtually eliminated in each of these portfolios (Portfolio 4 is invested in all cash, so there is no risk), assuming they own a diversified mix of securities.

Listed in the table are the expected annual returns for each asset class. As expected, the greater the risk, the greater the expected return. Bonds are more risky than cash, real estate generally has more risk than bonds, and stocks encompass more risk than all of the three other portfolios. The more risk assumed, the greater should be the expected returns.

Table 4.1 uses the term *probability* to reflect the risk of each asset class. For example, Portfolio 1 is invested completely in stocks and is expected to earn an annual return of 15 percent. However, the probability of earning a 15 percent annual return is only 60 percent. This is because stock prices, when measured on an annual basis, are very volatile. As discussed, stocks are long-term investments, and their prices will often move up and down dramatically when measured on a short-term basis. In this example, the annual return may be substantially higher or lower than 15 percent in a given year.

Due to the high amount of volatility and risk associated with a 100 percent stock portfolio, a prudent investor will want to diversify some of this risk away by investing in additional asset classes. Now let us look at Table 4.2 and see

Table 4.1
Nondiversified Portfolios

	Portfolio 1	*Portfolio 2*	*Portfolio 3*	*Portfolio 4*
	Stocks	*Bonds*	*Real Estate*	*Cash*
Percentage of Portfolio	100.0%	100.0%	100.0%	100.0%
Expected Annual Return	15.0%	7.0%	12.0%	5.0%
Probability	60.0%	80.0%	70.0%	100.0%

Table 4.2
Diversified Portfolio

	Portfolio 5			
	Stocks	*Bonds*	*Real Estate*	*Cash*
Percentage of Portfolio	40.0%	35.0%	20.0%	5.0%
Expected Annual Return	12.5%			
Probability	85.0%			

how the risk and expected return parameters change when a more diversified portfolio is created using multiple asset classes.

Table 4.2 shows the additional benefits of diversifying a portfolio by combining different asset classes. Portfolio 5 holds investments in stocks, bonds, real estate, and cash. By combining these different assets classes into one portfolio, the market risk associated with each individual asset class can be reduced.

Notice the key differences between the portfolios shown in Table 4.1 and the portfolio shown in Table 4.2. If you invested solely in bonds (Portfolio 2), you would have an 80 percent probability of earning a 7 percent annual return. If you invested only in real estate (Portfolio 3), you would have a 70 percent probability of earning a 12 percent annual return. However, when you combine asset classes in Portfolio 5, you now have an 85 percent probability of earning a 12.5 percent annual return. By diversifying among asset classes, your portfolio now has lower risk and a higher expected return than had you invested solely in bonds or real estate. In addition, while the expected return of Portfolio 5 is not as high as the expected return of Portfolio 1, from a risk versus return perspective, you have given up a relatively small amount of expected return in exchange for a substantial reduction in risk.

ACTIVE AND PASSIVE INVESTING

Two primary investment strategies include active and passive management approaches. An *active* investment strategy is employed when an investor or fund manager uses forecasting tools, assumptions, and research to determine which securities to buy and sell and when. Active investing is intended to *beat the market,* meaning that by choosing individual securities, an investor can earn greater returns than a general benchmark or market index. Active investors tend to buy and sell securities more often than passive investors as they focus more on timing investment opportunities (i.e., buying low and selling high).

Actively managed funds have professional managers with staffs of analysts that select specific securities to buy and sell at specific times. For example, a large cap stock fund manager may view the financial sector as being undervalued and choose to buy the stocks of certain banks that she feels will have superior performance. In addition, she may feel that the auto industry is overpriced and may choose to sell or not purchase any stocks of automobile manufacturers.

Specific companies and industries are constantly being reviewed by active fund managers in an attempt to determine which companies to buy, sell, and avoid at certain times. Active investing is the art of security picking and market timing.

A *passive* investment strategy is based upon a buy and hold approach. Passive investors own the same securities that make up a market index. Passive investors generally believe that they have a better chance of earning higher returns by investing in a general market index than by trying to select specific securities. These investors believe that most active investors and fund managers will not consistently beat the market. There is little buying and selling of securities under a passive investment strategy.

A passive investment strategy relies on the purchase of index funds. Because market indexes are designed to simply track a group of securities without attempting to identify more or less attractive securities, this investment strategy is passive. It is essentially a *buy and hold* approach to investing. The performance of a particular index fund is essentially equal to the performance of the general market that the index is tracking. For example, if you purchase shares in an S&P 500 index fund, and the S&P 500 Index earns 10 percent for the year, your index fund will earn approximately 10 percent as well.

Before talking more about the pros and cons of active versus passive management, let us discuss some specific investment products that will further differentiate these two strategies.

Active Investment Products

Managed Bond Mutual Funds—A managed bond mutual fund has a professional investment manager and staff that is responsible for researching and choosing which fixed income investments to purchase and when to buy and sell these securities. Depending upon the fund's investment objectives and the types of fixed income securities targeted, the fund's performance will be compared to a relevant index. For example, the performance of a broad-based, actively managed bond fund might be compared to the performance of the Barclays Capital U.S. Aggregate Bond Index.

Managed Stock Mutual Funds—A managed stock mutual fund has a professional investment manager and staff that is responsible for researching and choosing which stocks to purchase and when to buy and sell these securities. The performance of a managed stock fund is measured in comparison to a relevant index. For example, a managed stock fund that has a primary investment strategy of purchasing U.S. large cap stocks would most likely be compared to the S&P 500 Index. The investment manager responsible for this fund would strive to generate higher returns than the S&P 500 each year, which he may or may not achieve.

Managed Investment Portfolios—Many wealthy investors pay a money manager to manage a portfolio of investments for them. Such specialized attention usually requires a fairly large investment amount. In such cases, there is a specific money manager assigned to your account, and based on your investment parameters, he or she chooses appropriate investments that are targeted to maximize returns. Chosen investments usually include variations of international and domestic common stock and fixed income investments.

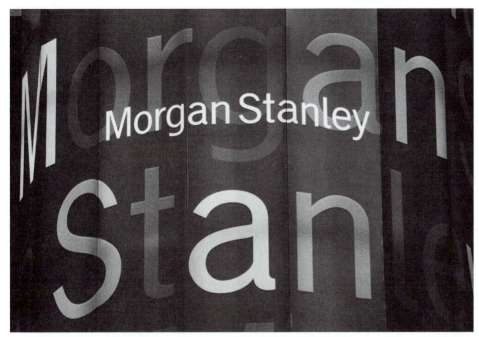

Investments firms such as Morgan Stanley offer numerous active investment products and strategies to clients. AP Photo/Mark Lennihan.

Certain investment sectors may be targeted based on the money manager's outlook for specific industries and the general economy. For example, she may invest more or less of your money during a certain period in companies operating in sectors such as natural resources, health care, financial services, or technology.

Passive Investment Products

Bond Index Funds—A bond index fund is a mutual fund or exchange traded fund that attempts to mirror the performance of a specific bond market index. A bond index fund will buy the same bonds and in the same percentages as the targeted index. Indexes created by investment banks, brokerage houses, and financial reporting entities serve to measure the performance of specific markets.

Consider the Barclays Capital U.S Aggregate Bond Index. You cannot buy shares in this index directly, but you can buy shares in index funds that attempt to hold the same securities and allocations and mirror its performance (less a small administrative fee). While the Barclays Capital U.S. Aggregate Bond Index is a very broad bond market index, you can also buy shares in other index funds that focus on narrower markets (i.e., solely on short-term government notes and bonds, mid-term investment grade corporate notes and bonds, high yield bonds, international fixed income, etc.).

Stock Index Funds—A stock index fund is a mutual fund or exchange traded fund that attempts to mirror the performance of a specific stock market index. A stock index fund will buy the same stocks and in the same percentages as the targeted index. Stock market index funds own the same stocks as indexes like the Dow Jones Industrial Average, the S&P 500, the Nasdaq Composite, and the Morgan Stanley Country Indexes.

Active Versus Passive Management

There are literally thousands of investment funds available that seek passive and active investment strategies. The majority of all mutual funds are actively managed, but there is a wide selection of mutual index funds. Most ETFs track specific indexes. While such indexed funds are normally considered passive investments, ETFs can be purchased at any time throughout the trading day at current market prices. This allows investors to buy and sell them quickly and use these vehicles for more active strategies when betting on market directions. Alternatively, ETFs can be held long term as passive investments.

Because of the varying investment strategies, fee structures, and performance results, a significant amount of time and effort should go into the selection process when choosing an active and/or passive investment strategy and specific funds.

Fees—The fees charged by actively managed funds are usually substantially more expensive than those charged by index funds. Actively managed funds require a substantial amount of resources to review specific countries, sectors, and companies when deciding which securities to buy and sell. An index fund does not require the services of a professional money manager or any research analysts and, in general, requires a significantly lesser support staff. Computers do most of the work matching the fund to the targeted index.

Tax Obligations—Index funds usually generate less taxable income when compared to actively managed funds. If securities are held and never sold, even if they have substantially increased in value, investors are not required to pay any income taxes on the appreciation until the securities are sold.

Because the investment strategy of an index fund is to essentially buy and hold a portfolio of securities long term, there is much less buying and selling and gain recognition, which results in fewer taxes being due. As will be discussed later, the differing tax implications between active and passive investment strategies can be minimized when using tax-deferred accounts such as 401K plans and individual retirement accounts (IRAs).

Performance—People are usually surprised to hear that most actively managed mutual funds underperform their benchmark indexes. Over the long term more index funds outperform active funds on a consistent basis. This means that more often than not, fund managers are being paid higher fees to actively manage funds that generate higher taxable income and lower returns when compared to the index that they are trying to beat. This is not

🗣 GUESS WHAT?

According to benchmarkfunds.com, the first index portfolio is attributed to Samsonite pension fund, which was created by Wells Fargo Bank in 1971. The creation of the first index fund has been credited to The Vanguard Group in 1976. Since then, index-based investing has gained wider acceptance among all classes of investors.

to say that there are not exceptional actively managed funds that have consistently outperformed their relevant benchmark indexes. However, studies have proven that the majority of actively managed mutual funds do not.

Diversification—When attempting to outperform their index benchmarks, professional fund managers often invest more dollars into specific sectors or industries than their comparable benchmark indexes based on their belief that these companies will perform better than the general market. After all, professional fund managers are getting paid a fee based on their perceived ability to pick better investments than those passively included in a general index fund. In order to do so, they need to buy securities that they think will perform better than the general market and sell or not purchase those securities that they think will underperform the general market. In doing so, active fund managers can have less diversified portfolios when compared to a market index fund, and thus, in some cases, they are assuming more risk.

PERSONAL INVESTMENT OBJECTIVES

One of the first things a professional financial advisor will do is get to know his customer. You cannot recommend specific investments to people until you understand their personal financial objectives. Each of us is different. We all have specific views of the world, and we each have individual circumstances that need to be considered before choosing any investment.

Whether you plan to employ the services of a financial advisor to help you manage your money, or whether you choose to make your own investment decisions, the first step is to understand your unique investment objectives. Here are some of the key factors that every investor should review and assess before making any investment.

Risk Tolerance—We have talked about managing and mitigating risk through diversification so that an investor can earn greater profits while minimizing risk. In addition, investors with longer investment horizons can assume greater risk than those with shorter investment horizons. As investors become older and the time period preceding retirement becomes shorter, more and more assets should be allocated to more conservative investments.

These are the general guidelines for prudent investing. However, each investor must make his own decisions when it comes to risk assumption. For example, while you are aware that the ownership of stocks and other forms of equity can significantly enhance your long-term returns, maybe you do not feel comfortable having most of your money in equity investments.

I certainly do not want anyone laying awake at night worrying about their portfolio. Even though some things may make sense on paper, it is up to each investor to assess his proper comfort level. There is a personal side to investing that must feel right to each investor. Only you can determine your true level of risk tolerance.

Preservation of Capital—Investors need to evaluate their need to preserve invested capital. For example, if you invest $1,000, do you always want your investment to be worth at least $1,000, or are you willing to let it fluctuate in order to achieve higher long-term returns? If you need the money in a day, week, month, or even year, you should invest the money conservatively and focus on preservation of capital. If you do not need the money for 5, 10, or 20 years, you might want to invest in something having more potential risk but greater expected long-term returns.

As a general rule, riskier investments should provide higher returns than investments having less risk. An investment has greater risk when the chances of repayment become less likely and/or when the expected value of an investment has greater volatility. For example, a high-yield bond pays a much higher return to an investor than a bond issued by the U.S. government. This is because the risk to the investor of losing all or a portion of his investment is substantially greater when owning a high-yield bond.

Consider a mutual fund that buys the common stock of small companies operating in less-developed countries (a small cap international fund). One would assume that this investment carries significantly more risk than a mutual fund owning the common stock of large U.S. companies. An investor might purchase shares in this small cap international fund as a means of adding diversification to her total portfolio and to pursue higher expected long-term profits when compared to most of her other investments. However, the investor must realize that the investment value will most likely fluctuate more widely when owning the small cap international fund when compared to owning a large cap U.S. fund.

Current Income—Do you need current income from some or all of your investments? For someone that is retired and relying on monthly income, there should be a strong focus on earning and receiving current and stable income. But if you are young with decades to go before retirement, you can focus more on trying to increase the value of your portfolio over time through capital appreciation. Any income received from your portfolio through sources such as dividends and interest payments can be immediately reinvested and allowed to compound.

When investors spend all of the earnings from their investment portfolio, there is no portfolio appreciation. For example, if an investor's portfolio earns an average return of $5,000 a year and the investor spends an average of $5,000 a year, then her portfolio will remain fairly static each year and not increase or decrease in value. But even though the portfolio is not decreasing in size, it is technically declining in value each year due to the effects of inflation continually eroding the purchasing power of a dollar.

Capital Appreciation—Capital appreciation is a form of profit or return that is derived from an increase in the value of a particular investment or portfolio. For example, if you invested $1,000 two years ago by buying shares in a mutual fund, and your shares are worth $1,200 today, you earned $200 through capital appreciation.

The more capital appreciation that a portfolio experiences, the more earnings that can be generated from the portfolio in the future. This is one of the key reasons why compounding and investing your money over long periods of time is so important. This is also why choosing the right investments is so important as well. If you have 20 or 30 years until retirement, consider investing a significant portion of your portfolio into diversified equity investments rather than lower earning bank and other fixed income products. To state the obvious, a portfolio worth $1,000,000 can generate a lot more income for you to spend before and during retirement than a portfolio worth $500,000.

Liquidity—If you need money in the near term, you should preserve your capital and invest in something short term, such as a money market account, bank certificate of deposit, or short-term bond fund. Such cash savings should be used to prepare for the expected and reserve for the unexpected. We all know that cash shortfalls can arise out of the blue for a variety of reasons. For example, if you need money in the next year to buy a car, you should not put your money into a three-year real estate investment or a stock mutual fund. You want the cash to be available when the time comes to buy the car, and you want to know that there will not be any loss on your investment. If you saved $10,000, you want assurance that you will have at least $10,000 when you need the money.

Monies that are not needed for longer periods of time can be invested in more volatile investments so that higher long-term returns can be targeted. For most young people and those having significant time before retirement, longer-term investments (i.e., equity, real estate, longer-term bonds, etc.) should be considered for at least a portion of their total portfolios.

Prudent investors avoid selling mid- and long-term investments to cover short-term cash needs. This is because longer-term investments tend to have much more price volatility, and there is a significantly greater risk that you could be forced to sell assets when prices are down and even at a loss. A balanced portfolio holds short-, mid-, and long-term investments.

Tax Considerations—By properly deferring and avoiding tax payments to the government, investors can invest more dollars for longer periods of time. This will lead to greater wealth more quickly. Investment vehicles such as individual retirement accounts (IRAs) and 401K plans allow earnings to accumulate on a tax-deferred basis (i.e., no taxes are paid until money is withdrawn from the account). We will further discuss tax considerations in a later chapter.

PORTFOLIO ALLOCATION EXAMPLES

Tables 4.3 to 4.5 show three hypothetical portfolios that vary in terms of investor risk tolerance from conservative to aggressive. Each portfolio is diversified among several asset classes. While actual investor portfolios may consist of more funds and more asset classes, these examples are intended to illustrate asset allocation and risk.

It is important to note that for simplicity purposes, I have chosen index funds for these examples. In reality, you may want to use all index funds, some index funds and some actively managed funds, or just all actively managed funds depending upon your specific investment objectives. In addition, I have tried to keep the analysis simple by limiting the defining characteristics of each fund. For example, you could be targeting small cap growth funds, small cap value funds, or a balance between the two. Depending on your risk profile, you may choose short-, medium-, and/or long-term government or

Table 4.3
Portfolio Allocation with Conservative Risk Profile

Fund	Category	Portfolio Allocation
S&P 500 Index Fund	Large U.S. Stocks	10.00%
Mid Cap Index Fund	Mid-Sized U.S. Stocks	5.00%
Small Cap Index Fund	Small U.S. Stocks	2.50%
Emerging Markets Index Fund	Foreign Stocks	2.50%
REIT Index Fund	Real Estate Stocks	5.00%
Long-Term Bond Index Fund	Fixed Income	20.00%
Mid-Term Bond Index Fund	Fixed Income	40.00%
Money Market Fund	Money Market	15.00%
		100.00%

Table 4.4
Portfolio Allocation with Moderate Risk Profile

Fund	Category	Portfolio Allocation
S&P 500 Index Fund	Large U.S. Stocks	25.00%
Mid Cap Index Fund	Mid-Sized U.S. Stocks	10.00%
Small Cap Index Fund	Small U.S. Stocks	10.00%
Emerging Markets Index Fund	Foreign Stocks	10.00%
REIT Index Fund	Real Estate Stocks	15.00%
Long-Term Bond Index Fund	Fixed Income	10.00%
Mid-Term Bond Index Fund	Fixed Income	15.00%
Money Market Fund	Money Market	5.00%
	Total	100.00%

Table 4.5
Portfolio Allocation with Aggressive Risk Profile

Fund	Category	Portfolio Allocation
S&P 500 Index Fund	Large U.S. Stocks	10.00%
Mid Cap Index Fund	Mid-Sized U.S. Stocks	10.00%
Small Cap Index Fund	Small U.S. Stocks	20.00%
Emerging Markets Index Fund	Foreign Stocks	20.00%
REIT Index Fund	Real Estate Stocks	20.00%
Long-Term Bond Index Fund	Fixed Income	10.00%
Mid-Term Bond Index Fund	Fixed Income	5.00%
Money Market Fund	Money Market	5.00%
	Total	100.00%

corporate bond funds. You may want an international bond fund, one that focuses on asset-backed and/or mortgage-backed securities, and so forth. The fund categories in these tables are just generalizations used to provide examples of how some investors might allocate their portfolio across asset classes and subasset classes based on their specific personal investment objectives.

Table 4.3 shows a portfolio representation that would be viewed as being fairly conservative. Notice that the allocation to fixed income versus equity is 75/25 percent. In addition, of the 75 percent fixed income allocation, the majority is allocated to short- and mid-term funds (the Money Market and Mid-Term Bond Funds). In addition, while there is an allocation to riskier assets such as small cap stocks and foreign stocks, these portfolio positions are small. This is to provide diversification benefits and the potential for capital appreciation, while limiting risk and portfolio volatility.

Table 4.3 might represent an older investor that is getting closer to retirement and who wants to limit his portfolio volatility, while allowing some equity allocation to enhance diversification and to protect against a reduction in purchasing power caused by inflation.

Table 4.4 shows how an average investor that is willing to assume moderate risk might allocate her portfolio. The fixed income versus equity allocation in this example is 30/70 percent, and there is a greater asset allocation to riskier funds with greater historic volatility, but higher expected returns.

A typical investor having a moderate risk profile might be someone that has a significant time period remaining until retirement (i.e., 10 years or more) and wants to grow the value of her portfolio materially before she reaches retirement. She can sustain short-term volatility to pursue greater expected long-term returns. Such an investor would focus on the benefits of diversification and the value that a portfolio of investments having varying risk and return characteristics can provide.

An investor having a more aggressive risk tolerance level might choose a portfolio like the one shown in Table 4.5. The fixed income versus equity allocation for this portfolio is 20/80 percent. The primary objective for such a portfolio is capital appreciation, while maintaining proper diversification

GUESS WHAT?

Rebalancing can help investors to "buy low and sell high." Many investors tend to let fear and emotion dominate their investment decisions, which often results in "buying high and selling low." For example, when markets are rising, investors feel comfortable about investing, and they do not want to miss opportunities to make money. But when markets are declining, investors tend to panic, sell, and avoid investing. This results in many people selling their investments in declining markets at low prices and buying their investments in rising markets at high prices. Rebalancing causes you to sell assets that have appreciated and buy assets that have maintained low or declining values.

and balance. Notice that there is a greater allocation to riskier categories that have historically shown more volatility, but greater returns such as real estate, foreign equities, and small cap stocks. This portfolio might be appropriate for young investors in their 20s and 30s.

PORTFOLIO REBALANCING

Portfolio rebalancing entails reallocating the investments within a portfolio to better meet current financial objectives. For example, as people become older and move through additional life stages, they will begin to lower their risk profiles by gradually selling longer-term, higher risk investments and buying shorter-term, lower risk investments. As investors age, they tend to increase their portfolio allocations toward more fixed income investments, while reducing their allocations to equity investments.

Another reason to rebalance your portfolio is due to market performance. Investors need to continue monitoring the percentages allocated to each type of investment and determine if further rebalancing is needed. For example, you may have allocated 15 percent of your initial portfolio to small cap stocks. Over time, small cap stocks may become 25 percent or more of your total portfolio due to strong performance in specific periods. In response, you may choose to sell a portion of your small cap stock investments and purchase other types of investments so that your overall targeted portfolio allocations match your current objectives.

Using another simplistic example, assume that 60 percent of your portfolio is in stocks, and 40 percent is in bonds. Over time, stocks should perform much better than bonds. If stocks earn an average annual return of 12 percent and bonds earn an average annual return of 6 percent, in five years your portfolio will be allocated over 66 percent to stocks and less than 34 percent to bonds. In this case, the portfolio's risk has increased due to more exposure to stocks and less exposure to bonds.

GUESS WHAT?

Studies have shown that disciplined portfolio rebalancing can reduce an investor's risk exposure, while also improving investment returns.

Rebalancing is simply the process of periodically realigning a portfolio back to its targeted asset allocation. In the example noted, an investor would sell a portion of her stock investments and buy more bonds. This would reduce her percentage of stock holdings back to around 60 percent and increase her bond holdings back to around 40 percent.

One way to rebalance is to do so based upon movements in asset classes rather than at specific points in time. For example, your portfolio may have 30 percent allocated to large cap stocks. You may decide that a range of 25 to 35 percent is acceptable. If your portfolio allocation falls outside of this range, you will either buy or sell large cap stocks. At the same time, you will look at all the other assets within your portfolio, and buy and sell as needed depending upon where their values fall within their designated ranges.

Rebalancing is routine for institutional investors such as pension and hedge funds, insurance companies, and money management firms, but many individual investors are unaware of this investment tool. In addition, of those investors that are aware of the concept, few actually spend the time to rebalance. Part of the reason may be that selling appreciating assets is often counterintuitive. Greed tends to focus people on keeping their best performing investments in hope of further gains rather than selling them to rebalance. This can lead to investments declining in value before investors are willing to sell them. In addition, many investors are unwilling to sell investments that have lost money until values return to at least breakeven levels. Investing based on emotion rather than logic usually leads to lower returns and higher risk.

I am not suggesting that you rebalance your portfolio on a short-term basis such as daily, weekly, or monthly. Doing so excessively can be counterproductive. In addition, and as will later be discussed, selling assets that have increased in value can generate recognized gains that trigger tax payments to the government. Rather, rebalancing should be gradually performed over time as performance trends materialize and solidify and when personal circumstances change.

5

Debt

It is far too easy for people to assume too much debt and get into financial trouble. Excessive debt can become an overwhelming burden and take years and even decades to resolve. Credit card offers constantly come across the television, in the mail, and through other media sources targeting people of all ages. Students and young adults present a particularly attractive market for credit card companies, which try to exploit the financially illiterate as much as possible. The ability to go to a store and charge something just by swiping a card is too easy and too enticing. The "play now and pay later" mentality often begins at a young age, and breaking the habit becomes harder and harder as time goes on.

Companies are more than happy to provide financing so that you can buy a new or used automobile, camper, boat, motorcycle, and so forth. In fact, many of the companies selling you that car or boat also own finance companies to help facilitate your purchase. These "one-stop-shopping" operations often make more money on financing your purchase than on the actual sale.

The residential housing market is currently (2009) in a state of chaos due to excessive borrowings used to purchase larger and more expensive homes than could reasonably be afforded. While much of the ultimate blame belongs to banks and other lenders, a prudent consumer should not agree to borrow an unmanageable amount of money no matter how much a lender is willing to provide.

But debt can be a helpful tool to assist people in achieving their goals and enhancing prosperity. Without inexpensive and long-term financing, most people would not own their own homes. Credit cards can be an efficient

According to Destroydebt.com, approximately 40 percent of Americans spend more than they earn.

means of bridging periods between paychecks. In addition, most people do not have enough cash to buy a new car. Paying for such an item over time allows them to own reliable vehicles and get to and from work and other places everyday. Debt can also enhance the profitability of many types of investments for individuals, small businesses, and large corporations. Companies throughout the world rely on various forms of debt financing to increase their earnings and stock prices. The key is to be selective and prudent before considering the assumption of debt.

GOOD DEBT VERSUS BAD DEBT

I used the terms *Good Debt* and *Bad Debt* in my first book to alert people to specific features of debt that can be more or less attractive. There are characteristics of differing types and uses of debt that can generally fall within one category versus the other. Whether an appropriate amount or form of debt is sensible will vary based upon the specific circumstances and individual.

When considering the use of any type of debt, you should always plan for the unexpected and remain confident that you can make the scheduled payments under favorable and unfavorable conditions. In addition, when considering high interest bearing loans such as those associated with most credit cards, consider the amount of interest being paid and ensure that a speedy repayment is achievable. It will always be safer to have less debt than more debt, but debt can be beneficial, and everyone needs to develop their own risk parameters and comfort levels. Only you know what you can and cannot afford.

Good Debt

Characteristics of Good Debt might include a low interest rate, desirable terms without excessive or unexpected fees, the ability to prepay without penalty, and interest that is tax-deductible.

A perfect example of Good Debt could be a home mortgage loan. One advantage to this type of debt is the available tax deduction. The interest expense paid on most home loans is tax deductible, meaning that the federal government is willing to give you free money as an incentive to purchase a home with the use of debt. Also, home mortgage financing is usually inexpensive with minimal transaction costs. Being able to borrow to cover the majority of a home purchase for 30 years or more is a rare and attractive source of financing.

It is important to note that Good Debt can become Bad Debt if abused. Good Debt is not debt that cannot be repaid or that places a severe strain on a person or business's financial position. Debt that is used to finance a foolish activity like a gambling trip to Las Vegas does not qualify as Good Debt. Good

🗨 GUESS WHAT?

Consider someone that earns $50,000 per year and rents his home. Because payments made for rent are not tax deductible, this person would be required to pay income taxes on the entire $50,000 (ignoring any other tax deductions). Now assume that the same person owns a home and pays $5,000 in annual interest to a bank on a home loan. Because the interest payments are tax deductible, he now only has to pay income taxes on $45,000 ($50,000 less the $5,000 tax deduction). Assuming a 20 percent tax rate, this person just saved $1,000 in tax payments for the year ($5,000 times 20%).

Debt is only Good Debt when the proceeds are spent or invested wisely, the terms of the debt are attractive, and you feel comfortable that you can make the required payments under reasonable assumptions.

Consider an example of when Good Debt could turn into Bad Debt. Let us assume that you want to purchase a rental property as an investment. You plan to buy a single-family home and rent it to a tenant. Using mortgage financing from a bank or other lender to buy the house can greatly increase the profitability of the investment and allow you to purchase the property. The property is expected to generate rental income that can be used to make the payments on the debt and to cover other ongoing expenses. The interest payments made to the lender are tax deductible, and you are able to obtain long-term financing with a low interest rate. There are minimal transaction costs associated with closing the loan, and the loan can be prepaid at anytime without penalty. But what if the property were to remain vacant for a few months, or if one or more large repair bills were needed, such as a new roof? Would you be able to continue to make the necessary payments? If not, this seemingly Good Debt could quickly become Bad Debt.

Bad Debt

Bad Debt has characteristics opposite of Good Debt. Features of Bad Debt could include high interest rates, prepayment penalties, and the inability to deduct interest payments for tax purposes.

One of the most common forms of Bad Debt is debt associated with credit cards. Millions of people carry high credit card balances from month to month and pay double-digit interest rates. This is how credit card companies make most of their money. They encourage consumers to overextend themselves so that they are forced to pay exorbitant sums of interest. In fact, for many card users, the interest payments are so significant that they are unable to repay any meaningful amount of principal each month. In such cases, the consumer keeps making monthly payments on debt that never gets repaid or even materially reduced. People living in such situations need to evaluate whether they are living beyond their means. To pay interest on such Bad Debt is counterproductive to the goals of budgeting, saving, compounding, and increasing one's net worth.

Other forms of Bad Debt often include loans to purchase consumer products such as cars, boats, home furnishings, and countless other items. These types of loans generally have high interest rates, and the interest paid is

---

✗ BEWARE!

The term *negative carry* means that your cost of borrowing is greater than your expected return on investment. If someone is paying double-digit interest rates on a credit card, they should not be saving any money until this high cost debt is fully repaid. If you are paying 10 to 20 percent interest rates on a credit card, there is no reason to put money into a savings account, stocks, bonds, or any other type of investment. By doing so, you are essentially borrowing on your credit card so that you can save money. This will most likely result in negative carry.

As an example, if you are paying a credit card company 15 percent annual interest on a $6,000 balance, and at the same time, depositing $500 a month into a bond fund that earns 5 percent annual interest, you are essentially losing 10 percent on the money that you are saving each year. As an alternative, why not stop saving for 12 months and pay off the credit card debt? This way, you eliminate the negative carry and a substantial cash drain. In the second year, you will no longer have any credit card debt and can again begin saving $500 a month plus the saved interest from the old credit card debt.

---

normally not tax deductible. Sometimes the financing terms for such loans can be attractive, such as when automobile dealerships offer 0 percent financing. However, usually the cost of the car or other product being purchased is substantially higher when you accept these types of promotional loans in order to compensate the dealer for the loss of interest.

OTHER PEOPLE'S MONEY

When you borrow money, you are essentially using someone else's money to finance a portion of your purchase. When using other people's money to invest, you can make money on your lender's money and avoid using as much of your own cash. Buying an asset with borrowed funds is referred to as "leveraging" your investment. The use of leverage can increase the profitability of an investment dramatically. However, leverage can also magnify losses when an investment does not perform well.

Let us look at the examples provided in Table 5.1 to illustrate the benefits and risks of using other people's money to leverage an investment. The scenarios presented assume that an investor is considering the purchase of real estate as an investment. The investor has $25,000 to invest and is considering whether to buy a $25,000 property (Scenarios 1 and 2) or use her $25,000 as a down payment, borrow $100,000 from a bank, and purchase a larger property for $125,000 (Scenarios 3 and 4).

Scenarios 1 and 2 assume that no leverage is employed and that the investor pays cash to buy a small piece of property. Under Scenario 1, if the investment increases in value by 10 percent during the year, the investor will earn a 10 percent profit. Under Scenario 2, if the investment loses 5 percent of its value during the year, the investor will lose 5 percent of her initial investment.

Scenarios 3 and 4 assume that the investor borrows money from a bank, which allows her to purchase a much larger property. If the investment increases in value during the year by 10 percent as indicated in Scenario 3,

Table 5.1
Non-Leverage Versus Leverage Scenarios

	Scenario 1	*Scenario 2*	*Scenario 3*	*Scenario 4*
Investment Amount	$25,000	$25,000	$25,000	$25,000
Amount of Bank Loan	–	–	100,000	100,000
Property Purchase Price	$25,000	$25,000	$125,000	$125,000
Interest Rate on Bank Loan	N/A	N/A	6.0%	6.0%
Annual Appreciation of Property	10.0%	–5.0%	10.0%	–5.0%
Property Value in One Year	$27,500	$23,750	$137,500	$118,750
Repayment of Bank Loan	–	–	(100,000)	(100,000)
Payment of Bank Interest	–	–	(6,000)	(6,000)
Remaining Cash	27,500	23,750	31,500	12,750
Less: Original Investment	(25,000)	(25,000)	(25,000)	(25,000)
Total Profit	$2,500	$(1,250)	$6,500	$(12,250)
Return on Initial Investment	10.0%	–5.0%	26.0%	–49.0%

the investor will earn a 26 percent profit on her initial investment amount of $25,000. The profitability under Scenario 3 is so much higher than the profitability assumed in Scenario 1 due to the benefits of leverage. In Scenario 3, the investor was able to make money on her $25,000 investment, but also earn profits on the money that she borrowed from the bank.

But leverage can also result in significant losses when an investment does not perform well. Scenario 4 shows the investor losing 49 percent of her $25,000 investment when the property declines in value by only 5 percent. This is because the investor not only loses 5 percent on her $25,000 investment, but she also loses money on the money lent to her by the bank. Scenario 4 highlights the fact that leverage can cause devastating results when abused or when poor investments are chosen.

THE IMPORTANCE OF YOUR CREDIT SCORE

The quality of a person's credit is viewed by virtually every lender when being considered for any type of loan. In addition, landlords, insurance companies, and other service providers may also check your credit history. Some employers check the credit history of potential employees before making hiring decisions.

A credit report is a listing of your credit history and includes debts outstanding and payment status. For example, if you never paid the last power bill for your apartment during college or if you were late with a car loan payment,

🎤   GUESS WHAT?

The law allows each consumer to obtain one free report from each credit agency every 12 months. Instead of going to each credit reporting company separately, you are able to contact one source to obtain copies of your credit report from any or all of the three agencies (visit www.annualcreditreport.com or call (877) 322-8228).

these items will show unfavorably on your credit report. A credit report is something that can haunt a person for life.

There are three national credit reporting agencies (Equifax, TransUnion, and Experian). These companies track your credit history as data gets reported to them by lenders. Sometimes lenders do not report information to all three agencies, so you could have differing credit reports from each reporting company.

If you know you are going to be applying for a significant loan in the future, such as for the purchase of a home, you should check your credit report at least six months in advance. This will allow you time to correct inaccuracies, pay off overdue balances, or perhaps to pay down large loans.

The data in your credit report is factored into the calculation of your credit score. A low credit score implies a high credit risk, which can lead to more fees and higher interest rates from lenders or the rejection of loan applications. While lenders and other third parties should consider other factors such as current income, length of steady employment, and a person's total amount of debt, a credit score is a key consideration when extending credit.

The most common type of credit score used by lenders is the FICO score (created by Fair Isaac Corp.). FICO scores range from 300 to 850. Following are a few ways to maintain and improve a FICO score:

- Pay your bills on time. This is the most important thing you can do to maintain good credit. Ensure that bills are received by (not mailed to) the billing parties by the stated deadlines.
- Avoid nearing the maximum limits on credit cards. At a minimum, keep your card balances below 50 percent of your maximum borrowing ability.
- Continue to grow the length of your credit history. This just takes time. One piece of advice is to not continually switch credit cards because this limits the length of credit history you have for each account.
- Avoid too much new credit. Each time a retailer or lender pulls your credit report can have an adverse effect on your credit score. The number of recent inquiries and how many new accounts have been opened will factor into your score.
- Build a repayment history. Having a diverse amount of debt and showing a successful payment history can help credit scores. This does not imply that you should take on debt just for the sake of improving your credit score, but some people with no debt have weak credit scores simply because they lack a recorded history.

For more information on credit scoring, check out www.myFICO.com and www.Bankrate.com.

PREVENTING IDENTITY THEFT

Financial identity theft is a crime in which someone steals your personal information and pretends to be you in order to charge and borrow money at your expense. Criminals impersonate you by using your name, social security number, birth date, and other information. People often do not find out that their identities have been stolen until being denied for loans and other forms of credit or after being contacted by collection agencies for past due amounts. Other times, people can be alerted sooner by being proactive and reviewing their personal credit reports. A victim's credit report and credit score will reflect stolen charges until they can be successfully disputed and removed. This process can takes months of frustration and personal expense.

In most cases, financial identity theft begins with obtaining personal information about a potential victim. This can be done by stealing mail, wallets, and purses; automobile and home break-ins; retrieving information from discarded personal computers; hacking into computer databases and wireless networks; and getting people to respond to bogus advertisements.

Based on growing identity theft problems, experts often suggests that a free credit report be ordered every four months from one of the three credit agencies to monitor your credit activity. In addition, the following suggestions can help to secure your personal information:

- Do not carry your Social Security number, passport, or birth certificate unless absolutely necessary, and keep these documents locked in a safe place. Also, only provide your Social Security number when absolutely necessary. Many firms and services that request this information can do without it. Do not be afraid to ask if a Social Security number is absolutely necessary.
- Avoid carrying a checkbook when unnecessary, and keep all used and unused checks in a safe place.
- When given the opportunity, use credit and bank debit cards with personal photographs on the cards.
- Consider using postal lockboxes for incoming mail, or at least take mail from your mail box as soon as possible. Place outgoing mail, including sensitive information like checks and formal documents, directly into postal collection boxes.
- Consider shredding mail and documents having personal information before throwing them away.
- Be very careful when retiring old computers. Make sure that data cannot be retrieved from hard drives.
- "Opt out" of allowing banks, brokerage firms, and insurance companies from sharing your personal information. Federal law requires

⚡ BEWARE!

According to a report by WIFR.com, the average time before someone realizes that their identity has been stolen is 12 to 18 months. Even worse is that 20 percent of Americans have reported some type of identity theft, and it takes people up to 600 hours and $1,400 to fix their identity and clear their credit (www.organizedaudrey.com). The periodic review of personal credit reports can help discover problems much sooner and minimize damages.

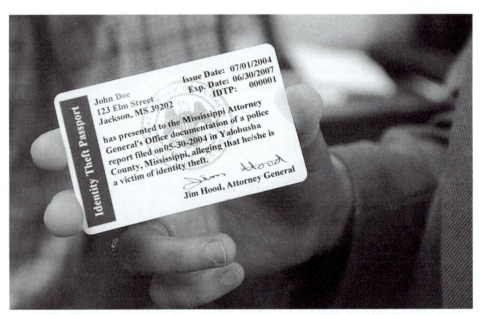

A sample identity card used by victims of identity theft to prove their identities to law enforcement, government agencies, and other third parties. Once your identity is stolen, it becomes expensive, timely, and extremely frustrating to correct the problem. AP Photo/Rogelio Solis.

these companies to provide you with the option to opt out of having your information shared.

• Change computer passwords frequently, and use complex passwords. Ensure that any wireless networks are secure and password protected.

CREDIT CARDS

When a credit card is issued to someone, the credit card provider is granting a line of credit to the cardholder. The user can borrow money from the credit card company to make payments to merchants and to receive cash advances. Balances can be carried from month to month as long as minimum required payments are being made.

Credit card offers can plague people of all ages, and credit card abuse can result in serious financial problems for years to come. It is easy to make purchases impulsively and spend beyond your means. Once this happens, balances are usually carried from month to month at exorbitant interest rates that can be as high as 30 percent. With such excessive financing costs, it often becomes difficult to make large enough payments each month to materially reduce the outstanding balance. The card user becomes trapped in a perpetual cycle that results in huge ongoing fees to the credit card company and a long-term obligation by the card owner.

While credit cards present risks, particularly to those individuals lacking in willpower and a proper understanding of the mechanics and various fees, they also provide an effective way to purchase goods and services. In addition, a credit card can reduce the need for cash, which can be more easily lost or stolen.

Credit cards are favored by stores and other merchants because the charges are paid quickly by the credit card company, and the credit card company is responsible for collecting funds from the credit card user. Also, the elimination of cash transactions greatly reduces the threat of employee theft.

Credit cards, such as MasterCard and Visa, are sponsored by individual banks and can be used to charge items at most locations. Credit cards such as those issued by stores, gas stations, and other retailers allow purchases at specific brand locations and are more limited. Other card providers such as American Express are often used by businesses so that their employees can pay for company travel and entertainment expenses.

Applying for a credit card is a fairly simple process. A person must be 18 years or older and have income, such as a part-time job. For those people lacking a credit history or having weak credit, a parent or other willing person can cosign an application. If you are unable to pay your bills, the cosigner will be responsible for payment. Any credit card provider will give you an application to complete. Usually such applications can be found in your local bank branch or on card providers' Web sites. The information required is easy to provide, such as name, current and prior addresses, employment status, and current income.

When you are given a credit card, you are given a specific spending limit. For example, a $5,000 limit allows you to have up to $5,000 of unpaid charges outstanding. You can make periodic charges over time or charge the entire $5,000 at once. As you make payments and reduce the outstanding balance, you are entitled to make additional purchases. Credit cards serve as revolving lines of credit, meaning that their balances can go up and down with borrowings and repayments.

You will be targeted by credit card companies as soon as you turn 18 years old. Credit card companies collect and purchase data on people so that they can send card applications and pursue other marketing tactics. There are thousands of different credit cards available in the United States. When considering which card to use, you need to seriously evaluate all the terms and conditions of each card. Maintaining the same credit card for an extended period of time can help to build a favorable credit history, so choosing the right first card is an important decision.

Credit cards come in all colors, shapes, and sizes with varying terms, pricing, and features. It is important for applicants to read and understand every word of a credit card agreement before committing. AP Photo/Mark Lennihan.

Credit Card Fees and Terms

Annual Percentage Rate (APR)—A key consideration when reviewing differing credit cards is the annual percentage rate or APR. This is the interest rate charged for the dollars borrowed stated on an annual basis. While credit cards should be repaid in full each month to avoid costly interest expense, the APR of a specific card should be considered in case balances need to be carried from time to time.

Periodic Rate—When applying an interest rate to your outstanding balances each billing period, the periodic rate is the interest rate applied to compute the monthly financing charges.

Annual Fees—Many credit cards charge annual fees that commonly range from $0 to $50 a year. Cards that offer more benefits (i.e., gold and platinum cards) may require annual fees of up to $150. Many card benefits are not used by cardholders or they may come with limitations or inconvenient terms that do not justify such higher costs. For people with limited spending needs, seeking the lowest annual fee is often the best approach.

Table 5.2 illustrates a simplistic example of how an annual fee can result in higher financing costs even when accompanied by a lower APR.

Table 5.2
Credit Card Financing Cost Examples

	Card A	Card B
Average Monthly Balance	$1,000	$1,000
Annual Percentage Rate (APR)	× 15%	× 12%
Annual Finance Charges	$150	$120
Annual Fee	–	50
Total Annual Cost	$150	$170

Financing Charge Calculations—Because credit card interest rates can be so substantial and the total financing costs so excessive, it is important that credit card users understand how interest is computed on outstanding balances. Different cards can have differing calculation methods.

- *Average Daily Balance* is the most commonly used method when computing interest charges. Interest is computed based upon the average outstanding balance for the prior month. Any payments received are given credit when received by the card issuer.
- *Adjusted Balance Method* subtracts payments received from the balance owed at the end of the prior period. This results in the most favorable outcome for card users because interest is computed on lower balances.
- *Previous Balance Method* results in an unfavorable outcome for consumers and tends to be the most expensive approach. Interest is computed based upon the balance owed at the end of the previous billing period. Payments made during the current billing cycle are not included, which results in greater interest costs.

Transaction Fees—Credit card companies often charge fees for services such as cash advances, late payments, and when credit limits are exceeded. These fees can significantly increase total financing costs, particularly for smaller purchases.

Payment Grace Period—Some credit card companies provide a certain number of days after the payment due date before they begin charging interest.

Reward Programs—To attract customers, many credit card companies offer reward programs to consumers and businesses that provide benefits such as cash rebates based on purchases. For example, a credit card company may provide a rebate of 1.5 percent of purchases at the end of each month. If you charge $10,000 during the year, you could receive rebate checks for $150. Other programs accumulate points that can be redeemed for items such as airline tickets, vacation packages, and countless retail products, including video and sound systems and appliances. Often each dollar spent equates to one reward point. As reward points are accumulated, they can be used to make purchases.

Because of the numerous and differing features associated with so many credit cards, making an appropriate choice can be difficult. Following are a few factors to consider:

- Card users should always strive to fully repay outstanding balances each month to avoid costly financing charges. Paying double-digit interest rates to credit card companies is contrary to any type of rational savings plan. However, when evaluating different credit cards, the interest rate and financing charge calculations should be seriously reviewed and compared in case monthly balances are carried. So look for low interest rates, but realize that these rates are not fixed and may be adjusted over time by the credit card company.
- Weigh the costs versus benefits when considering reward programs. For example, normally such cards require annual fees. Consider whether the rewards earned will offset this fee and any other differing features when comparing cards with and without reward programs.
- Evaluate and consider any punitive transaction fees. For example, some cards charge fees each time a card is used or when payments are late.
- Read all credit card disclosures. Credit card companies disclose their fees and calculations with extremely small print. It is not stimulating reading, but do yourself a favor and read every word. Ask the card company or someone you know to explain any language that is unclear or confusing.
- Sometimes self-discipline is the best discipline. Just because a credit card company is willing to provide you with a $10,000 credit limit does not mean that you need to take it. If you feel more comfortable with a $1,000 limit, tell the card issuer that you only want $1,000. While using a small fraction of a larger credit limit can help to build your credit history, you need to determine what will be an appropriate credit limit.

Other Types of Charge Cards

Secured Credit Cards—Secured credit cards are credit cards backed by a special deposit account. For example, if someone deposits $2,000 into a special savings account, a credit card with a borrowing limit of anywhere from $1,000 to $20,000 may be issued depending upon the person and the lender. The bank account serves as collateral for the credit card company and cannot be accessed by its owner until the credit card account is fully repaid and closed. Secured credit cards are often used by people having weak or no credit history.

✎   BEWARE!

There are approximately 1.2 billion active credit cards in the United States and about 60 percent of active credit cards are not paid off monthly. The typical credit card purchase costs 112 percent more than if cash had been used due to the interest paid to credit card companies (Destroydebt.com).

The fees and interest rates on secured credit cards are often higher than those on normal credit cards, but they can provide a way for people to rebuild credit history and to make purchases in a more timely and convenient fashion.

Charge Cards—A charge card requires the balance of the card to be repaid in full each month. Because there is no ability to carry balances from month to month, there are no interest charges associated with a charge card (although there are often annual fees). Charge cards often have higher and sometimes unlimited spending limits when compared to credit cards. American Express and Diner's Club are examples of charge cards.

Prepaid Cards—A prepaid card is not a credit card because there is no "credit" being provided to the cardholder. Rather, an amount of money is paid in advance to the credit card issuer. This amount, less any required processing fees, can be charged on the card as needed. For example, an employer or parent may not want an individual to have unauthorized spending access. Instead, a dollar amount such as $500 or $1,000 may be paid to a card issuer, and the prepaid card user may charge this amount on the card.

Debit Card—A debit card is linked to a user's bank account. The word *debit* means "subtract." When a debit card is used to make a purchase, you are subtracting money from your own bank account. When using a debit card, you are only able to spend up to what is in your bank account. If you order a $50 lunch and you only have $40 in your account, you will be unable to pay the check. Debit cards allow users to avoid carrying cash or checks, and debit cards are easier to obtain than credit cards.

KEY FINANCING TERMS

While not all-inclusive and not relevant to all types of borrowings, the following summarizes most of the key terms to consider when evaluating different lenders and financing options.

Interest Rate—In return for providing you with financing to purchase a home, automobile, or other asset, banks and other lenders are compensated by charging you interest on your loan. Often times, you are given a choice between a fixed rate of interest and an adjustable (also called a "variable" or "floating") rate of interest. A fixed rate loan has a fixed rate of interest for the life of the loan. For example, the interest rate on a 6 percent, 30-year, fixed rate loan will be 6 percent for the entire 30 years.

An adjustable rate loan has an interest rate that is reset at certain points in time that can go up or down depending on the terms of the loan agreement and where comparable interest rates are at the specific reset dates. The interest rate at each reset date is usually determined based upon a fixed margin and some type of variable index. For example, assume that you enter a 15-year adjustable rate loan. Let us also assume that the fixed margin is 2.5 percent and that the index is 12-month LIBOR. The interest rate for the first year on this hypothetical loan might be set at 5 percent when the loan is closed. Going forward, each year the interest rate will be adjusted based upon the margin and the index. If at the beginning of the second year 12-month LIBOR is 4.5 percent, then the interest rate for the following year will be set at 7 percent (the 2.5% fixed margin plus the current 12-month LIBOR of 4.5%).

Some adjustable rate loans have limits or "caps" to protect the borrower from rapid increases in interest rates. These caps can be periodic or for the full term of the loan. For example, a typical adjustable rate loan might have an annual interest rate cap of 1 percent per year, which means that under no circumstance can the interest rate on the loan increase by more than 1 percent every 12 months. Assume that the loan referenced in the prior paragraph has a cap of 1 percent per year. In this case, the 5 percent initial interest rate would only be reset to 6 percent rather than 7 percent in the second year due to the annual cap.

A lifetime interest rate cap limits increases in interest rates over the life of the loan. For example, a loan may have a lifetime cap of 10 percent. This means that the interest rate on the loan can only go as high as 10 percent on each reset date. Once the overall interest rate resulting from the combined fixed margin and index exceeds 10 percent, the loan will be capped at 10 percent for that period. If the margin plus the index is less than 10 percent in later periods, then the interest rate on the loan will be reset below the cap for the related period(s).

Usually, adjustable rate loans have lower initial interest rates when compared to fixed rate loans. However, with adjustable rate loans, the borrower runs the risk that future interest rates will rise significantly and that the cost of borrowing will dramatically increase.

Many borrowers have lost property to lenders, been forced into bankruptcy, and have experienced other financial difficulties due to rising payment amounts caused by adjustable rates loans. The rise and fall of the residential housing market that has recently taken place can be substantially blamed on the aggressive lending policies employed by lenders and the ignorance or denial of many borrowers. Creating loans that borrowers could only afford with very low initial interest rates, knowing that these rates would rise dramatically in the near future, was imprudent. Both lenders and borrowers should have ensured that higher payments, that in many cases were certain to occur, could be afforded.

Loan-to-Value Ratio—Lenders limit the amount of money that they will lend based upon a loan-to-value or LTV ratio. When determining how much to lend, lenders start by assessing the value of the property that you own or are preparing to purchase. Value can be determined by the purchase price for items such as automobiles, boats, and other consumer products or by ordering an appraisal, which is a third party's opinion of value. Appraisals are almost always used by lenders when valuing commercial and residential real estate.

If a home is appraised at $150,000 and a lender is willing to lend using an 80 percent LTV ratio, then $120,000 (80% times $150,000) can be borrowed

✏ BEWARE!

A study performed by economists Brian Bucks and Karen Pence found that 35 percent of people with adjustable rate mortgages did not know how much their interest rates could increase at one time, and 41 percent did not know the maximum interest rate they could face.

In aggressive lending markets, some lenders may be willing to lend up to 100 percent against the value of an asset. In tighter and more conservative lending environments, such as the one now underway due to the current financial crisis, it becomes much more difficult to obtain financing, and LTV ratios tend to be lower and more conservative.

against the property. The remaining $30,000 must come from the borrower's down payment.

Loan Maturity Date—Every loan will have a scheduled maturity date on which the final payment is due to fully repay the loan. Traditional home mortgage loans are usually 15 or 30 years in length. Consumer product loans tend to be much shorter. Generally, when looking at a specific type of financing, the shorter the term of the loan, the lower the interest rate. This is because when banks and other lenders get repaid more quickly, they are assuming less risk and can charge lower interest rates. However, the faster repayment required on shorter-term loans results in greater monthly payments.

Some people that are debt averse like to payoff their home loans as soon as possible. Such people might choose 15-year mortgages and buy cheaper homes so that they can afford the larger payments each month. Doing so will lower their loan balances more quickly when compared to 30-year loans. In addition, these borrowers will pay substantially less interest over the life of a 15-year loan when compared to a 30-year loan. But home loans are often a source of Good Debt. Some people might choose 30-year loans so that they can afford larger homes based on the lower payments when compared to shorter-term loans. Also, the lower loan payments on longer-term loans can leave more money available each month to be invested into other types of investments.

Amortization Schedule—The amount of any scheduled principal amortization on a loan will affect the amount of your periodic payments. As mentioned, a shorter-term loan results in larger payments, but also reduces the amount of your loan balance more quickly. A longer amortization schedule reduces your payments, but results in a higher loan balance over time.

Traditional residential housing loans have the most simplistic amortization schedules. A 15-year, fixed rate loan has a 15-year amortization schedule. A 30-year loan has a 30-year loan amortization schedule. If a borrower makes his monthly payments for 15 or 30 years, on the last payment date, his loan will have a balance of zero and be completely repaid.

A 30-year mortgage loan carries a fixed interest rate today of about 6.5 percent. A 15-year loan to the same borrower has a fixed interest rate of around 6 percent. Assuming these interest rates, over the life of a $150,000, 30-year loan, a homeowner would pay approximately $173,757 in total interest payments, while only paying about $77,841 in total interest over the life of the 15-year loan.

The payments on fixed rate loans are normally calculated so that at the end of the loan, the entire principal balance has been repaid. Table 5.3 shows an example of the annual payments for a 15-year fixed rate loan. While almost all home mortgage loans require monthly payments, Table 5.3 assumes annual payments for simplicity.

As can be seen in Table 5.3, the total payments remain the same each period. However, the composition of the payment changes over time. As the loan principal balance gets reduced, a lesser portion of each payment is allocated to interest and more to principal.

Other more complex loan products will allow longer amortization schedules with earlier loan maturity dates, which result in substantial principal balances being due in lump sums. For example, a seven-year loan might have an amortization schedule of 20 years. The maturity date of the loan would be after seven years, and the outstanding principal balance of the loan would be due in full at this time. This results in what is referred to as a "balloon" payment, which is essentially the unamortized portion of your loan balance that is due to your lender on the loan's maturity date.

Loans with balloon payments can subject borrowers to refinancing risks. If a homeowner does not have the remaining loan balance on the balloon date or is unable to find another lender to provide a new loan at such time, she may default on the loan. In addition, there is the risk that a new loan needed to refinance the balloon payment will be at unfavorable terms, including a much higher interest rate. But shorter-term loans having balloon payments

Table 5.3
Amortization Schedule Example

	Beginning Loan Principal Balance	Total Payment	Interest	Principal	Ending Loan Principal Balance
Year 1	$150,000	$15,444	$9,000	$6,444	$143,556
Year 2	143,556	15,444	8,613	6,831	136,725
Year 3	136,725	15,444	8,203	7,241	129,484
Year 4	129,484	15,444	7,769	7,675	121,808
Year 5	121,808	15,444	7,308	8,136	113,672
Year 6	113,672	15,444	6,820	8,624	105,048
Year 7	105,048	15,444	6,303	9,142	95,907
Year 8	95,907	15,444	5,754	9,690	86,217
Year 9	86,217	15,444	5,173	10,271	75,945
Year 10	75,945	15,444	4,557	10,888	65,057
Year 11	65,057	15,444	3,903	11,541	53,517
Year 12	53,517	15,444	3,211	12,233	41,283
Year 13	41,283	15,444	2,477	12,967	28,316
Year 14	28,316	15,444	1,699	13,745	14,570
Year 15	14,570	15,444	874	14,570	0

can also come with lower interest rates when compared to longer-term loans. If a borrower plans to sell the asset being financed prior to a loan's scheduled maturity date, such savings can be substantial.

Some loans have no scheduled amortization for a period of time, and then principal payments begin at some point in the future. These loans result in lower initial payments while the loans remain interest only, but substantially larger payments result once monthly principal payments are added. Such loans have caused problems for many borrowers that could not afford their loans after their payments increased.

Sometimes borrowers are offered loans that can have negative amortization. Such features usually accompany certain types of adjustable rate mortgages. For example, based on a certain interest rate, your monthly loan payment may be $1,200. However, based upon the terms of your loan, your payment may be capped so that it is never greater than $1,000 per month. In this case, the additional $200 is applied to your loan balance. If your loan balance was $100,000 prior to this payment, after the payment you would now owe $100,200. Loans with negative amortization features can allow borrowers to control their monthly payments. In the example provided, the borrower's payment is limited to $1,000 per month regardless of how high interest rates get. However, such loans can add further financial stress to borrowers as loan balances and interest costs increase over time.

Loan Origination Fees or "Points"—Lenders will sometimes charge an up-front origination fee. These are most common on commercial and residential real estate loans. Origination fees are quoted as a percentage of the principal balance of the loan. For example, a loan origination fee of 1 percent (which equals "one point") on a $200,000 loan would equate to an upfront fee of $2,000. Every point equals 1 percent of the loan principal balance.

Small loan origination fees are generally used to cover a lender's administrative costs. Larger origination fees are to compensate the lender for providing the loan or for agreeing to a lower interest rate. But these fees vary based upon the type of loan, the current lending environment, and the specific lender.

Borrowers may avoid origination fees in competitive lending markets in which lenders are aggressively trying to lend money. In more conservative lending environments, lenders have more negotiating power and are able to charge higher financing costs.

Borrowers are sometimes presented with multiple financing options. Such choices can come from the same lender or from multiple lenders. In return

⚡ BEWARE!

Many loans made to home buyers prior to the national housing market collapse that took place during the late 2000s were interest-only, adjustable rate mortgages. These loans start with low interest rates and do not require any principal repayment for a certain period of time (usually 36 to 60 months). After this grace period expires, the interest rate resets and principal payments are required. According to realtytimes.com, monthly payments on these loans can increase overnight by 30 to 70 percent.

for higher upfront origination fees, lenders are often willing to accept lower interest rates on their loans.

Table 5.4 shows a simplistic example of what a lender might offer to a potential borrower. As you can see, for a $150,000 loan the lender is willing to lower the interest rate in return for higher origination fees. One of the reasons for this compromise is that many loans are prepaid before their maturity dates. As you can see, Option 3 results in the lowest financing cost when the loan remains outstanding for its full five-year term. However, Option 3 also has the highest financing cost if the loan is repaid after only one year.

Borrowers need to consider their financing needs when determining whether to pay higher loan origination fees, which is often referred to as "buying down the interest rate," because paying a higher upfront origination fee effectively buys a lower interest rate on the loan. In most cases, it is best to try and avoid or minimize any origination fees.

Borrowers should ask for multiple financing options, and the more options the better. So be sure to ask your lenders to provide as many choices as possible. Look for options regarding terms such as loan maturity date, the amortization schedule, and ranging interest rates and origination fees, and choose the best financing structure for your particular needs.

Personal Guarantees—In most cases, lenders will require you to sign a personal guarantee before they lend you money. It is important to understand what happens if you default on your loan when a personal guarantee is involved. Suppose that you borrow $10,000 to buy a car. After a few months,

Table 5.4
Loan Origination Fee Scenarios

Terms	Option 1	Option 2	Option 3
Loan Amount	$150,000	$150,000	$150,000
Points	0.00%	1.00%	2.50%
Interest Rate	7.00%	6.50%	6.00%
Loan Maturity Date	5 Years	5 Years	5 Years
Financing Costs - 5 years			
Points	$–	$1,500	$3,750
Interest for 5 Years	52,500	48,750	45,000
Total Financing Costs	$52,500	$50,250	$48,750
Financing Costs - 3 years			
Points	$–	$1,500	$3,750
Interest for 5 Years	31,500	29,250	30,750
Total Financing Costs	$31,500	$30,750	$34,500
Financing Costs - 1 years			
Points	$–	$1,500	$3,750
Interest for 5 Years	10,500	9,750	9,000
Total Financing Costs	$10,500	$11,250	$12,750

🗩   GUESS WHAT?

Assume that you borrow money to buy a commercial property as an investment. A bank may lend you $250,000 for 10 years at a fixed interest rate of 8 percent. After three years, assume that you can get a better loan from another lender with an interest rate of only 6 percent. If you use the new loan to repay the existing loan, you have lowered your interest rate from 8 to 6 percent. This is a great deal for you, but what about the bank that provided the first loan? This lender was earning 8 percent on your loan, and after the prepayment it can only relend the money at 6 percent. In order to protect the bank from this risk, the loan may require a prepayment penalty for a certain period (i.e., the first five years of the loan).

---

you lose your job and become unable to make the monthly loan payments. The first thing your lender is going to do is repossess the car and sell it in order to recoup as much of its loan amount as possible. If the car is sold for $8,000 and you owe your lender $9,500, there will be a shortfall. In this case, you will still owe the lender $1,500 and have no car! This amount owed will remain outstanding on your personal credit report until the lender is repaid.

In some cases, you may be able to avoid a personal guarantee when borrowing money to purchase assets such as commercial real estate. Without a personal guarantee, lenders will only take the underlying property, and you will not be obligated to pay for any shortfall between the value of the collateral and your loan amount.

Prepayment Penalties—Sometimes a lender will charge a borrower a fee when a loan is repaid prior to its maturity date. When lenders are repaid, they need to relend the money to continue earning profits. Prepayment penalties are intended to compensate lenders for being repaid earlier than expected. In addition, prepayment penalties can serve to help offset lower interest rates.

A simplistic prepayment penalty might be a fee of 1 percent times the outstanding principal balance of the loan at the time of prepayment. For example, if you owed $250,000 and prepaid your loan, you would be forced to pay a prepayment penalty of $2,500. Other prepayment penalty calculations can be much more complicated.

Most loans do not have prepayment penalties, particularly standard consumer type loans. But some loans used to finance business and investment activities may have such provisions. Be sure to read loan documents carefully, and if you feel unqualified to do so, ask someone qualified for help.

CONSUMER PRODUCT LOANS

When making expensive purchases for things such as automobiles, motorcycles, recreational vehicles, boats, furniture, and other consumer products, buyers often borrow a portion of the sales price to spread their payments out over time and to make these items more affordable. Consumer product loans are provided by banks and other lenders. Often times, specialty finance companies owned by large corporations focus on specific types of loans. For example, the automobile companies have financing subsidiaries that assist consumers in purchasing their products by providing automobile loans.

Most consumer product loans are short term when compared to loans secured by assets such as real estate because the underlying collateral tends to depreciate in value over time. Because short-term loans require the entire loan amount to be repaid within a fairly short period of time, the monthly payments can be quite large.

Most loans require a down payment ranging from 10 to 20 percent. However, special offers and particular lenders will sometimes provide up to 100 percent financing. Usually lenders are compensated with higher interest rates and fees when greater amounts are being financed. Other times, dealers are trying to move inventory, and consumers may be able to receive very favorable terms.

Consumer product loans are usually three to seven years in term depending on the underlying collateral. If a borrower defaults and misses his payments, the car, boat, or other product will be repossessed by the company that provided the loan. The collateral will be sold, and any shortfall between the lender's loan amount (including back interest that is often computed using a higher default interest rate) and the sales proceeds will be an obligation of the borrower. In addition, the borrower's credit report will be damaged.

The interest paid on consumer product loans is not tax deductible unless the product is being used for business purposes. In addition, these loans often carry high interest rates when compared to other financing sources such as home equity loans, which will be discussed later in the chapter. When buying the underlying products, customers can often become excited and more focused on having the car, boat, or other item than on the specific financing terms. Many consumer product loans are a source of Bad Debt.

Sometimes retailers will offer special financing terms such as 0 percent interest or no payments for a certain period of time. Usually retailers look at the total selling price of the product and the financing terms when determining total profitability. In order to convince buyers that they are getting a great deal, retailers may alter the terms between the sales price and the financing. For example, a car dealer may offer 0 percent financing, but charge you a higher price for the car than if you had paid in cash. Alternatively, you may be offered a discounted price if the car is financed at a higher interest rate.

When considering consumer product loans, buyers need to determine whether the item being purchased fits within his or her budget. For example, most of us need a car to get to and from school or work, but purchasing a Saturn versus a Mercedes is clearly more economical. In addition, perhaps a buyer should delay or pass up new furniture, a Jet Ski, and other discretionary purchases.

⚡ BEWARE!

Depending on the specific model, a new car might depreciate in value by 20 to 25 percent in the first month after purchase. This means that a $30,000 car bought today might be worth around $22,500 soon after being driven off the lot. When the collateral securing a loan is going to depreciate, lenders want to be repaid relatively quickly.

Buyers should ensure that they are maintaining a prudent savings program and that they are not carrying credit card balances from month to month. Before entering any financial obligation, people should ensure that bills can be managed and paid on time. In addition, when considering the purchase of such high-cost products, the total purchase price including any financing costs should be considered and compared to different financing alternatives.

FINANCING YOUR FIRST HOME

As discussed, when buying a home the majority of the purchase price is normally borrowed from a bank or other lending institution. A lender will provide a loan to a home buyer in return for a mortgage on the property. A mortgage provides a security interest in real property and is granted to the lender to serve as collateral for the loan. If the homeowner fails to make one or more scheduled payments on the loan, the lender can foreclose on the mortgage. Upon foreclosure, the lender becomes the new owner of the property. At this point, the borrower no longer owns the home and is forced to vacate the premises. The lender will sell the home to recover all or a portion of the amount due on the loan. Upon foreclosure, the home buyer will very likely lose his down payment and any other money invested in the home.

The value of a home less the current amount of debt outstanding on the property is referred to as *home equity*. When you first buy a house, your down payment is considered equity. For example, if a house costs $100,000 and a borrower puts down $20,000 and borrows $80,000, she has $20,000 of home equity in the property. Any changes made to a home that adds value will increase homeowner equity, such as the remodeling of a kitchen or bathroom. Also, as the loan balance on a property declines over time due to the portions of monthly payments that are allocated to principal repayment each month, home equity increases as well. Using the same example, if a home remains worth $100,000, but the balance on the original loan declines from $80,000 to $75,000 over time as monthly payments are made, the homeowner now has $25,000 (instead of $20,000) of home equity. Building home equity is a powerful savings tool for people. It allows you to borrow more money over time against your home, and it provides you with greater cash proceeds when a property is sold.

As you begin to think about buying your first home, it is helpful to know what type of home you can afford. It would be rather pointless to spend time looking at $500,000 houses when you can only afford one that costs $200,000. In addition, during aggressive lending cycles, you may find banks and other financial institutions willing to lend you more money than you should be willing to borrow. There are literally hundreds of thousands of people losing their homes under bank foreclosures today because they borrowed more money than they should have to buy homes that they really could not afford. Be prudent when considering the cost of a home. Losing your home and any invested equity to a lender can dramatically lower your net worth and ruin your credit history.

It is helpful to know what banks and other lenders will be looking for when considering whether or not to grant you a loan. When someone

🗣 GUESS WHAT?

Using a general rule of thumb, most home buyers can afford a home that costs between two to three times their annual incomes. For example, if you have a salary of $50,000, this would suggest that you can afford to buy a home costing up to $150,000. But be careful when using such an approach. Each home buyer is different. The amount of the down payment, the level of current interest rates on home loans, and any additional financial obligations of each borrower must be considered.

lends you thousands and even hundreds of thousands of dollars, you can bet they want a high degree of confidence that they will be repaid. When considering lending you money to purchase a home, lenders want to ensure that you have a stable source of income. They also want to know that you earn enough money to cover your loan payments and any other debt obligations.

But how much debt is too much? This is a question that varies by individual circumstances. However, when reviewing a potential borrower's personal finances, many lenders focus upon the person's *debt-to-income ratio* (often referred to as a borrower's DTI). There are two types of debt-to-income ratios that lenders normally compute when determining if a potential borrower will qualify for a home loan.

A *front-end ratio* indicates the amount of gross income that is needed to cover housing related expenses. For renters, this would include the amount of monthly rent paid to a landlord. For a homeowner, this would include principal and interest payments, insurance and property tax expenses, and any homeowners' association dues. Most lenders like to see a front-end ratio of less than 28 percent, but some will go higher. Often exceptions above 28 percent result in higher interest rates to borrowers.

A *back-end ratio* indicates the amount of gross income that is used to cover housing-related expenses as calculated in the front-end ratio, but it also includes other monthly debts including payments for student loans, credit cards, automobile loans, child support payments, and other forms of debt. Most lenders like their borrowers to have back-end ratios of 36 percent or less. Some lenders may go higher on back-end ratios, but doing so can also result in higher interest rates.

In order to qualify for a housing loan, a lender may require a borrower to have a debt-to-income ratio of 28/36. This means that the borrower's front-end ratio should not be greater than 28 percent and the back-end ratio should not be more than 36 percent. To further clarify this point, Table 5.5 shows an example of the calculations of these two ratios.

⚡ BEWARE!

Studies have shown that when a person's debt obligations are greater than 40 percent of their monthly gross income, they become substantially more prone to miss payments and are considered a greater credit risk.

Table 5.5
Debt-to-Income Ratio Examples

Annual Gross Income	$45,000	
	Front-end Ratio	*Back-end Ratio*
Monthly Gross Income	$3,750	$3,750
Monthly Home Mortgage	875	875
Monthly Property Insurance	45	45
Monthly Property Taxes	90	90
Monthly Homeowner Association Dues	15	15
Monthly Student Loan Payments		100
Monthly Credit Card Payments		100
Total Monthly Expenses	$1,025	$1,225
Debt-to-Income Ratios	27.3%	32.67%

Conforming Loans and Nonconforming Loans

When applying for a loan to purchase a home, you will need to complete a loan application with one or more lenders. Each lender will either approve or reject your application based upon criteria such as your credit history, your current income and employment status, and the size and type of home that you are attempting to purchase.

The easiest home loans to get approved are called *conforming mortgage loans.* A conforming mortgage loan meets specific criteria established by federal agencies. Most times, when your local bank provides a home loan to a customer, the loan is later sold to a federally sponsored entity such as Fannie Mae (the Federal National Mortgage Association) and Freddie Mac (the Federal Home Loan Mortgage Corporation). By selling their loans to such entities for a profit, local banks and other lenders are able to recoup money lent and recycle capital so that they can continue to make more loans to other customers.

Conforming loans have maximum dollar limits. Loans above this amount are considered to be *nonconforming* or *jumbo* mortgage loans. As part of the Economic Stimulus Plan of 2008, the U.S. Congress raised the amount of a conforming home loan from $417,000 to 125 percent of the median home price in each county or $417,000, whichever is greater. In addition, conforming loans require specific borrower debt-to-income ratios and documentation such as proof of employment.

When borrower debt-to-income ratios fall outside of the allowable ranges, specific documentation is missing, loan sizes are too large, or the properties being financed do not meet required conforming guidelines, such loans are considered to be nonconforming. Because nonconforming loans are less generic and are considered to have greater risk than conforming loans, they are in less demand and harder to sell. Therefore, nonconforming loans tend to have higher interest rates and other less favorable terms when compared to conforming loans.

Private Mortgage Insurance

Purchasing private mortgage insurance (PMI) allows home buyers to avoid the normal 20 percent down payment when purchasing a home. Such insurance is provided to qualifying home buyers from insurance companies in return for an insurance premium paid each month. This insurance covers lenders in case home buyers default on their loans. For example, assume that you qualify for private mortgage insurance and that you purchase a home. Instead of having to make the normal down payment of 20 percent, having private mortgage insurance allows you to make a lesser down payment that can be as low as 5 percent and borrow more from banks and other lenders. In return for the lower down payment, you agree to pay an insurance company a monthly fee. If you default on the bank loan, the insurance company will repay the bank for any losses up to approximately 20 percent of the loan amount.

The costs to the home buyer for PMI vary depending on the amount of down payment. For many borrowers, once the loan-to-value ratio reaches 80 percent or less, meaning that there is now 20 percent or more borrower equity in the home, the PMI payments may be discontinued. Some high-risk borrowers will be required to continue to make PMI payments until a lower loan-to-value limit is reached. Good ways to avoid being labeled as a "high-risk" borrower include maintaining a good credit history and reasonable debt-to-income ratios. Although the home buyer typically bears the costs of PMI, the lender is the insurance company's client and will normally approach PMI providers on the home buyer's behalf.

80-10-10 Financing

One way that some borrowers get around using PMI is to finance their home purchases using what is referred to as 80-10-10 financing. Using such a structure, a home buyer borrows 80 percent of a home's purchase price under a traditional mortgage loan. Then an additional "second" mortgage loan is provided by the same lender or even a different lender for another 10 percent of the purchase price. The home buyer purchases the home with two mortgage loans, and now only needs a 10 percent down payment and no longer requires any PMI.

A second mortgage loan is a loan that is put on a property after an existing mortgage has already been in place. For example, traditional bank loans to home buyers are "first" mortgage loans. Second mortgages are subordinate to first mortgages. If a borrower defaults on his loan payments, the first mortgage provider can foreclose on the property. Once the property is sold, the second mortgage lender will only receive proceeds if the first mortgage provider has been fully repaid. As you can imagine, second mortgages have

✊ GUESS WHAT?

Some lenders may be willing to provide 80-15-5 financing structures. In such cases, a traditional mortgage loan is provided for 80 percent of the home purchase price, a second mortgage loan is provided for 15 percent, and the home buyer is required to provide a 5 percent down payment. An 80-15-5 structure also eliminates the need for PMI.

more risk than first mortgages. Therefore, lenders will usually require higher origination fees and interest rates for second mortgages.

Federal Housing Administration Loans

The Federal Housing Administration (FHA) serves to help home buyers that cannot afford conventional down payments or that do not qualify for PMI. The FHA does not make loans. Rather, it insures loans made by lenders. Borrowers receiving FHA assistance can qualify for down payments as low as 3 percent. The cost of insurance under an FHA loan is similar to the cost of PMI insurance and usually amounts to about 0.5 percent of the loan balance per year.

FHA insurance premiums must be made until you have repaid about 22 percent of a loan's principal balance. This differs from most PMI loans, which allow insurance premiums to be discontinued once a borrower's home equity reaches 20 percent, which can result from both loan repayments and from property appreciation.

HOME EQUITY LOANS

An efficient source of financing for homeowners is to borrow against the equity within their homes. Banks and other lenders provide loans secured

Home equity loans and lines of credit can be an efficient and attractive source of consumer financing. AP Photo/Ben Margot.

🗣 GUESS WHAT?

The interest paid on home equity loans and home equity lines of credit are tax deductible regardless of how the loan proceeds are spent or invested. If you borrow to take a vacation, buy a car, or to invest in the stock or real estate markets, the interest paid is still tax deductible. For homeowners having sufficient equity in their homes, using loans secured by home equity having low interest rates and tax deductible interest payments is an attractive source of financing.

by home equity to homeowners in return for a second mortgage on their properties. Loans secured by home equity can be less than 5 years and up to 20 years in length, but normally they do not have maturity dates longer than the first mortgage loan on a specific property. The interest rate on a loan secured by home equity can be fixed or adjustable depending upon the type of loan.

It is important to differentiate between a *home equity loan* and a *home equity line of credit*. A home equity loan has a fixed dollar amount that must be borrowed at once. The interest rate on a home equity loan is usually fixed, and there is a predetermined repayment schedule. Any principal payments made by the borrower reduce the outstanding balance of the loan and cannot be reborrowed.

A home equity line of credit has a revolving credit limit that can be borrowed and repaid without penalty during the life of the loan. These loans serve as lines of credit and usually have adjustable interest rates that reset over time. Interest rates on home equity lines of credit are usually tied to the lender's prime rate. Many home equity lines of credit have annual interest rates that are equal to the lender's prime rate and are adjusted from time to time. Others have annual interest rates ranging from the lender's prime rate less .75 percent to the prime rate plus 1.00 percent. Banks and other lenders usually have the same prime rate, which can be viewed on financial Web sites such as Bloomberg.com.

Home equity loans provide less flexibility when compared to the revolving nature of a home equity line of credit. Being able to borrow when needed and repay when cash is available allows borrowers to lower interest costs by paying down debt, knowing that they can reborrow when needed. However, borrowers using home equity lines of credit are subject to interest rate risk. Home equity loans having fixed rates of interest ensure a specific monthly payment that will not change over time. Interest rates on home equity lines of credit can go up and down and be more or less favorable when compared to the fixed interest rates on home equity loans. This uncertainly can place greater risk on borrowers.

6

Tax Considerations

A knowledgeable investor focuses on increasing the value of his investments while minimizing the amount of taxes paid to one or more governments. Different types of investments have different tax consequences. In addition, the same investment held for different lengths of time can result in significantly different tax amounts being paid. Delaying the payment of taxes until some point in the future is also a valuable investment tool. Sophisticated investors consider and understand tax implications before making investment choices.

ORDINARY VERSUS CAPITAL GAIN TAXES

People in the United States are required to pay taxes to state and federal governments based upon the amount of income that they earn. The tax revenues earned by governments are the primary source of income used to maintain local, state, and national infrastructures, including public schools and transportation systems and health care and social security programs. All taxpayers are required to pay the federal government taxes on income earned through wages, self-employment, investments, and most other sources. However, some states do not require residents to pay income taxes, while others do. When you live in a state with income tax requirements, you are often paying income taxes to both the state and federal governments on the same income.

The items taxed, the allowable tax deductions, and the specific tax rates vary by state. However, the tax rate calculations for taxes owed to the federal government are based on scaling schedules that are applicable to all

According to NetScientia Web Concepts, the Internal Revenue Service (IRS) sends out eight billion pages of tax forms and instructions each year. Laid out end to end, they would stretch 28 times around the earth! American taxpayers spend $200 billion and 5.4 billion hours working to comply with federal tax regulations each year, more than it takes to produce every car, truck, and van in the United States!"

Income tax rates and rules can change often and be very complicated. The subject of raising or lowering consumer and business taxes is an ongoing political debate. AP Photo/Chris Carlson.

taxpayers. There are several tax schedules created each year to reflect the status of each taxpayer. For example, unmarried individual taxpayers are subject to a specific tax schedule, while a separate tax schedule is applicable to married taxpayers that choose to file a joint tax return. Another tax schedule applies to married taxpayers that choose to file separate tax returns. Federal tax schedules also provide tax concessions to individual taxpayers that are widowed or that have one or more dependents and serve as the head of a household.

Ordinary Income Taxes

Federal tax rate schedules are applicable for each specific year and can change from year to year. Table 6.1 shows the federal tax rate schedules for the year 2009 by taxpayer status. The federal tax rates provided in these annual schedules are referred to as "ordinary tax rates" and are applied to what is referred to as "ordinary" income. Ordinary income is income received from wages, bonuses, tips, commissions, and other forms of compensation earned from being employed. Other forms of ordinary income can include interest and

Table 6.1
2009 Federal Tax Rates

Tax Rate	Single Filers	Married Filing Jointly or Qualifying Widow/Widower	Married Filing Separately	Head of Household
10%	Up to $8,350	Up to $16,700	Up to $8,350	Up to $11,950
15%	$8,351–$33,950	$16,701–$67,900	$8,351–$33,950	$11,951–$45,500
25%	$33,951–$82,250	$67,901–$137,050	$33,951–$68,525	$45,501–$117,450
28%	$82,251–$171,550	$137,051–$208,850	$68,526–$104,425	$117,451–$190,200
33%	$171,551–$372,950	$208,851–$372,950	$104,426–$186,475	$190,201–$372,950
35%	$372,951 or more	$372,951 or more	$186,476 or more	$372,951 or more

Table 6.2
Federal Income Tax Calculation

Tax Rate	Income	Taxes Due
10%	$16,700	$1,670
15%	51,200	7,680
25%	7,100	1,775
Totals	$75,000	$11,125

dividends received on investments, net income on rental properties, and self-employment income from business ownership. Ordinary income differs from "capital gain" income, which will be discussed next.

Let us use an example to further illustrate how the scaling federal tax rates work. Assume a married couple earned taxable ordinary income of $75,000 for the year 2009 and that they file a joint tax return. Using the schedule in Table 6.1, the couple would compute their tax obligation for the year as shown in Table 6.2.

The couple benefits from the lower 10 percent and 15 percent tax rates for most of their income, and only $7,100 is taxed at the higher 25 percent tax rate. By using these scaling tax rates, the couple is paying an actual tax rate of 14.8 percent ($11,125/$75,000) on $75,000 of ordinary income. The scaling nature of the federal tax rate schedules is intended to subject wealthier taxpayers earning greater amounts of income to higher tax rates, while providing tax relief and reduced tax rates to those earning lower incomes.

Capital Gain Taxes

A capital gain results when an asset is sold at a price greater than an investor's cost. For example, if an investor purchases shares of General Electric

Company common stock for $1,000 and later sells the same shares for $1,500, a $500 capital gain results.

A capital loss results when an asset is sold at a price that is less than an investor's cost. If a Ford Motor Company bond is purchased for $500 and later sold for $300, the investor will realize a capital loss of $200. Capital gains and losses result from the sale of stocks, bonds, mutual funds, ETFs, real estate, and other investments and financial assets.

It is important to note that there are short-term capital gains and long-term capital gains. When an investment is bought and sold within a 12-month period, a short-term capital gain results. When an investment is held for greater than 12 months and later sold, there is a long-term capital gain. A long-term capital gain results when an investment is sold after 1 year, 2 years, 20 years, or at any other time as long as the investment is held for at least 12 months. Short-term capital gains are currently taxed by the federal government at ordinary income tax rates, while long-term capital gains are often taxed at a lower federal tax rate. The federal tax rate for long-term capital gains in the United States for the year 2009 was 15 percent.

Depending upon your level of income, receiving long-term versus short-term capital gain treatment can be important. Consider the couple referenced in Table 6.2. Let us assume that in addition to the couple's $75,000 of ordinary income, during the year 2009 they also sold an investment that had appreciated by $30,000. If they held the investment for less than 12 months, they would report a short-term capital gain and be taxed at the ordinary federal tax rate of 25 percent. Therefore, the couple's tax bill would increase by $7,500 due to the $30,000 short-term capital gain. But what if the couple had held the investment for 12 months or longer? In this case, a long-term capital gain would have resulted leading to the more favorable 15 percent capital gains tax that was in effect during 2009. Now the couple's tax bill has only increased by $4,500. By holding the investment for a longer period in order to receive long-term capital gain treatment, the couple saved $3,000 in taxes ($4,500 versus $7,500).

Certain mutual funds tend to buy and sell securities more often than others. When stocks, bonds, and other investments are sold, either a capital gain or capital loss will be recognized by the mutual fund and passed on to its investors. The more securities that have appreciated in value and that are sold by a specific mutual fund, the more taxes that the fund will generate for its investors. The amount of securities sold by a fund can be measured by its *portfolio turnover rate,* which measures how many times the dollars within a particular mutual fund are reinvested. A fund's turnover rate is one of the best indications of the general level of investor tax liabilities that will be generated by a specific fund when compared to other funds. The more times a fund buys and sells assets or turns its portfolio, the more chances that capital gains will be recognized leading to greater investor tax payments.

If a mutual fund has a portfolio turnover rate of 100 percent, this means that the fund is selling and buying a completely new set of investments each year. Each time an investment is sold at a gain, investors will have to pay capital gain taxes. In addition, if investments are held by the fund for less than 12 months, the sales generate short-term capital gains, which often result

For the year 2007, the federal government collected $2.5 trillion in tax revenue. Of this amount, 45 percent was from individual income taxes, 35 percent was from payroll taxes, and 15 percent was from corporate income taxes (www.taxpolicycenter.org).

People become very vocal and passionate when it comes to the subject of paying taxes. AP Photo/Stephan Savoia.

in higher tax payments when compared to long-term capital gains. When looking at mutual funds with high portfolio turnover rates, investors need to evaluate whether the additional tax burden being generated from such funds is being offset by better investment performance.

THE TIME VALUE OF MONEY

It is important to understand why paying taxes at some point in the future is better than paying the same taxes today. If someone were to offer you $1,000 today or $1,000 a year from now, which would you take? I would take the $1,000 today for two reasons. First, having the money now eliminates any risk that I might not be paid in one year. Second, I can take the $1,000 today, invest it, and hopefully have more than $1,000 in one year. Assume I purchase a one-year, $1,000 certificate of deposit from a bank that pays interest of 5 percent. In one year when the CD matures, I should have $1,050.

In the previous example, the future value of $1,000 one year from today assuming a 5 percent interest rate is $1,050. Conversely, assuming the same 5 percent interest rate, the value today (the "present value") of $1,050 to be received in one year is $1,000. Therefore, if someone offers you the choice of receiving $1,000 today or $1,000 a year from now and you feel that you should earn 5 percent on a one-year loan to this person, then the $1,000 payable in one year is really only worth $952.38 today. I backed into this number by using a simple formula ($1,000/1.05 = $952.38). It can be tested by multiplying $952.38 times 1.05 (1 plus the assumed interest rate) to get back to $1,000.

These examples serve as the basis for one of the most important concepts of investing, which is referred to as "the time value of money." Now we can use this principal to further explore why paying taxes in the future is better than paying taxes today.

TAX DEFERRAL

Holding investments long term can result in the deferral of income taxes, which is an important investment strategy. Consider someone who bought shares in a mutual fund. If the shares were purchased in 1990 for $100,000 and sold in 1992 for $125,000, the investor would be forced to pay a capital gain tax on the $25,000 profit on his 1992 federal tax return. However, if the investor held the shares until 2010 before selling them for $400,000, a capital gain tax would not be due until the filing of his 2010 federal tax return. Even though the mutual fund investment more than tripled in value over a 20-year period, no taxes would be due on this appreciation until the time of sale. Federal tax laws allow capital gain taxes to be deferred and not recognized until the time when an investment is sold.

As another tax deferral example, consider Tables 6.3 and 6.4. Table 6.3 shows what happens to an initial investment of $10,000 over a 20-year period. In this example, the investor earns 8 percent annually and pays taxes on the income each year. At the end of 20 years, the investment of $10,000 has grown to be worth $32,071.

Now let us look at Table 6.4, which assumes the same investment as in Table 6.3 with one exception. Instead of the investor paying taxes to the government each year, Table 6.4 assumes that the investor can defer the payment of taxes until the 20th year. By doing so, the investor is able to earn 8 percent on the money that would have been paid to the government each year. After 20 years, this investment is worth $37,457 or $5,386 (17%) more than the investment shown in Table 6.3.

Table 6.4 is an example of the benefits provided by the government when tax payments can be deferred. Rather than being paid to the government, this money can be reinvested and any earnings belong to the investor. The government is essentially providing investors with interest-free loans. Tax deferral is one of the primary benefits of investment retirement accounts, which will be discussed later in the chapter.

Another example that highlights the benefits of deferring taxes applies to real estate investing. Internal Revenue Code Section 1031 allows qualifying

Table 6.3
20-Year Investment with Annual Tax Payments

	Beginning Investment Value	8% Earnings	Taxes Paid (25% tax rate)	Ending Investment Value
Year 1	$10,000	$ 800	$(200)	$10,600
Year 2	10,600	848	(212)	11,236
Year 3	11,236	899	(225)	11,910
Year 4	11,910	953	(238)	12,625
Year 5	12,625	1,010	(252)	13,382
Year 6	13,382	1,071	(268)	14,185
Year 7	14,185	1,135	(284)	15,036
Year 8	15,036	1,203	(301)	15,938
Year 9	15,938	1,275	(319)	16,895
Year 10	16,895	1,352	(338)	17,908
Year 11	17,908	1,433	(358)	18,983
Year 12	18,983	1,519	(380)	20,122
Year 13	20,122	1,610	(402)	21,329
Year 14	21,329	1,706	(427)	22,609
Year 15	22,609	1,809	(452)	23,966
Year 16	23,966	1,917	(479)	25,404
Year 17	25,404	2,032	(508)	26,928
Year 18	26,928	2,154	(539)	28,543
Year 19	28,543	2,283	(571)	30,256
Year 20	30,256	2,420	(605)	32,071

investors to sell an investment property and defer the payment of income taxes if they purchase another investment property within a predefined period of time. For example, suppose you paid $100,000 for a property, and five years later it was worth $150,000. Let us also assume that the capital gain tax rate is 15 percent. Therefore, if you sell your property for $150,000 you will owe the federal government $7,500 in taxes (($150,000 – $100,000) × 15%).

Using the previous example, if you decided to purchase another qualifying investment property within the permitted time frame (currently 180 days) of selling your existing property, Section 1031 allows you to defer the payment of any capital gain taxes and roll the gain into your next purchase. Such a transaction is often referred to as a "like kind exchange" or a "1031 exchange." Assuming that you sell your property and buy another, you will no longer be required to pay the $7,500 in taxes. Rather, this tax payment is deferred and paid at the time you sell the second property (unless you enter another like kind exchange). If you continue to buy and sell real estate investments,

Table 6.4
20-Year Investment with Deferred Tax Payments

	Beginning Investment Value	8% Earnings	Taxes Paid (25% tax rate)	Ending Investment Value
Year 1	$10,000	$ 800		$10,800
Year 2	10,800	864		11,664
Year 3	11,664	933		12,597
Year 4	12,597	1,008		13,605
Year 5	13,605	1,088		14,693
Year 6	14,693	1,175		15,869
Year 7	15,869	1,269		17,138
Year 8	17,138	1,371		18,509
Year 9	18,509	1,481		19,990
Year 10	19,990	1,599		21,589
Year 11	21,589	1,727		23,316
Year 12	23,316	1,865		25,182
Year 13	25,182	2,015		27,196
Year 14	27,196	2,176		29,372
Year 15	29,372	2,350		31,722
Year 16	31,722	2,538		34,259
Year 17	34,259	2,741		37,000
Year 18	37,000	2,960		39,960
Year 19	39,960	3,197		43,157
Year 20	43,157	3,453	(9,152)	37,457

you can continue to defer more and more taxes. A broad range of real estate investments qualify under Section 1031 including houses, condominiums, office buildings, restaurants, hotels, and so forth. Before considering such an exchange, you should consult a tax advisor for full details relevant to your particular situation.

TAX AVOIDANCE

There is a difference between deferring income taxes and receiving tax deductions that reduce your income tax expense. The key difference is that tax deferrals result in the delaying of tax payments, while tax deductions result in permanent tax savings. A prudent investor makes the most of the tax deferral and tax deduction opportunities provided by governments. Remember, each dollar saved in taxes is a dollar that can be invested, compounded, and used to increase your net worth. Let us consider a couple examples to illustrate the benefits of tax deductions.

When you borrow money to purchase an investment, any interest paid on a loan is usually tax deductible. The tax deductibility of interest expense actually lowers your cost of borrowing. Consider the following formula:

After tax interest rate = (Before tax interest rate) × (1 – investor's tax rate)

Assume that you borrow money from a bank to purchase an investment property. A bank may charge you an interest rate of 7 percent. If you can deduct the interest payments on the loan, you will either lower your tax bill or receive a tax refund from this benefit. If your tax rate is 25 percent, your after tax interest rate on the loan becomes 5.25 percent based upon the following:

After tax interest rate = (7%) × (1 – 25%)
After tax interest rate = 5.25%

This means that while you are paying the bank a 7 percent interest rate, after your tax deduction for the interest expense, you are really only paying about 5.25 percent on your loan due to the permanent tax deduction provided by the interest paid.

Many real estate investments generate tax losses year after year even when they are appreciating in value. This is because the interest on borrowed funds, depreciation expense, and repair and maintenance costs are shown as expense items on an investor's tax return. The deductibility of these expenses can help to generate substantial tax losses. So while investors know that their investments are increasing in value, they are receiving substantial tax savings each year.

Using another example, taxpayers are currently allowed to deduct their home mortgage loan interest for both primary and secondary residences on up to $500,000 ($1,000,000 for married filers) of mortgage debt assuming certain income thresholds are not exceeded. In addition, interest on up to $50,000 ($100,000 for married filers) on home equity loans and lines of credit can also be deducted. This means that interest on up to $1,100,000 of combined debt can be deducted on a homeowner's tax return for both his primary residence and any vacation home as well. Also, remember that the interest paid on a home equity loan is tax deductible regardless of how the money is used. This is why it often makes sense to use home equity loan financing to purchase items rather than nondeductible consumer product loans. In addition, the interest rates on home equity loans are often more attractive even before the tax deduction is considered.

Other meaningful tax deductions include qualifying investment expenses. For example, fees paid to financial advisors are tax deductible. So are the costs associated with renting safe deposit boxes for storing investments like gold, diamonds, and stock certificates. The costs of financial publications can also be taken as a deduction against any investment income.

THE BENEFITS OF RETIREMENT ACCOUNTS

The government encourages people to save for their retirement by providing tax benefits when money is invested within certain types of retirement accounts. The concept is based upon savings that are accumulated during a person's working years and then later withdrawn over time and used to aid the investor with his or her financial needs during retirement. Beginning the use of retirement accounts at a young age can reap tremendous rewards later in life and lead to great wealth and financial comfort.

The two most common types of personal retirement accounts include the 401K plan and the Individual Retirement Account (IRA). Each of these investment structures can provide significant benefits and should be seriously considered as your first long-term savings vehicles. Let us talk about 401K plans first.

401K Plans

An employer-sponsored 401K plan can provide investors with significant benefits that should not be ignored. The specific type of investments that 401K dollars are invested in can either be chosen by the employer or by the employee depending upon how the plan is structured. Normally, periodic deductions are made from an employee's paycheck and are invested within an assortment of stock, bond, and money market mutual funds. The dollars that investors invest from their paychecks into such plans are not taxed as income.

Let us assume that your job pays $40,000 a year and that your paychecks are reduced by 20 percent for federal income taxes. This would result in you receiving net paychecks for the year of $32,000 ($40,000 gross pay less $8,000 in taxes). Now let us assume that you contribute 15 percent of your gross pay into a qualified 401K plan sponsored by your employer. You would still earn $40,000 for the year, but now $6,000 will be deducted from your gross pay and invested into the 401K plan. Now your tax burden will be $6,800 (($40,000 salary less the $6,000 401K contribution) times 20%) instead of $8,000. Your net pay will be $27,200 instead of $32,000, but you now have an investment of $6,000 in the 401K plan that should continue to grow in value over time. Put another way, you now have $33,200 of net pay ($27,200 take home plus $6,000 invested in the 401K plan) rather than the $32,000 that you would have had if you had chosen not to participate in the 401K plan. For saving money for *your* retirement, the government just gave you $1,200!

Another attractive 401K plan feature that cannot be ignored is the fact that many employers will often match a certain percentage or dollar amount on your behalf based upon the amount that you save each year. Typically, employers will contribute a certain amount of an employee's savings into a 401K plan, and the contribution will vest over a specified period. For example, let us assume that your employer has agreed to match the first 3 percent of your salary that you contribute into its 401K plan and that this matched amount vests over five years. If you earn $40,000 for the year and contribute 3 percent to the 401K plan, you will have invested $1,200. In addition, your employer will contribute another 3 percent or $1,200 into the 401K plan on your behalf. Based on the five-year vesting schedule, you will be entitled to 20 percent or $240 of the $1,200 contributed by your employer (plus any earnings on these amounts) for each of the next five years.

When an employer matches your contribution into a 401K plan, assuming you remain employed for the entire vesting period, you essentially just doubled your money at the time of your contribution. Instead of having $1,200 invested, you now have $2,400. In addition, the value of the entire $2,400 should continue to grow and compound over time.

The earnings from your investments in a 401K plan continue to accumulate over time. However, investors are not required to pay income taxes on these earnings until later in life when the proceeds are being withdrawn. This means that you get the benefit of investing more dollars for longer periods of time when you can defer the payment of income taxes. The earnings on your contributions and any contributions made by your employer are not taxed until you begin to withdraw funds from the plan. This form of tax deferral can benefit investors for many decades.

In most circumstances, investors should use their employer-sponsored 401K plans as their first investment vehicle. This is particularly true when an employer is matching a portion of their savings. At a minimum, investors should try to contribute at least enough to receive the maximum amount of their employer contribution. For example, if your employer matches up to the first 3 percent of your salary, then you should contribute at least 3 percent of your salary to maximize this benefit. If you contribute only 2 percent of your salary, your employer will only contribute 2 percent, and you will have given up the opportunity to receive free money. Over time investors should strive to contribute the maximum amount of annual savings permitted by law ($16,500 per year in 2009 or $22,000 if you are age 50 or older) to take advantage of the substantial tax benefits.

If you are self-employed, there are ways that you can set up a retirement plan for yourself and your employees that are based on the same principals as an employer-sponsored 401K plan. Examples of such plans include Simplified Employee Pension (SEP) and Keogh plans. If you are self-employed and are not using such a tool, I strongly recommend that you meet with a tax advisor to learn more about your options and the benefits that can be achieved.

Individual Retirement Accounts (IRAs)

An IRA allows earnings to compound over time on either a tax-free or a tax-deferred basis depending on the type of IRA chosen. Investors can usually choose investment alternatives from a vast array of mutual funds, stocks, bonds, and other securities that are offered by the brokerage firm handling your account. The two primary types of IRAs are the Traditional IRA and the Roth IRA. Both accounts can offer substantial benefits to specific

🎤 GUESS WHAT?

Most companies offer their employees the ability to participate in a 401K plan. Some employers require waiting periods of up to 12 months before new employees can join, but most allow participation within the first few months of employment. The average employer contribution is 3 percent of its payroll expense (www.bpp401K.com).

◉ GUESS WHAT?

When using both actively managed and passively managed mutual and exchange traded funds, investors should consider using tax-deferred retirement accounts to hold actively managed funds. Because actively managed funds tend to buy and sell securities much more frequently than passive investments, such as indexed mutual funds, the higher tax obligations generated from selling securities can be avoided in tax-deferred retirement accounts because no taxes are due until the time of withdrawal. Passive investments that generate minimal tax obligations can be held outside of retirement accounts. The same logic applies to bond funds that generate interest income. Holding these types of investments in retirement accounts helps to lower investor tax burdens.

---

individuals, but each has its own income limitations and tax benefits that must be considered when evaluating each person's needs.

With a Traditional IRA, you may be able to deduct your annual contributions (limited to a maximum annual amount of $5,000 in 2009 or $6,000 if you are age 50 or over) on your income tax return depending upon whether or not you participate in other retirement plans and your income level. Just like with 401K plans, this means that the government is actually reducing your annual income tax bill each year when you decide to save money in a Traditional IRA. Earnings within a Traditional IRA accumulate over time on a tax-deferred basis. This means that you do not pay any income taxes on your account earnings until you begin to make withdrawals during your retirement years.

Contributions to a Roth IRA (also limited to a maximum annual contribution of $5,000 or $6,000 if you are age 50 or over) are not tax deductible, but the earnings grow on a tax deferred basis. In addition, if you retire after the age of 59½ and the account has been held open for at least a five-year period, the distributions you take in retirement are tax-free. This means that you never have to pay taxes on income that has been earned and compounded over decades!

I recommend that you research which IRA is most suitable for your personal needs. As the first step, I suggest going to the Web site of any major brokerage company (i.e., The Vanguard Group, Fidelity Investments, Morgan Stanley, Merrill Lynch, etc.) and searching for IRAs. Most firms will provide a comparison of Traditional and Roth IRAs in a simplistic form that will enable you to choose the right plan for your specific circumstances.

◉ GUESS WHAT?

For the year 2008, there were almost 90 million tax refunds provided by the IRS in the United States that totaled over $214 billion. The average tax refund for the year was $2,383. It typically takes six to eight weeks to receive a federal tax refund when a tax return is mailed to the IRS. When tax returns are "e-filed" and submitted to the IRS over the Internet, the average time of receiving refunds is within 10 days (www.hrblock.com).

THE TAX GEEK

Tax advisors have a reputation for being anal, boring geeks that wear conservative suits (and sometimes bow ties) and crunch numbers in small offices. Admittedly, most of the tax specialists that I have met fit this description. However, it takes a certain type of person to maintain interest in tax regulations and to stay on top of new and pending tax rules. State and federal governments are constantly changing tax laws, and it is important to understand how these changes affect your investments and financial planning decisions. While not a job for everyone, the tax advisor plays a key role for the financially literate.

Tax is a complicated field that requires specialists that focus solely on tax matters and nothing else. I meet with my tax advisor frequently. Rather than looking for qualifying tax deductions and deferrals after the tax year is over like many taxpayers, I meet with my advisor and determine which deductions I should be aware of and targeting before the tax year even begins. To do so after the fact is counterproductive. There is little a taxpayer can do once the year is over.

It is important to differentiate between a true tax advisor and the franchised CPA firm whose primary focus is to spit out thousands of tax returns as quickly as possible. In many cases, these people are serving a robotic role of entering numbers and printing your tax return after the tax year has ended. What you need is someone that you can meet with at the start of each year, perhaps as he or she is completing your prior year tax return, and talk about what savings and deferrals can be achieved in the coming year. You want someone that you can build a relationship with. Many of the national firms will assign a different tax preparer to your account each year, which results in a passive versus proactive approach to building wealth and maximizing tax benefits.

The primary objectives for investors when it comes to taxes should be to pay as little as possible and as late as possible (within the confines of the tax regulations). Tax is a complex topic, and all investors can benefit from a relationship with a good tax advisor.

7

Insurance

How would you like to work really hard for many years, wisely save and invest your money, and then lose it all in a day? I am not referring to a stock market collapse or a real estate market depression. Rather, the type of financial devastation that I am describing can be more easily avoided and would be unnecessarily tragic if to occur unprotected.

Imagine that you get into a car accident and severely injure someone or someone's property and that you have no automobile insurance. Or consider a situation in which your pet attacks a child or another animal or causes significant harm to personal property. What about if someone falls down in your home or yard? If you have investments, a house or other assets, you may likely be sued for damages that could amount to hundreds of thousands of dollars. You might be worth $1 million today and nothing tomorrow. We live in a society in which people constantly sue one another. You have seen the steady stream of television commercials with greedy lawyers and law firms that beg for the opportunity to sue people and businesses for any conceivable reason.

Using another example, assume that you buy a home for $200,000 and that you borrow $160,000 to make the purchase. Your lender will require that you insure the property for at least $160,000 so that it will be repaid if the home is ever destroyed by fire or other unexpected event. Let us also assume that over time the property appreciates and becomes worth $500,000. If your amount of insurance coverage was never increased to account for this added value and the home is destroyed, your lender will receive the insurance proceeds and you will have a potentially worthless piece of property.

⚡ BEWARE!

It is important to realize that if you lose a lawsuit and you have no insurance or the amount of your insurance is insufficient, you might need to sell many or all of your assets. In addition, if the value of your assets is not sufficient to pay the required settlement, your future wages and income could be garnished for many years into the future. Under such a circumstance, one unexpected event could wipe out your entire financial net worth!

It is important to have insurance when it comes to protecting your assets. When you own something, think about all the things that could go wrong that would reduce its value (i.e., theft, vandalism, fire, wind, earthquake, flood, explosions, etc.) and determine if you have adequate protection.

WHAT IS INSURANCE?

Insurance can be defined as a risk management tool that allows people and businesses to transfer certain risks from themselves to one or more insurance companies. Insurance companies provide insurance to protect people and businesses from certain negative events in return for fees, which are referred to as *insurance premiums*. In return for the payment of a certain premium each period (i.e., monthly, quarterly, semi-annually, or annually), an insurance company will provide you with an insurance policy. An insurance policy is a legal contract that specifies the period covered by insurance, the types and amounts of insurance coverage, and the amount of the premium.

Many of the risks covered by insurance companies have very low probabilities of occurring, but if they do happen, tremendous financial losses can result. For example, if a person's home were to burn to the ground, an insurance company may need to pay the homeowner thousands of dollars. However, the insurance company may have only collected a few thousand dollars in insurance premiums from this particular client. But hundreds of thousands of other clients have been paying premiums to the insurance company for years and have never claimed any losses. By pooling and sharing the risks among thousands of insurance policies, an insurance company greatly reduces its chances of losing money. This allows insurance companies to provide insurance to individuals at relatively cheap prices.

Also covered in most insurance policies is the amount of any deductible. An insurance policy deductible is the amount that the insured person must pay out-of-pocket before the insurance company begins to pay for any loss. For example, if your automobile policy has a deductible of $2,500 and you hit a tree with your car and cause $3,000 worth of damages, you will be obligated to pay the first $2,500 and your insurance company will pay the additional $500.

Some insurance deductibles are measured by each event or occurrence, while others are based on cumulative events. For example, if the deductible referenced in the previous paragraph is measured by occurrence, each time that you crash your car, you will be required to pay the first $2,500 of any damages. If a policy deductible is based upon cumulative events, then you will continue to make all payments until the deductible is reached. Going

In 2005, Hurricane Katrina slammed the Gulf Coast of the United States as a Category 3 hurricane. The Commerce Department estimated over $100 billion of property losses would not be covered by insurance.

forward, the insurance company will make all payments until any policy limits are reached. For example, a dental insurance policy might require that the insured person pay the first $200 for dental services during the year. After the $200 deductible has been paid by the insured for one or more visits to the dentist, the insurance company will begin to pay for future visits and services costing more than this amount. In this example, the insurance company may limit the total amount of expenses that it will pay during the policy period to an amount such as $10,000.

Insurance policies will have some type of policy exclusions that specify certain circumstances and events of loss that an insurance company will not cover. For example, a home insurance policy may not cover the theft of jewelry and other excluded items unless the insured agrees to pay a higher premium. A medical insurance policy may not cover emergency and other types of care without your primary physician's approval. Your home and rental property may not be insured against losses caused by mold or terrorist acts. Some events of loss are not insurable, while others are depending upon the insurance company, the specific policy, and the amount of premium paid.

It is important that people read every word of each insurance policy to fully understand what is covered and what is not covered. Each insurance policy may differ in material respects. Policy limitations should be considered before entering an insurance policy, and additional policy coverage or additional policies may be desirable. Many people find out what their insurance policies do not cover after a loss occurs and it is too late.

LIABILITY INSURANCE

As mentioned, people like to sue one another, and it is not that difficult to find a reason to file a lawsuit. Some people make a living out of suing others. Even if a lawsuit is frivolous and unfounded, it is very expensive to hire one or more lawyers to defend yourself. Oftentimes it makes more sense to settle out of court by making payment to the person that filed the lawsuit. In either case, you risk losing a substantial amount of money if you are not insured against such risks.

Liability insurance is a broad type of insurance that covers the insured from legal claims. Such insurance is intended to cover the costs of defending a lawsuit and the payment of any settlement depending upon how the insurance company wants to proceed. Many types of insurance include some type of liability insurance. For example, a homeowner's insurance policy normally covers not only the home itself and much of its contents, but it also covers events such as when someone gets injured on the property or within the home and sues the insured. An automobile insurance policy should also include liability coverage for instances when an automobile is used to cause personal injury or property damage. For example, if you crash your car through your neighbor's house, they might sue you for the cost of the property damage plus a more subjective cost for their personal injury and even any mental duress caused by the accident.

Professional liability insurance is another form of liability insurance that protects doctors, lawyers, builders, architects, accountants, and other professionals against legal claims by their clients. Professional liability insurance often covers risks that are not covered by general liability policies such as negligence, misrepresentation, and inaccurate advice.

HOMEOWNERS' INSURANCE

If someone owns a home and it gets destroyed along with everything in it, most people do not have the ability to rebuild and replace its contents. Such an event could take a lifetime to recoup. A homeowners' insurance policy protects the insured from such a devastating event. If a home is damaged or destroyed by a covered peril such as fire or wind, a homeowners' insurance policy provides the homeowner with the money to rebuild or repair the home and to purchase new appliances, clothing, furniture, kitchen supplies, electronics, and other items as needed. A homeowner's policy should also provide loss of use provisions. If your home is damaged and unlivable for a period of time, the policy should pay for temporary housing while your home is being repaired or rebuilt.

If you own a condominium, usually the condominium association will cover damages to the exterior of the building, but not the interior even when losses result from events outside of your control. If a water heater bursts or an electrical fire takes place, the owner of the condominium will be responsible for any interior damage. A homeowners' insurance policy protects the owner from such risks.

Homeowners' insurance also provides liability protection. If someone gets injured on your property, such insurance protects you from lawsuits. Your insurance company will either pay to settle or defend such legal actions on your behalf. Homeowners' insurance provides dual protection by providing coverage of both property and general liability.

If the time comes to file a claim for damaged, lost, or stolen property, an insurance company will require a list of the specific items and an estimate of their net worth. Doing so is a lot easier when you still have your things. Consider taking pictures or a video recording of your insured items. Keep this information in a secure place, such as a safe or safety deposit box.

It is important to understand whether your insurance policy covers the actual cash value or the replacement cost of your property. For example, if your living room furniture that was purchased 10 years ago is destroyed and your policy covers the actual cash value, you will be paid far less than the amount needed to buy new furniture. If the policy covers replacement cost, you should receive enough money from your insurance company to buy new living room furniture at today's prices.

If you rent an apartment, house, or even a dorm room, you still want to consider protecting your personal property. Renters' insurance can cover the costs of your personal property and provide liability protection in case someone gets injured within the home.

Many weather-related accidents, fire, vandalism, and theft are covered under most homeowners' insurance policies. Some of the common events that are not covered include flood, earthquake, nuclear incidents, acts of war, and terrorism. Flood and earthquake insurance can usually be obtained under separate insurance policies or as addendums to existing homeowners' insurance policies, and sometimes coverage for such events is required by lenders depending upon a property's location. However, other possible events that are difficult to predict, such as war and terrorism, may not be insurable.

You should monitor any material increase in value to your property over time. Just because you had proper insurance coverage several years ago does not mean that you are properly insured today. Stay on top of your coverage and your asset values. You might want to keep a file or spreadsheet updated periodically that lists your assets and any corresponding insurance policies, coverage amounts, limitations, and other relevant information.

AUTOMOBILE INSURANCE

Another type of insurance that should be considered mandatory is automobile insurance. No one should be driving a vehicle without proper insurance. In almost all states, a minimum amount of automobile insurance is required by law, and failure to comply can result in hefty fines and penalties. Automobile accidents can result in huge costs for damages involving your own vehicle, one or more other vehicles, personal and business property, and personal injury. Remember that even if your car is only worth $200, you can still cause $1 million worth of damages.

While most states require only varying levels of property and liability insurance, most drivers will want to purchase collision and comprehensive automobile insurance as well. As the name implies, collision insurance pays for damages to your automobile when you "collide" with something. For example, if you rear-end another vehicle, the costs to repair your car would

⚡ BEWARE!

According to the Insurance Information Institute, in the year 2007, the value of stolen motor vehicles in the United States was $7.4 billion. The average value of a motor vehicle reported stolen was $6,755, which means that about 1.1 million automobiles were stolen that year. The Federal Bureau of Investigation (FBI) estimates that an automobile is stolen in the United States about every 28.8 seconds.

be covered under your collision insurance policy. Without it, you would be forced to pay your own expenses out-of-pocket.

Comprehensive auto insurance covers auto theft, vandalism and weather-related and other unforeseen events that are not covered by collision insurance. So if your new car stereo system is stolen while shopping at the mall and you want your insurance company to help pay for a new one, you better have comprehensive insurance. If you purchase a vehicle with a loan from a bank or other lender, you will most likely be required to have collision and comprehensive insurance.

Like a homeowners' insurance policy, auto insurance includes liability coverage that protects the insured from accident-related lawsuits. Different states will require different minimum liability coverage amounts. In many cases, the amount required is far less than actually needed. For example, a state with weak enforcement laws might require liability coverage for drivers

Unfortunately, many people realize that they need insurance after an uninsured event, and it becomes too late. AP Photo/Frederick Breedon.

✗   **BEWARE!**

According to the Insurance Information Institute, during the year 2007, uninsured motorists ranged from 1 to 29 percent by state with New Mexico (29%), Mississippi (28%), Alabama (26%), Oklahoma (24%), and Florida (23%) leading the top five.

of only $10,000. A short stay in a hospital for the affected parties can vastly exceed this amount. Any shortfall between your insurance coverage and the amount of damage you cause is your responsibility.

HEALTH INSURANCE

A health insurance policy provides protection in case you become sick or ill. Such coverage includes routine doctor visits, emergency care, and many of the costs for medicines and prescriptions. Depending upon the specific policy, health insurance can cover the costs associated with dermatologists, chiropractors, optometrists, dental surgeons, psychotherapists, and other specialists. If you are alive and breathing, you need health insurance. A day should not go by without this type of protection.

Think about what happens if you get into a serious accident or have a prolonged illness. The dollar expenses associated with a hospital stay can quickly escalate into the tens of thousands over very short periods of time. For an injury or a disease that requires long-term treatment, medical costs can become astronomical. Even brief doctor visits for minor accidents can result in large dollar amounts. Not paying such bills can haunt a person's credit report for a lifetime and lead to an ongoing financial burden and even personal bankruptcy.

Health insurance can be purchased on a group basis, such as by a small business or corporation, or by individuals. The costs of such policies will vary by the amount of any deductible, the number of covered persons if a group policy, any coverage limits, and other specific features. Generally, the more people covered under one plan, such as when policies are purchased by large corporations, the cheaper the costs. In addition, the higher the deductible or the amount that the insured will be required to pay, the lower the premium. Policies for individuals are usually most expensive with costs increasing as the insured gets older and the need for greater medical care becomes more likely.

A societal problem today is that health insurance costs continue to rise quickly. In addition, many employers do not provide health insurance for their employees. The smaller the business, the more costly it becomes to obtain health insurance, so some businesses choose not to offer this benefit. Others are forced to pass on large costs to their employees. Not providing such insurance subjects business owners to the risk of being unable to attract and retain top talent. You should evaluate health insurance benefits before

✗   **BEWARE!**

According to daveramsey.com, medical bills are the number one cause of bankruptcy.

🗨 GUESS WHAT?

It is estimated that during the year 2007, 46 million Americans, or 18 percent of the population under the age of 65, had no health insurance, and nearly 90 million people, almost one-third of the population under age 65, spent some portion of either 2006 or 2007 without such insurance (National Coalition on Health Care).

accepting employment opportunities, and always ensure proper coverage with or without your employer's assistance.

Most businesses that offer health insurance will cover a portion of the costs and require employees to cover the remaining portion. The total cost and the split between employer and employee vary dramatically by company size and policy. Covered employees with families usually pay substantially more than single employees having no dependents.

DISABILITY INSURANCE

Most people do not consider themselves to be assets. Many people think of an asset as something that costs money. Others think of an asset as something that generates income or a profit. But by working you do generate income. By being able to work and receive a paycheck or by running a business, you become an asset to yourself, your family, and your employer and employees. If something serious were to happen to you, in most cases the level of income you produce would be drastically reduced or even eliminated. Such an event could cause a significant lifestyle change for both you and members of your family. So why not treat yourself like any other asset?

Disability insurance is a means of protecting a portion of your income when a disabling accident or illness no longer allows you to conduct your normal work activities. Imagine that you have an accident and are hospitalized or forced to remain at home for an extended period of time. Besides needing to pay for your medical treatment, you will also need to continue to pay your normal living expenses. When you get sick, the world keeps on moving and the grocery stores, the power and phone companies, and your landlords and lenders continue to expect timely payment. If you are supporting yourself or yourself and others, unless you have substantial savings, you may quickly run out of money. Disability insurance provides you with cash while you are unable to work.

Purchasing disability insurance to provide enough income to support a person and his or her family during times of distress should be strongly considered. Some employers provide varying types and amounts of disability insurance for their employees. Others do not. You need to evaluate whether such policies cover you while only on the job or if you are also covered outside

🗨 GUESS WHAT?

The chance of becoming disabled before the age of 65 is about 30 percent (www.disability quotes.com).

of work. In addition, employer-provided policies often only cover a relatively small fraction of a person's normal income. In such cases, it may be a wise investment to purchase an outside policy to increase the total dollar amount of coverage.

Disability insurance is often used to "bridge" a period of time until a person can begin working again. When determining how much disability insurance to purchase, a person needs to ensure that if he was disabled for the rest of his life, that the income paid by a policy is sufficient and that it will be paid for a long enough period of time.

The determination of how much disability insurance to purchase is a very personal decision. Each person needs to consider how much they are willing to pay in premiums each month or year in return for this type of security. However, unless you have a rich uncle willing to take care of you, I strongly suggest you maintain some level of disability insurance.

LIFE INSURANCE

Whenever you have people financially dependent on you, you need to consider purchasing a life insurance policy. While death may not be a focal point for many young adults, it can happen at any time. If you have children, a spouse, or other family members that rely on your income, think about how their financial situations would change without you. If you are married with children, think about how losing a spouse would affect your life and the lives of your children.

Life insurance should be considered to be a form of protection needed between now and the time that you are able to retire. As you get closer to retirement, life insurance becomes less necessary as your savings and investments increase and compound over time. It is in the earlier years of your life that you are most financially vulnerable.

If you die while covered under a life insurance policy, your insurance company will be obligated to pay your beneficiary, which will be one or more persons that you specify within your policy, a lump sum cash payment. Coverage amounts normally range from $250,000 to several million dollars. However, I have known wealthy individuals to insure themselves for $30 million or more. Life insurance proceeds can be spent anyway the beneficiary chooses unless there are stipulations specified by the insured in other documents. For example, a person's will may specify that his life insurance proceeds be used only for certain purposes. Common uses for life insurance proceeds include paying down debts and paying for college educations and ongoing bills.

A long-term life insurance policy can fix your payments for periods as long as 30 years. Younger applicants are normally provided with substantially lower premiums because the risk of making payments is reduced for insurance companies. Locking these lower costs for long periods of time can be a favorable decision. If your health deteriorates over the insured period, your premiums cannot be increased.

When purchasing life insurance, you will most likely be presented with a choice of buying variable life insurance (sometimes called "whole" or "universal" life insurance) or term life insurance.

Choosing the right amount of life insurance is a very personal decision that varies by individual circumstances. Factors to be considered include amounts and types of debt, the number of children and other dependents, other sources of income, and a person's overall lifestyle. Many professionals within the insurance industry suggest 5 to 10 times a person's annual salary.

Variable Life Insurance

Insurance salespeople make a significantly higher commission from selling variable life insurance when compared to term life insurance, which is often why they try to convince you that this is the better choice.

Variable life insurance pays a predetermined amount to the beneficiaries of the insured at the time of his or her death. In addition, variable life insurance allows a portion of the premiums paid to be invested in securities such as stock and bond mutual funds. The payment of income taxes can also be deferred on earnings generated from the invested funds until the time of withdrawal. A variable life insurance policy begins to have a redeemable or "surrender" value at some point that continues to accumulate over time from both additional premiums paid and from earnings on invested funds. The surrender value of the policy can be withdrawn and borrowed against by the insured.

Term Life Insurance

Like variable life insurance, term life insurance pays a predetermined dollar amount to one or more beneficiaries of the insured at the time of his or her death. However, unlike variable life insurance, a term life policy has no cash or policy surrender value unless the person insured actually dies during the term of the policy.

Upon first glance, one might be swayed toward purchasing variable life insurance so that a portion of the premiums are invested and future value is provided regardless of whether the person insured dies or not. However, variable life insurance is significantly more costly than term life insurance. In addition, it often takes many years before any of your premiums are actually invested. Also, an educated investor can most likely achieve higher investment returns than those generated by a variable life insurance policy.

It is always beneficial to compare quotes from several quality insurance companies to make sure that you are getting the best terms and the lowest premiums. You probably want to purchase insurance from an insurance company that has a rating of "A" (Excellent) or better. The most popular company that provides ratings on various insurance companies is A.M. Best Co. (www.ambest.com).

THE PROTECTION OF AN UMBRELLA

To insure against major lawsuits, I recommend the purchase of an umbrella insurance policy. An umbrella policy allows people to protect themselves

Significant discounts can be received when purchasing homeowners' and renters' insurance for items such as fire and burglar alarm systems, sprinkler systems, and fire extinguishers. In addition, worthwhile discounts can be received when you combine other types of insurance polices with the same insurance company (i.e., home, auto, and umbrella policies).

---

against lawsuits by providing additional coverage in addition to your existing insurance policies. For example, automobile and homeowners' insurance policies provide liability coverage in case you injure someone with your vehicle or in case someone is injured on your property. However, these policies have limits. If you get sued for $500,000 and your policy provides maximum coverage of only $300,000, you could be on the hook to pay the remaining $200,000. You may be forced to pay this amount by selling assets and/or through deductions from your ongoing paychecks. It is not uncommon today for successful lawsuits to require payments far in excess of normal policy coverage limits.

Another reason to have an umbrella policy is to obtain coverage for liabilities that may be excluded from your existing policies or for liabilities that are given minimal coverage under existing policies. For example, someone may sue you for false claims or slander based upon something that you or a family member said. An umbrella policy covers against such risks.

Normally, you will purchase an umbrella policy from the same insurance company that provides your automobile and homeowners' or renters' policies. Fortunately, the cost associated with an umbrella policy is fairly minimal (i.e., a couple hundred dollars a year for a $1,000,000 policy).

BUSINESS INSURANCE

If you are a business owner, you owe it to yourself and your employees to insure your business against certain risks. Most business insurance policies cover four general areas including property, liability, employees, and loss of income.

Property—Business property and casualty policies protect businesses against the risk of loss for buildings, inventory, machinery, equipment, and other assets used by a business. Such insurance can cover business assets inside and outside of the workplace, including goods in transit, such as when companies make deliveries or when goods are shipped to customers.

Liability—The more complicated the business and the more contact with the public, the greater the chances that accidents can occur leading to legal actions against a company. Business liability insurance can protect businesses from damages caused by employee errors and negligence, customer injuries, and other unfavorable events.

Employees—Business owners need to take care of their workers in order to remain competitive and to attract top talent. Many businesses provide health benefits such as medical, dental, vision, disability, and life insurance for their employees. Depending upon the size and specific type of business, the range

Property damage, loss of income, and other uninsured risks can ruin a business virtually overnight. AP Photo/Dave Martin.

of company health benefits provided and the level of cost sharing between employee and employer can vary significantly.

Workers' compensation insurance is required by state law to compensate employees for workplace injuries. Before workers' compensation insurance, employees could more easily sue businesses for injuries in the workplace. This led to substantial litigation between companies and their employees. Ultimately, states set up systems whereby all employers are required to purchase workers' compensation insurance for their employees. In return, workers are much less able to file successful lawsuits against employers for injuries.

Loss of Income—A business may be forced to stop or significantly reduce operations after a fire or other type of catastrophe takes place. Business interruption insurance provides payments that allow business owners to continue paying their bills and employees while buildings, equipment, and other key resources are being repaired or replaced.

A COST VERSUS BENEFIT ANALYSIS

There are costs and benefits associated with having insurance. The costs are straightforward and can be measured by the dollar amounts that you pay to your insurance company (or the payments that your bank or someone else makes on your behalf). The benefits of having insurance are far more subjective. When considering insuring yourself or an asset, ask yourself the following questions:

- What risks am I insuring against?
- What are the worst scenarios that can possibly happen?

- What is the likelihood of such events actually taking place?
- Could I and my family members comfortably survive such an event from a monetary perspective?
- How much does it cost to purchase insurance to gain protection from these risks?
- What dollar amount should I insure against and still feel adequately protected?
- What riders, exemptions, and limitations can I live with in my insurance policies to minimize costs?

Some businesses choose to self-insure because their owners or managers feel that it is more advantageous to remain uninsured for certain items and keep the cash rather than pay premiums to an insurance company. If an unexpected event takes place, they are willing to use the saved proceeds from not making periodic insurance payments plus any necessary out-of-pocket cash to cover any costs. You may come to a similar conclusion when evaluating particular risks. Just make sure that if an uninsured event were to take place that you have the proper resources to absorb it.

8

The Entrepreneur

An entrepreneur can be defined as a person that creates a business, company, or venture intended to provide a new or improved product or service. This person assumes the risks, benefits, and accountability for the direction and outcome of an endeavor.

The world has benefited tremendously from the entrepreneur. Many new technologies and greater efficiencies are available because someone took the initiative to create something. The entrepreneur is critically important to society and allows businesses to effectively compete and offer new and cheaper products, which is beneficial to consumers.

Consider the contributions of some of the most famous entrepreneurs. Donald Trump is a real estate tycoon, author, television host, and the founder of Trump University. He is also the owner of the Miss Universe, Miss USA, and Miss Teen USA pageants. Mr. Trump has lost and regained fortunes and has been responsible for some of the most well-known office buildings, resorts, casinos, and golf courses. Mr. Trump is one of the richest people in America. *Forbes* Magazine's prestigious Forbes 400 listed Mr. Trump as having a net worth of $2.7 billion!

Oprah Winfrey began her career as a radio broadcaster. She now hosts one of the most popular television shows. Ms. Winfrey is an established actor and founder of her own production company that focuses on television and film production, magazine publishing, and online media. Ms. Winfrey also formed the magazine *O, The Oprah Magazine,* which is one of the leading woman's lifestyle publications, and *O at Home,* a home design publication.

In addition, her book club is the largest in the world with over half a million members. Ms. Winfrey has also created charitable organizations that have awarded millions of dollars to people in need around the world.

Michael Dell started with a big idea and $1,000 from his dorm room in 1984. He dreamed of providing affordable computers to college students. Mr. Dell revolutionized the personal computing business by skipping the middle man and selling computers directly to users. Customers can now order personalized computers online and avoid additional mark-ups from distributors and other retailers. Dell Corporation is now the largest personal computer manufacturer and largest online computer retailer, employing over 40,000 people worldwide in over 170 countries. Michael Dell has a net worth of over $30 billion!

Contrary to popular belief, Henry Ford was not the inventor of the automobile. No single person has been credited with this discovery. However, Mr. Ford was instrumental in transforming the industry in a way that made automobiles available and affordable to the general population. His innovating designs of standardized interchangeable parts and assembly-line production techniques led to the creation of the first mass-production assembly plant.

Microsoft Corp.'s founder and Chairman Bill Gates is one of the most well-known entrepreneurs and one of the wealthiest people in the world. AP Photo/Ted S. Warren.

These people and numerous other entrepreneurs have improved the quality of life for billions of people around the world.

THE BIG IDEA

You may feel that you have an entrepreneurial spirit. You have the eagerness and perseverance to drive forward and never give up. You want to be your own boss and control your own destiny. You want to create something new that will benefit thousands, millions, or even billions of people. But where do you start? Advancing from a poor student with few resources to the CEO of a major company is no small step. But most entrepreneurs have faced similar adversity and made such a leap through hard work, determination, and a big idea.

Great business ventures begin with that first great idea. But many people have great ideas and never act on them. Others act and fail one or more times before giving up. A true entrepreneur has not only the foresight to identify a consumer need, but also the relentless motivation and vision to convert an idea into a new or improved product.

There must be passion behind an idea. Successful entrepreneurs have the ability to convey their vision within business plans, presentations, and other marketing materials. They are able to generate excitement and inspire others. Entrepreneurs lead by example and motivate themselves, their employees, and others with little effort.

Before you spend substantial amounts of money and time on developing your big idea, you need to be assured that no one else has already thought of a similar product. More importantly, you need to know that no one else has produced or patented the idea. As will be further discussed, entrepreneurs and inventors often file patents to prove and protect their ideas. You can search www.uspto.gov to see what patents have already been recorded. Alternatively, a patent attorney can research your idea and ensure that no one else has already patented a similar product.

Even if someone has filed a patent on a similar idea or product, you may be able to purchase the patent rights. Many patents are filed to secure an idea that is never developed. The patent holder may be willing to sell his rights under the patent. This can clear the way for you to develop your idea and also save a significant amount of time when trying to record your own patent, which can take two to three years to successfully file.

Once you have secured your big idea, there are several paths that you can pursue to develop it depending upon how involved you want to be in the process. For example, you can team up with another company that oversees the production and sales processes. In this case, you would assume a fairly passive role and be paid royalties or a percentage of any profits earned. This would

🗪 GUESS WHAT?

Microsoft Corporation began as a simple idea between Bill Gates and Paul Allen in 1975. Through dedication and by pursing their passions, they were able to create a company that has simplified the lives of anyone owning a computer. Microsoft Corporation is worth over $180 billion today, and its founders are two of the wealthiest people in the world!

GUESS WHAT?

According to Entrepreneur.com, approximately 85 to 90 percent of all recorded patents never get developed.

hand over most of the control of the venture to someone else. However, such an arrangement could provide financing, manufacturing facilities, distribution networks, and other resources that might be very difficult to obtain on your own.

Alternatively, you may want to oversee every aspect of the production process, including research and development, financing, marketing, sales, and so forth. This would give you more control over the product and might be an appropriate strategy for building a company. More work and assumed risk should also provide a greater portion of any profits.

Various types of arrangements can be formed with investors and partners to shift more or less of the responsibilities and profits among each of the parties. Part of the decision will be based upon your desired level of involvement. Other considerations include your access to capital and other required resources. Also, the type of idea and product may determine whether it would be best sold through an existing company as another product or product line or whether it can serve as the foundation for an entire business that can be built and expanded over time.

CREATING A BUSINESS PLAN

Once you have a big idea that has not been previously taken by someone else, the next step is to formalize your ideas, strategies, and objectives within a business plan. A business plan is a summary of how a person or company is going to carry out a particular set of initiatives in order to achieve specific goals. Business plans can provide varying degrees of value. Some companies prepare voluminous business plans that consume a hundred pages or more on an annual basis. The people responsible for managing the plan might read it once and never look at it again. Other key personnel may never read a page. In such cases, going to the effort of creating a business plan just to say that you have one can result in wasted effort.

A valuable business plan provides realistic insights and serves as a roadmap when executing the strategies of a business. As time unfolds, forecasted and projected outcomes often do not evolve exactly as expected. Businesses need to adapt quickly to changing environments and unforeseen events. Some businesses are more stable than others and easier to predict. For example, a utilities company may be able to accurately forecast its earnings for the next one to three years. But a startup company has no history and is often surrounded by uncertainty, so its operations and performance will be difficult to estimate.

For the entrepreneur, the process of creating a business plan can be more meaningful than the actual plan itself. By thinking through and documenting all the various aspects of a business, such as appropriate suppliers, production processes, location, management and personnel, and costs and sources of financing, business owners can envision potential problems and solutions. In addition, tracking the actual performance of the business plan over time and understanding why some components did not materialize as planned can be a valuable learning experience.

The content of a business plan will vary based upon the product and the target audience. A business plan should contain whatever information is necessary to evaluate and to pursue a specific venture. If the plan is being used primarily to generate ideas, then a formal written document becomes less important. However, most ventures rely on some type of financing, and investors and lenders will want to see a formal business plan before committing dollars to an investment.

When you plan to distribute a business plan to one or more persons, you should focus on a professional format. Consider including a table of contents and have each key subject fully discussed and broken out into chapters or sections. Graphs, charts, and other illustrations can also help to convey your message.

Be sure to proof and edit your business plan a couple times, and ask colleagues, friends, and family to read the plan and provide comments as well. If you need assistance, consider leveraging the skills of any potential partners or employees, or consider using consultants. For example, a graphic design specialist can assist with artwork, graphs, and charts and the creation of an overall professional appearance. A local accountant can help prepare or review any financial projections. If you need to hire one or more consultants, you should still be able to do most of the work yourself and minimize costs. Your final business plan may be a key factor for investors and lenders when determining whether to invest millions of dollars into your venture, so it can be very worthwhile to spend the time and money.

There is no specific format to a business plan. Each one is based on a particular business model and focuses on the most relevant business objectives, risks and opportunities as perceived by the person or management team assessing the business. However, there are some topics that are common in most business plans.

- *The Executive Summary*—Business plans can be tens and even hundreds of pages. However, excessively long plans tend to lose their impact; many people do not have the time to read so much information. An executive summary appears at the very front of a business plan and needs to capture the attention of the reader quickly.

  Most executive summaries are one to two pages long. Think of yourself as having two minutes to sell your idea to someone without this person knowing anything about your venture. What are the most important points that need to be heard? How can you best convey these points in written form? Remember, the person considering your project is only reading words off a page. You may not get the chance to personally present your ideas. The executive summary is often intended to help you obtain a face-to-face meeting. It needs to make a powerful impression and leave the reader wanting to hear more.
- *Product Details*—A new idea should translate into a product. A product can be something tangible, or it can be a provided service. Drawing a product and its components can be very helpful. Sometimes flow

diagrams that show inputs being transformed into outputs can aid in explaining and clarifying a process and can help to generate ideas for improvement.

A business plan should identify the need for a particular product. It should also address product pricing, any packaging features, and targeted distribution channels (i.e., direct mail, retailers, wholesalers, etc.). It is important to meet or create a need for a product and to generate consumer awareness. Why will ultimate users want this product? What is the best and most profitable means of making the product available to the broadest audience? What can be done to the product to capture more attention and to create greater demand?

- *Market Analysis*—Once you have envisioned a product, you should assess its potential demand. Consider who represents your target market, and determine where and how they normally shop. Will they need to modify their behaviors in order to buy or use your product? Is this a reasonable expectation? Will consumers find value in your product and perceive the price as being reasonable? Consider conducting focus group meetings that can be used to obtain feedback from a representative group within your target market of customers.

  Once a product is created, competitors may begin imitating it. Think about your current and potential competition. What can you do better than them? What will differentiate your product from theirs? Can your product be patented to protect against replication?

- *Production*—Some products may require a more complex production process than others. For tangible products, consider how you will produce a prototype that can be shown to potential investors, distributors, and customers, but also address how a larger production facility will be created and financed. Where will it be located? How large of a facility will be initially needed? Would you lease or buy the land and building? As the business grows, can this manufacturing area be expanded, or will additional facilities be needed? Who will design the required machinery to produce the product? Is there an ample supply of qualified employees?

  When offering a new service, the initial costs will most likely be significantly lower when compared to what is needed to produce a physical product. Such startups can usually begin operations with much lower overhead, fewer employees, lesser space, and much less capital. However, the supply and accessibility to any needed resources must be considered. This may include certain types of people, other products needed to provide the service, sources of transportation, and so forth.

- *Marketing*—Having a great product is a good start. But making people aware of your product and convincing them to try it is critical to your venture's success. Think about how other products are marketed to people. A traditional marketing campaign might include finding retail stores willing to sell your product. You provide the retailers with a discounted purchase price, and they apply a mark-up and sell the product for a profit.

  Other products are marketed by selling to wholesalers. A wholesaler would purchase your product and increase the price before selling it to a retailer, who would then increase the price again before selling it to the end user. This approach tends to result in the lowest profit margin because profits need to be provided to both wholesalers and retailers. However, using such distribution channels can lead to substantially higher sales volumes.

Some sellers use infomercials, radio, and other forms of advertisement to sell directly to the consumer. There are often higher profit margins in these types of sales because prices are not discounted and products are not sold through distributors and retailers.

Establishing a brand and having people remember your product or service favorably is necessary to generate repeat business. Customer satisfaction is critical. Brand awareness can be achieved by advertising and marketing campaigns, word of mouth, and repeat sales.

The marketing strategy for your product can change as production increases and it becomes more accepted. As your business expands, the costs to produce your product or service should decline. In addition, operational efficiencies should be targeted to help lower costs. When it costs less to produce a product, it can be sold at lower prices to increase sales, or the price can remain constant and higher profit margins will result.

- *Financing*—It takes money to make money. The best ideas often remain ideas without the proper financing to make things happen. Convincing people to provide capital for your venture is one of the most important steps required in launching a business.

  The text of the business plan should identify the amount of financing required for the various phases of the business. A condensed version of this information should also be referenced within the executive summary. In addition, any financial projections provided should also reflect when capital will be received and any periodic payments required on such monies (e.g., monthly interest payments). We will talk more about the types of financing that may be targeted in the next section.

- *Exit Strategy*—Investors will want to understand how they will be repaid their initial investment and any profits. The term *exit strategy* refers to some type of event that will allow investors to be repaid and to exit their investment. Examples of exit strategies include the ultimate sale of a business, the listing of a company's common stock on a national stock exchange so that it can be bought and sold quickly, or the liquidation of a company by selling its assets.

  Investors do not want to have their invested dollars tied up in an investment for excessive periods. For example, a debt provider that lends money to a business will impose a debt maturity date within the loan documents that will require the debt to be repaid by a certain date. If the money is not repaid on time and a new arrangement is not negotiated, the borrower will be in default on the loan. Most investors want their investment back within 5 to 10 years. Such investors may reinvest in a successful venture or choose to keep their money invested for longer periods of time, but they want to control such decisions.

- *Financial Projections*—Most businesses prepare financial projections to estimate future profitability. Simplistic financial projections will show general sources of revenues and expenses. For example, one line item might be labeled "office expense" and aggregate the costs of many small expenses such as postage, copier leasing, paper products, computer systems, rent, and other items related to running an office. More detailed financial projections might show each specific line item and be much more comprehensive. While it may be more appropriate to show a summarized version to third parties, going through the process of forecasting and evaluating each specific revenue and expense item can be very worthwhile.

Any money remaining after deducting expenses from revenue will reflect the profitability of the business. Many startup companies are unprofitable for a period of time while they grow, expand production and customers, and generate better operating efficiencies. But ultimately a business must show profits, or there is no reason for the business to exist (unless it is pursuing nonprofit activities, such as helping the less fortunate, and its funding is provided by donors).

The exercise of preparing financial projections can be very meaningful. Similar to the entire business plan creation process, thinking about and estimating each revenue and expense item can be a rewarding experience. Doing so may provide valuable insights into why a particular product is viable or unrealistic and lead to changes within the business plan itself. Designing an attractive product is a great start, but lacking customers willing to pay enough to justify its production presents a serious problem.

The finished output for financial projections should be financial statements, including an income statement, balance sheet, and some type of statement of cash flows for each projected period. If you have difficulty preparing these statements, seek assistance from potential partners and employees or from a local CPA or accounting firm. If the business moves forward, such financial statements will most likely need to be prepared on an ongoing basis to measure business performance and to report such results to lenders, investors, and other third parties.

You will also want to show some form of profitability measurement for your investors. You and your investors will want to know that your efforts are worthwhile and generating sufficient profitability. Investors will expect a minimum return on their investment to compensate them for the risk that they are assuming. For example, if $1 million is invested into your company and the company earns $30,000 for the year, this implies only a 3 percent profit ($30,000 in income divided by the $1 million investment). While such low profits and even losses would be expected in the early years of a startup venture, a 3 percent return would be unacceptable over the long term.

The profitability of most businesses and projects is measured by using some type of Internal Rate of Return (IRR) formula, which can be computed using an Excel spreadsheet. An IRR calculation indicates the expected profitability of an investment based upon when monies are invested and returned to investors. Most investors in startup companies will want to see forecasted IRRs that reflect average annual profits of 25 to 50 percent or more depending upon the risk and stage of the particular business. If there are losses or low profits in the early years of the business, huge profits in later years will be expected to offset the lower numbers.

Sophisticated investors are going to look at the expected IRR of your investment opportunity versus many other alternatives when deciding where to invest their money. For anyone preparing financial projections, I strongly suggest understanding the meaning and calculation of an IRR analysis. Your colleagues, a local accountant, or someone that has studied finance and capital budgeting may be able to assist you with these calculations.

Lenders and investors want to see that a business can generate enough cash and profits to protect their investments. Financial projections can help people to better understand the inputs and outputs of a venture and visualize its potential profitability. Numerical presentations within a business plan can also show that the entrepreneur has thought about the many variables that can affect the business and has a rational plan to deal with them.

Most financial projections cover periods of 1 to 10 years. Some are shown on a monthly basis. Others are presented quarterly or annually. It may be helpful to prepare monthly financial projections, but show a more summarized format (i.e., on an annual basis) to investors and other third parties. As you can imagine, the longer the period being forecasted, the less reliable become the assumptions and the projected results. But sometimes it is necessary to forecast 5- to 10-year periods in order to show lenders and investors one or more targeted exit strategies and how they will be repaid.

- *Personnel*—A key factor in convincing lenders to lend and investors to invest is the level of experience held by the management team of a particular endeavor. The less experience you have, the harder you will need to sell yourself and your ideas. Many entrepreneurs recognize their weaknesses and hire others to complement their skill sets. For example, an entrepreneur that is skilled in a particular industry may lack financial experience and hire a controller or a chief financial officer.

  A business plan should briefly list the relevant experience, achievements, educations, and other credentials of the founders and other members of management, any board of directors, and any other key personnel or service providers.

FINDING FINANCING

Most businesses will need money to get started and to expand, and most entrepreneurs starting out in the world have little to contribute. The two

✎ **BEWARE!**

According to a study by the U.S. Small Business Association, only about two-thirds of small businesses survive the first two years, and less than half make it to four years. Having a rational and sound business plan will help increase the odds of success.

primary types of funding for a business consist of debt and equity. Equity is subordinate to debt, which means that if a business experiences financial difficulties, the debt gets repaid first before any equity investors receive a penny. This makes equity much more risky than debt. Therefore, in order to attract capital, businesses must promise to pay their equity investors more than they pay their debt providers.

In order for someone to provide debt, they want to see enough equity to ensure that they will be repaid. For example, if a venture needs a million dollars to get started, a lender may want to see at least 50 percent of this amount provided by equity investors before being willing to lend to the entity. Many startup companies are unable to obtain debt financing until a successful track record is in place. In such cases, all of the initial financing is provided by equity investors.

The type of business and its targeted activities will also be a determining factor in the debt versus equity mix. Tangible assets such as real estate can serve as strong collateral for a lender. In contrast, a business investing in new technologies that have little residual value if the venture fails will provide much less assurance to banks and other lenders.

Sources of Equity Capital

The amount of equity needed will vary based upon the size and scope of a business venture. Those providing a service to customers will often need less capital than those producing a physical product. Large-scale production efforts and high-cost products will require more capital. For example, an entrepreneur focused on producing a new type of automobile will require a lot more money than someone planning to make garden hose attachments.

Partners and Members of Management—If the founders and management team of a business truly believe in its success, they may be willing and able to invest equity capital to get the business started. Normally, the first investors to invest within a business are the ones that make the most money when the business becomes successful. However, with such endeavors there is usually a high degree of risk that any capital invested will be lost forever if the business does not succeed.

Family and Friends—Depending on the needs of a new business and upon your circle of friends and family, you may be able to raise enough money to start your business through this network. The wealthier and larger the number of friends and family, the better your chances of raising a meaningful amount of capital. You will need to target people that like and trust you and that have faith in your abilities to execute your idea. Any partners or members of management on your team may also be able to provide investors through their network of family and friends.

Outside investors like to see money personally invested by the entrepreneur, members of management, and family and friends because this shows a level of personal commitment. If the business fails, not only do founders and members of management lose their own money, they also lose dollars invested by close personal relationships. This can be a motivating force. No one wants to lose money, nor do they want to disappoint the people closest to them.

Angel Investors—An angel investor is usually a sophisticated and affluent individual that invests in startup companies. Sometimes individual angel investors organize into angel networks or angel groups to pool capital, expertise, and resources. Angel investors usually invest their own money versus venture capitalists (to be discussed) that are usually investing and managing other people's monies. Funding from angel investors typically comes after money is invested by family and friends. This source of funding will often serve as financing between the time that capital is raised by family and friends and the time that venture capital can be attracted. Angel investors usually invest smaller dollar amounts when compared to venture capitalist firms. This may be a few hundred thousand dollars versus a million dollars or more that a venture capitalist might invest.

Because angel investors often invest in the earliest stages of a venture, they have a greater chance of losing their investments in many companies. For the ones that succeed, an angel investor typically expects to earn 10, 20, or more times their original investment over a 5- to 10-year period. This capital tends to be very expensive and requires that a substantial ownership position in the company be provided to the investor.

Venture Capitalists—Venture capital is equity provided by institutional investors and high net worth individuals that is used to invest in startup companies and businesses having limited operating history. In return for an ownership position in a company, a venture capitalist firm will pool capital from many investors and select investment opportunities expected to have high growth and profitability potential. These firms normally expect some type of viable exit strategy so that they can cash out of their investments within a 3- to 10-year period. Some companies chosen by the venture capitalist will fail and money will be lost; others will generate huge profits. The goal of the venture capitalist is to minimize its poor performing investments and provide high profits to its investors.

The downside to the entrepreneur when utilizing angel and venture capital is the ownership portion of the business that is given to one or more investors in return for the money raised to launch and grow the business. In addition, the activities of the venture will be closely watched by any participating investors. One or more seats on a company's board of directors may be taken by angel investors or members of a venture capitalist firm, and ongoing reporting is normally required and monitored. Entrepreneurs need to ensure that they are not giving up too much control and too much of an ownership position in return for capital.

Financing Stages

There are several financing stages that a new business venture moves through, and its ability to attract capital changes with each stage. In addition, as a

🐾 GUESS WHAT?

A study conducted in 1996 by Freear and Wetzel estimated that approximately 250,000 angel investors invest between $10 and $20 billion in roughly 30,000 companies per year.

company advances through the different stages, it should become more able to borrow money (debt capital), and the costs of new debt and equity capital should begin to decline as the company continues to develop a history of success and shows less risk.

Seed Stage Financing—At this point, one or more entrepreneurs have a big idea, but a product or service has not been fully developed. Investors at the seed stage usually provide capital to be spent on designing a prototype product, market research, patent applications, and legal costs. Finding capital at this stage is most difficult because there is no proven concept, and the business is considered to be very risky. Obtaining debt capital can be nearly impossible. Equity capital for seed financing is often provided by family and friends. Attracting outside financing is very difficult, and when achieved at this infancy stage, a substantial amount of control and ownership is often provided to capital providers.

Startup Stage Financing—During the startup stage, the actual business is in operation. People are hired, production processes are designed and implemented, product testing may be underway, and relationships with potential distributors are established.

Some venture capitalists may agree to invest during the startup stage, but angel investors are more likely candidates. Finding willing lenders at this stage will still be extremely difficult.

First Stage Financing—By the time a company is two or three years old, its sales volumes have hopefully continued to trend upwards, and the product begins to receive wider acceptance and greater demand. Usually, any cash being generated from sales is being reinvested into the business. The company may be profitable or hovering around breakeven at this point. A management team and employees are in place, and ways to reduce costs and increase efficiencies are targeted.

Venture capitalist firms willing to invest in early stage business operations are likely candidates to provide the first stage financing needed to further grow the business. This is still considered an early entry point for venture capitalists, so businesses needing such capital will likely pay a high price in terms of any ownership interests and control granted.

Second Stage Financing—By the time a business is ready for second stage financing, sales should be growing rapidly and capital limitations are constraining growth. Sales that are made on credit to distributors tie up cash, and more dollars are needed to invest in inventory and infrastructure. Capital is needed to expand production, facilitate sales, and increase marketing efforts and enter new markets.

Third Stage Financing—When a company reaches the third stage, the business continues to grow, and the product is well accepted. Demand continues to exceed supply, and production capabilities are often constrained. The enterprise needs more capital to expand production, which may mean the enlargement of existing facilities, the creation of one or more new manufacturing plants, or the addition of new service providers depending upon the specific product. The layers of management continue to increase, and more employees continue to be added.

Venture capitalist firms willing to invest in a third stage company become more abundant as the business's level of risk continues to decline. In addition,

🗣 GUESS WHAT?

Venture capital financing has helped launch successful companies like Amazon.com, Amgen, Federal Express, Microsoft, and Starbucks.

---

business owners can usually maintain a greater ownership percentage and maintain more control of the company than when seeking venture capital in the earlier stages. The company's chances of finding banks and other lenders willing to lend to the company become more likely as well. Money raised can be used to better the product, increase and improve production capabilities, and further marketing efforts to maintain a rapid growth trend. The venture may begin exploring and developing new products and improved versions of its existing product(s).

Bridge/Pre-Public Stage Financing—During this stage, the company begins to focus on its exit strategy. The business now has an established product and continues to build a successful track record. The company wants to repay its original investors and be able to attract new investors on a larger scale. Potential exit strategies can include the listing of the company's stock on a stock exchange, a sale of the company, or a merger with another company.

During this stage, business operations remain very active. The company may be focused on staying ahead of its competitors and upon continual product improvement and new product development and release. Venture capitalist firms are usually more than willing to provide financing during such a mature phase. In addition, banks often become very interested in the company due to the potential investment banking fees that can be earned by taking the company public, serving as an advisor to potential mergers and acquisitions, and for debt and equity issuance as a public company.

PROTECTING YOUR INVESTMENT

Once you have a big idea, you want to make sure that no one steals it. Having someone replicate your product after you have invested substantial dollars and hours into its development would be devastating. Registering your product with the government can protect you from others stating that you are copying their ideas. This is where the services of a qualified attorney become invaluable.

Some entrepreneurs will ask potential investors to sign a legal form stating that they will not discuss or disclose any business ideas to anyone else. This is to prevent people from listening to your presentation or seeing your business plan or other marketing materials and deciding to pursue the opportunity themselves. Alternatively, they could casually discuss your idea with a friend, neighbor, client, or colleague, who might decide to steal the concept. However, signing such agreements might conflict with the activities of other clients or limit future business opportunities, so many angel investors and venture capitalist firms are unwilling to sign such documents, leaving the entrepreneur at risk.

An intellectual property attorney can represent clients in protecting product trademarks, service marks, business ideas, and technology ownership.

🗣 GUESS WHAT?

In 2006, marketing consultant Interbrands collaborated with *Business Week* to publish the values of the top international trademarks of 40 companies. The Coca-Cola brand was valued at $67 billion, Microsoft was worth $56.9 billion, Disney's value was $27.8 billion, and McDonalds came in at $27.5 billion.

Hundreds of thousands of inventors and entrepreneurs file for protection each year under patent, trademark, and copyright laws. However, it can be hard to decide which type of filing is appropriate for your particular product. It is possible that a product or service may warrant protection under several filings, but each category offers its own specific benefits and security.

Patents—A patent is a grant provided by a government that provides the creator of an invention the exclusive rights to make, use, and sell a particular product for a specified period of time. An entrepreneur that invents a new process, machine, product, or useful improvement can be patent eligible. Obtaining a patent on your product protects you and prevents others from replicating your idea and selling or using your product.

To have your patent application accepted, your claims defining the invention must be new, inventive, and useful. You must prove that your idea is new and not an altered version of someone else's product and that it is beneficial to the public. A patent usually protects your product for a period of up to 20 years.

Copyrights—For authors, playwrights, composers, and other artists, a copyright provides the legal right to exclusively produce, sell, and distribute a form of

A McDonald's restaurant in downtown Tokyo demonstrates the worldwide recognition of the company's trademark. AP Photo.

literary or artistic work. Copyrights can cover creations such as books, movies, computer code, graphic images, music, and architecture. A copyright protects others from copying, reprinting, producing, selling, or using the copyrighted material.

Registration with the U.S. Copyright Office is no longer required for something to be legally copyrighted. As long as a "work" is in written or electronic form, it is copyrighted for the life of the author plus 70 years. However, formally registering can help to avoid or more quickly resolve potential disputes.

Trademarks—When a person or company owns a symbol, logo, or name that identifies a product, people tend to identify the product by a specific name or image. Such trademarks distinguish particular products from their peers and can have substantial value. For example, the names and logos of Exxon, the Pillsbury Doughboy, and Coca Cola are strongly associated with the products that these companies sell and are great marketing tools.

A trademark does not need to be legally filed with a government agency in order to be protected. However, if not formally registered, a trademark may only be enforceable in the geographic areas in which it is used and recognized. For example, if your product is sold and well-known by its logo only in the Northeastern United States, unless you file your logo as a trademark, others will be able to use it in other regions of the country. Owners can maintain trademark rights by simply using the trademark. If a trademark is not in use for a period of time, normally five years, then others may begin using it.

Service Marks—A service mark is very similar to a trademark except that the logo, symbol, or design represents a service rather than a product. Examples of service marks include Wendy's (restaurant services), COMPUSA (retail and wholesale computer services), and Citibank (banking and financial services).

Intellectual property right laws will vary among countries. It is best to employ the services of a capable intellectual property rights attorney or consultant when considering the need for one or more patents, copyrights, trademarks, and service marks. If your idea is truly unique and worth protecting, preserving the value of your product, service, or any relevant attributes is money well spent.

9

Economics

THE ECONOMY

An economy can be defined as the economic-related activity within a certain area. When people speak about the economy, they are usually referring to the economy for a particular country. However, an economy can be narrowed to include the activities within a region or local area. An economy relates to all aspects of the production and consumption of goods and services.

A country's *gross domestic product* (GDP) is an economic measurement of the country's output and an indicator of how well a country is performing. GDP is calculated by taking the value of all the goods and services produced by a specific country during a specific period of time, which is usually based upon a calendar year.

The field of economics is broken down more generally between macroeconomics and microeconomics. *Macroeconomics* focuses on the behaviors of the overall economy, such as the effects of unemployment, inflation, and product and service imports and exports with other countries.

Microeconomics focuses on narrower segments of an economy, including consumer, business, and government behaviors and the cause and effect relationships that exist when decisions are made. For example, if the price of a particular product is raised, the change in demand for the product can be assessed. Microeconomics focuses on more granular pieces of an economy, while macroeconomics is centered on a larger scale and looks at the economy as a whole.

Most U.S. economists agree that GDP growth of 3 to 5 percent per year is favorable for the overall economy.

The global economy refers to the integration and interconnectedness of the economies of many countries throughout the world. Most countries trade goods and services with one another based upon the availability and costs to produce certain products. Some products and resources are only available in certain regions of the world. Some countries have better production facilities and lower labor costs that allow them to produce more efficiently.

Multinational companies have operations in hundreds of countries. Such businesses have production facilities and sell their products throughout the world. By expanding businesses internationally, companies are able to diversify their sources of income and target growth opportunities. For example, the U.S. market for a particular product may have matured with little future growth opportunities. However, markets in China and India may offer tremendous demand.

RECESSIONS AND DEPRESSIONS

A government is responsible for keeping its economy stable and for providing opportunities and employment for its citizens. When an economy is stable and growing at a reasonable rate, enough of the population is employed, household income tends to grow each year, and people generally have a favorable quality of life.

If an economy grows too quickly, inflation can result. Inflation leads to higher prices for the goods and services that consumers buy on a daily basis. In essence, a dollar today will be worth less than a dollar in the future in terms of what it will be able to buy due to inflation.

High inflation also leads to higher interest rates, which can result in poor economic performance over time. When high inflation persists, interest rates on credit cards, automobile, home and business loans, and other borrowing sources rise. Higher interest rates make it more expensive for consumers and businesses to borrow money, which leads to lower spending. Lower spending leads to greater unemployment, lower GDP, and lower economic growth.

If the economy grows too slowly, stagnates, or experiences negative growth, a country runs the risk of moving into a recession or even a depression. The term *economic recession* can be measured in different ways. A common definition of a recession is two or more quarters of negative growth in GDP. This means that instead of growing for a six-month or longer period, the economy

The U.S. economy is the largest in the world. For the year 2007, its gross domestic product was estimated to be $13.8 trillion.

🗣 GUESS WHAT?

During the economic depression of the 1930s, one out of every four persons wanting to work could not find a job. In addition, the stock market declined by almost 90 percent from peak to bottom. Many businesses filed bankruptcy, and many people lived in poverty in need of shelter, food, and clothing.

contracts. During periods of recession, people spend less and businesses make lower profits. This causes companies to reduce their workforces, and unemployment rises. As unemployment increases, people tend to spend even less, which places further strain on households and businesses.

A depression is much more severe than a recession. There is no formal definition for an *economic depression,* but a depression includes a longer period of declining economic performance. During a depression, unemployment reaches very high levels, and many companies are forced to file bankruptcy. The last depression in the United States began in 1929 and lasted through the early 1930s. Other U.S. depressions occurred in the 1870s and 1890s.

The depression of the 1930s resulted in millions of Americans being out of work. Long lines of hungry people waiting for food to feed their families formed daily across the nation. AP Photo.

BUDGET DEFICITS AND SURPLUSES

When you spend more than you earn, you will generate a deficit. If your household budget allows you to spend $1,000 a month and you spend $1,200, you will have a budget deficit. Somehow you will need to cover the $200 shortfall for the month. One way would be to borrow the money through a loan from a parent, friend, or bank. You could also borrow the money from a credit card company and carry a balance of $200 into the next month.

When you spend less than you earn, you generate a budget surplus for the period. If during the next month your budget allows $1,000 in spending and you only spend $750, you will have a budget surplus of $250 for the month. Periodic budget deficits and surpluses are combined to determine a cumulative budget position. For example, if your household budget has a deficit in January of $200 and a surplus in February of $250, you would have a $50 budget surplus for the first two months of the year.

The same rules to budgeting apply to governments, but on a much larger scale. A government's budget deficit is caused when the government spends more than it receives in income. A government budget surplus results when tax revenues and other sources of income exceed government spending.

Budget deficits tend to arise when economies are experiencing slow growth or when they are in a phase of contraction. When an economy is performing poorly, tax revenues fall due to greater unemployment and lower consumer income and business profits. Under such circumstances, a government's source of income declines because people and companies are paying less taxes. In addition, governments may also lower tax rates and provide tax incentives to consumers and businesses so that they spend more, which is a fiscal policy (discussed later) tool that leads to lesser tax revenues. Lower income leads to budget deficits.

Not only does a government's income decrease during a slow or declining economic cycle due to lower tax revenues, its spending often increases as well, which leads to an even greater budget deficit. In order to stimulate an economy and move a country away from recession, governments tend to spend more during economic downturns. Government costs can increase substantially when an economy is sluggish. The expense associated with unemployment insurance and other social welfare programs increases as a greater portion of the population is unemployed. In addition, governments can spend more discretionary dollars under fiscal policy initiatives to try to stimulate an economy, as further discussed later.

So where does a government get the money to cover its deficits? Normally, a government will borrow money by issuing notes and bonds to investors. Individual states issue municipal securities to raise money. The U.S. Treasury sells treasury bills, notes, and bonds on a monthly basis to finance the federal government's activities. As deficits grow, countries are forced to issue more and more debt. When the economy is performing well and budget deficits are declining, then a greater amount of debt is repaid and less new debt is issued.

Governments can also print new currency to help pay off debt and to reduce budget deficits. However, a major problem associated with printing new currency is that a country's supply of money increases. When more

In 2002, the governor of California projected the state of California's budget deficit to reach a staggering $34.8 billion. The 2009–2010 budget deficit is expected to grow to almost $42 billion, which is placing the state of California on the verge of bankruptcy. AP Photo/John Decker.

currency is created, more money makes its way to the banks and banks are able to lend more money. When more money is printed, the chances of inflation increase and the value of a country's currency becomes less. More money within an economy leads to inflation, so countries tend to rely much more on debt issuance to finance their deficits.

When an economy is performing well, a greater number of people are employed and consumers spend more. This leads to greater demand from businesses to meet increased consumer spending. Businesses then employ more people and invest more capital into new equipment and other resources, which helps to further stimulate an economy. In such cases, personal and corporate incomes rise and lead to higher income taxes being paid to the government. In addition, during periods of economic expansion, governments

GUESS WHAT?

The U.S. government currently has a budget deficit of almost $500 billion in early 2009. Due to the deep recession that started in 2007 and the amount of economic stimulus needed to revive the economy and to bailout banks and other companies, forecasts are estimating a budget deficit of over $1 trillion by the year 2010!

can spend less. Greater tax and other sources of revenue and lower government spending lead to reduced deficits and budget surpluses.

The general goal of government is to accumulate budget surpluses in times of economic prosperity. When an economy begins to slow or slip into recession, such surpluses can be used to help stimulate the economy. The objective over the long term is to maintain a balanced budget without severe accumulated and prolonged deficits and the large debt obligations needed to cover them.

FISCAL POLICY

Governments use an array of tools to try to move an economy in a certain direction. For example, if an economy is expected to slow down and the risk of recession is on the horizon, a government may try to stimulate the economy and increase its growth. If an economy is beginning to overheat and inflation is on the rise, a government may try to slow down the economy.

Most government actions regarding economic policies can be grouped under either *fiscal policy* or *monetary policy*. Fiscal policies include actions by a government directed toward moving an economy through changes in (1) the levels of business and consumer taxes and (2) the amount of government spending.

Governments are supported by tax revenues. State governments receive monies from state income, sales, property, and other taxes. The U.S. federal government earns tax revenue primarily from federal taxes paid by people and businesses on earned income. Anyone with a job most likely pays some type of federal income tax. These payments are made to the federal government and used to help support the country's health care, education, military, and other vital programs.

When people and businesses are forced to pay higher taxes, they have less money to spend. This means that businesses will hire fewer employees and invest less money into expanding operations, or they may even scale back their activities. Consumers will also spend less on goods and services, which will lead to lower demand from businesses for the products and services that they produce. When there is less spending and lower demand, there is less growth in the economy. Therefore, raising tax rates for consumers and companies results in lower economic activity and slows the growth rate of the economy.

When consumers and businesses are allowed to pay lesser taxes to the government, they have more cash available to spend. People will buy more goods and services, and businesses will invest capital and increase production and labor in order to expand and meet the greater demand. This leads to more employment, greater economic activity, and a growing economy.

U.S. governments spend money on military and defense, health care, research, education, welfare, roadways, and transportation and other programs. Of the total amount of government spending, about two-thirds is mandatory spending that is needed to maintain the country's infrastructure. But the remaining one-third of the government's overall spending is discretionary. This discretionary spending is what is used by the government to help stimulate or slow down economic growth through fiscal policy. Just like when consumers and businesses spend more money, an increase in the government's spending also tends to stimulate the economy. When the government slows its spending, economic growth begins to decline.

The three separate stances taken by the federal government regarding fiscal policy include neutral, expansionary, and contractionary. A neutral position implies that tax revenues received by the government approximate the amount of government spending for a specific period. When a government employs an expansionary policy, tax revenues are usually less than the government is actually spending due to lower tax rates, higher government spending, or both. This will lead to a larger budget deficit or a smaller budget surplus because the government is spending more than it is earning.

If a government is focused on contractionary fiscal policy, the tax revenues it receives are usually more than the amount it is spending due to higher tax rates and greater tax revenues being received from consumers and businesses, and/or lower discretionary government spending. Such a policy will result in a smaller budget deficit or greater budget surplus depending upon the state of the country's budget.

When inflation is rising to uncomfortable levels, a government may choose contractionary fiscal policies, including raising income taxes and spending less, in order to cool the economy and lower inflation so that the prices of goods and services keep from escalating. If economic growth is slow and the potential for a recession exists, a government may choose to employ expansionary fiscal policies and lower income taxes, spend less, or utilize a combination of both strategies.

MONETARY POLICY

The government uses monetary policy as a means to stabilize the economy. A government's central bank is usually responsible for a country's financial and banking systems and for making and implementing monetary policy decisions. The U.S. Federal Reserve (often called "the Fed") serves as the central bank for the United States. Examples of other central banks include the Bank of England, the People's Bank of China, and the European Central Bank, which is responsible for the monetary policies for numerous countries in Europe. The Fed has several monetary policy tools available to help it promote economic stability.

Open Market Operations

The Fed's Open Market Committee (FOMC) is able to manipulate the supply of money in the U.S. financial system by buying or selling government securities. When purchasing government securities, such as treasury bonds, the FOMC is increasing the money supply by providing more money to the banking system that can be lent to consumers and businesses, which helps lead to economic expansion. When the FOMC sells government bonds, they take money from the banking system, leaving banks with less money to lend, which results in economic contraction.

Bank Reserve Requirements

The Federal Reserve requires banks and other depository institutions to maintain a minimum amount of funds on reserve in case they have unexpected cash outflows. These reserves can be kept in cash in their vaults or on deposit with the Fed. Reserves refer to the amount of deposits that each bank must have on hand at all times. For example, if banks are required to maintain a 10 percent reserve, this means that they can lend $100 to their customers for every $10 they have in deposits.

When the reserve requirement is raised, banks are forced to retain more cash, and they cannot lend as much. With fewer loans to customers, this makes banks less profitable and also lowers the amount of available credit to consumers and businesses. Therefore, raising the reserve requirement leads to reduced economic growth. Lowering the reserve requirement allows banks to lend more dollars and leads to greater availability of credit and economic growth.

Each time the Federal Reserve changes the reserve requirements for banks, the banks incur costs to make the corresponding changes to their policies. To avoid this disruption, the Federal Reserve rarely changes bank reserve requirements.

The Cost of Money

When the cost of money is increased, people and businesses tend to borrow less and an economy will contract. Conversely, when the cost of money is cheap, consumers and companies borrow and spend more, leading to economic expansion. One way that a central bank can control the costs of money is by indirectly changing the interest rates that consumers and businesses pay to borrow money, which is the most frequently used tool when implementing monetary policy. The U.S. government accomplishes this by increasing or reducing two key interest rates. Any changes flow through the economy and lead to increased or reduced economic growth, depending on the direction of the interest rate changes.

When banks and other depository institutions need money on a short-term basis, they are permitted to borrow from the Federal Reserve through its "discount window" at an interest rate called the *discount rate*. The discount window is a lending program that allows banks to borrow money from the Federal Reserve by pledging collateral such as loans and securities. Why would banks want to borrow from the Federal Reserve? Because sometimes banks lend out more money than they should, and their reserve requirements become insufficient. In such cases, banks are allowed to borrow money from the discount window to remain in compliance.

Banks can also borrow amongst themselves at an interest rate known as the *federal funds* interest rate. A target federal funds rate is set in the United States by the FOMC, and most banks stick closely to this rate when lending

🗣 GUESS WHAT?

There is a lag time between when a central bank changes interest rates and when the change is felt through the economy. Most estimates for the U.S. economy are somewhere between 6 to 18 months.

---

to one another. Banks can borrow from other banks to remain in compliance with their reserve requirements. The Federal Reserve prefers that banks borrow money from one another at the federal funds rate rather than using the discount window and borrowing at the discount rate. In fact, the discount rate is usually about one percentage point higher than the federal funds rate to encourage banks to use the discount window as a last resort borrowing mechanism.

When banks pay more to borrow money, they charge their customers more to borrow money. Through changes in the discount rate and the federal funds rate, the government indirectly alters the rate of interest that consumers and businesses pay on credit cards, loans, and other forms of borrowings when seeking to stimulate or slow the economy.

FOREIGN CURRENCIES

Currency is the paper and coins used within an economy to purchase goods and services. Just as the people within different countries often speak differing languages, each country often has its own financial currency. The currency used within the United States is the U.S. dollar. The currency used by England is the British pound. Japan uses the yen. The European Union consists of 15 European countries that have all agreed to use the euro as their currency.

The value or purchasing power between the currencies of different countries changes frequently and often within seconds. When people travel to foreign countries for vacation or business, they sometimes need to buy the local currency so that they can pay for things within the visited country. One currency is converted to another country's currency at the current exchange rate. An *exchange rate* is the price of one country's currency when compared to the price of another country's currency. Most currencies are priced against the U.S. dollar. For example, if one Canadian dollar is worth 0.80 U.S. dollars, one U.S. dollar can be converted into 1.25 Canadian dollars.

Just because one currency buys more of another currency does not mean that you can buy more of the same product in the other country. For example, it may cost four U.S. dollars to buy a gallon of milk in the United States. If four U.S. dollars converts into five Canadian dollars, a gallon of milk may cost five Canadian dollars in Canada, which would result in the same cost for milk in the United States and Canada.

Sometimes one currency can be weaker than another. In such cases, more products or services can be bought in one currency versus another. When the U.S. dollar is strong compared to another currency, U.S. citizens can buy more goods and services in the other country than they can in the United

A woman walks past a foreign exchange rate information panel in central Milan, Italy, displaying currency conversion rates. Financial institutions earn fees by converting currencies for consumers and businesses. AP Photo/Luca Bruno.

States by converting U.S. dollars into the foreign currency. When one country's currency is weaker than another country's currency, the country with the stronger currency has a buying opportunity when purchasing products and services from the country having the weaker currency. Products and services within the country having the weaker currency are cheaper than the same products and services within the country having the stronger currency. When the United States has a strong currency, it tends to import more products and services from other countries.

On the other hand, when a country has a weak currency compared to the currency of another country, the products and services of the other country are more expensive. For example, when the U.S. dollar is considered to be the weaker currency, its citizens and businesses tend to buy more goods and services within the United States and less from countries having stronger currencies. In this case, foreign countries having stronger currencies will buy more goods and services from the U.S. at cheaper prices, which will lead to a greater number of U.S. exports.

Table 9.1 is intended to show the effects of weaker and stronger foreign currencies:

When companies buy and sell products from one another, they often need to transact in foreign currencies. When doing so, companies run the risk of losing money due to currency fluctuations. For example, assume that a U.S. corporation sells 5,000 hairdryers to a salon company in England for $25,000. If the exchange rate between the United States and England at the time of sale

Table 9.1
Weaker Versus Stronger Foreign Currencies

	Country A	Country B
Currency Value	Weak	Strong
Cost of Importing Goods and Services	Higher	Lower
Volume of Exports	Increases	Decreases
Volume of Imports	Decreases	Increases

was 0.80 British pounds for every U.S. dollar, $25,000 would equate to 20,000 British pounds. Let us assume that payment is due by the British Company 30 days after receipt of the hairdryers and that based upon the sales agreement, the English company will pay for the shipment in British pounds based upon the currency conversion rate at the time of sale (rather than at the time of payment).

But the U.S. corporation needs U.S. dollars to pay its suppliers and employees and will therefore need to convert the British pounds into U.S. dollars upon receipt. This means that the U.S. corporation is assuming the currency risk of the transaction for a period of 30 days until the British pounds can be received and converted into U.S. dollars.

Now say that 30 days later the British company pays the 20,000 pounds but the conversion rate is now 0.90 British pounds for every U.S. dollar (the British pound has weakened). The U.S. company will convert the 20,000 British pounds into only $22,222. In this case, the U.S. company just lost $2,778 due to currency fluctuations (20,000 British pounds divided by 0.90 equals $22,222). Had the value of the British pound strengthened during the 30-day period to 0.70 British pounds for every U.S. dollar, the U.S. company would have made a profit of $3,571 due to currency fluctuations (20,000 British pounds divided by 0.70 equals $28,571).

Currency risk is the risk that the value of one currency will change versus the value of another currency. When companies have monies owed to them in foreign currencies that need to be converted into the home currency, there is currency risk. Many companies eliminate or reduce currency risk by using financial derivatives such as foreign currency swaps, options, and futures contracts.

BOOMS AND BUSTS

Government policy makers target a stable economy that can be maintained for the long term. Slow growing economies can result in high unemployment

🗣 GUESS WHAT?

The foreign exchange market is one of the largest markets in the world. By some estimates, when expressed in terms of U.S. dollars, about $3.2 trillion of currency changes hands each day (Wikipedia.com).

and a lower quality of life for the general population. Rapidly growing economies that are unsustainable can lead to inflation and economic decline as well.

An *economic boom* can be defined as a period of rapid economic expansion. Such periods include high employment, greater consumer demand, and increased production and expansion by businesses. Economic booms are viewed as periods of prosperity.

While economic booms are generally discussed on a national level, specific regions, cities, and towns can experience above average growth based upon population increases, the growth of certain industries, and other location-specific activities that do not occur across the country. In addition, certain sectors of the economy can experience abnormal growth spurts. Examples include the residential housing market boom that took place in the early to mid-2000s and the technology boom of the 1990s. The Roaring Twenties, which refers to the economic prosperity of the 1920s, can also be characterized as a booming period.

But sometimes economic and sector booms are unsustainable and lead to pricing collapses, market corrections, economic declines, and even recessions. The bursting of such "bubbles" can happen very quickly. The residential housing market collapse that began in 2007 has led to a severe global recession. Many houses are now selling for prices that are half the values of two or three years earlier. The technology boom of the 1990s led to a Nasdaq stock market crash and a loss of wealth that has never recovered. The economic boom of the 1920s was followed by a stock market crash and the Great Depression.

An *economic bust* can result in times of high unemployment, lower consumer demand, reduced expansion or contraction by businesses, and low inflation. As history has indicated, an economic bust can result in recession or even depression. Sector and industry busts usually occur after abnormal and unjustified expectations and price increases.

While great wealth can be earned during booming periods, massive financial losses can result even faster when bubbles burst. Even though unwarranted prices are often recognized by many investors and industry professionals, prior to the bursting of many industry and sector bubbles, greed tends to be the dominating factor. People become so consumed with making easy money in a rapidly rising market and so afraid of missing "the deal of a lifetime," that rational thought seems to be ignored.

When U.S. housing prices were rising at double-digit rates in the early and mid-2000s, it became obvious to many people that such values were unsustainable and that a market correction was needed. Fewer and fewer people could afford to buy houses, yet real estate speculators continued to buy and

🗨 GUESS WHAT?

Tulip Mania was a period in Dutch history during the 1600s when tulip bulb prices reached an extraordinary all-time high before rapidly collapsing. By many accounts, this was considered to be the bursting of the first economic bubble in history.

GUESS WHAT?

Due to the bursting of the residential housing market and two years of declining home prices, in May of 2009, Zillow.com reported that almost 22 percent of all U.S. homeowners were "underwater," meaning that their homes were worth less than the money owed on them.

---

force prices upward. During the technology boom of the 1990s, the stock prices of many companies having irrational business plans and no earnings potential for years to come were rapidly rising to unprecedented levels. Many investors knew this false wealth creation was too good to be true, yet they continued to pump more money into technology stocks. Finally, investors realized that these ridiculously high stock prices made no sense and panicked. Fear took over and more and more people began to sell, forcing the Nasdaq stock market to suddenly collapse.

It is important to maintain prudent investment strategies and discipline to avoid massive financial losses when bubbles burst. Adhere to the principals of diversification, and never put too much of your money into one investment, industry, or sector. Do not always feel the need to follow the crowd. There are countless examples of when smart people made stupid decisions and thousands and even millions of people were right behind them. Also, do not invest blindly. Understand the history and current stage of economies, industries, and markets. When things seem too good to be true, they probably are, and it may only be a matter of time before others come to the same conclusion. You may miss some upside potential, but you may also miss a devastating and irreversible financial loss.

LEADING ECONOMIC INDICATORS

When economists attempt to predict the future direction of the economy, they rely on numerous sources of economic data. The most telling information can be categorized as leading or lagging economic indicators. A *leading* economic indicator tends to move ahead and in the same direction as the general economy. When economists see enough leading economic indicators increasing and reflecting growth, they usually conclude that the overall economy is growing as well.

GUESS WHAT?

In July of 2008, the price of oil reached over $147 a barrel. Some analysts were predicting a price of $200 a barrel due to concerns over limited supplies within the earth and excessive demand from rapidly growing countries such as China and India. The price of gasoline escalated to $5.00 a gallon in some U.S. cities. However, by the end of 2008, the price of oil quickly fell to under $40 a barrel due to the global economic recession of the late 2000s.

🗣 GUESS WHAT?

According to Wikipedia, the Index of Leading Indicators was able to accurately predict seven of the recessions between 1959 and 2001. However, it also predicted five recessions during this period that did not occur.

An aggregate, well-known leading economic indicator is a composite of 10 variables. The Index of Leading Indicators is released monthly by The Conference Board, a nongovernment agency, and includes the following:

1. The interest rate spread between long- and short-term interest rates
2. The inflation adjusted supply of money
3. The average weekly hours worked by manufacturing workers
4. Manufacturers' new orders for consumer goods and materials
5. The S&P 500 stock market index
6. How quickly new merchandise is delivered from supplies to vendors
7. The average number of initial applications for unemployment insurance
8. The amount of new residential housing building permits
9. Consumer sentiment
10. Manufacturers' new orders of nondefense capital goods

This list is ordered by importance based upon the predictive ability of each of the 10 variables. For example, historically the spread between long- and short-term interest rates has been the greatest predictor of the direction of the economy. Manufacturers' new orders for capital goods unrelated to the defense industry have proven over time to be the weakest indicator of economic activity.

Investors, economists, and economic policy makers watch these and other indicators closely when attempting to assess the direction of the economy. The index has historically turned downward prior to a recession and upward prior to an economic expansion.

LAGGING ECONOMIC INDICATORS

Lagging economic indicators have a tendency to trail movements in the general economy. Because lagging economic indicators move after the economy, they add little value when trying to forecast future economic activity. However, lagging indicators do provide insight into the performance of the economy and can aid economists in measuring and revising prior forecasts.

The Index of Lagging Indicators measures the performance of seven key variables that have historically had strong correlations with movements in the general economy. The Index of Lagging Indicators is released by The Conference Board each month and includes the following data sources:

1. The average length of time that people are unemployed
2. The amount of outstanding commercial loans

3. Price changes for the service sector
4. The change in the cost of labor for each unit of manufactured output
5. The ratio of trade and manufacturing inventories to sales
6. The ratio of consumer credit outstanding when compared to consumer income
7. The average prime interest rate charged by banks

10

The 10 Most Common Mistakes to Avoid

1. CHOOSING THE WRONG CAREER

Spending the majority of your waking hours in a job that brings you unhappiness or little pleasure is counter to life's purpose. Some people choose a job or career because of money. Others do so because of the wishes of their parents or other people of influence. Many just follow the herd. But doing something you do not enjoy for long periods of time can severely dampen your level of happiness and lead to varying levels of depression, personal and marital problems, and unnecessary stress.

People should match their personalities and skill sets when considering specific jobs and an overall career. I am not saying that you should avoid jobs just because you are lacking in specific requirements; part of taking a new position is the excitement of learning new things. But do not, for example, take a career in sales when you dislike working with people. Focus on your strengths, weaknesses, and gifts. Most weaknesses can be improved. Try to match your current and desired skills and personality traits with careers that leverage these characteristics.

2. NEVER LEARNING TO SAVE

Learning to save money prudently is truly a skill that can provide financial security and long-term wealth and comfort. Teaching children and young adults this lesson at an early age will yield the most benefits. The sooner that people can start saving, properly investing, and minimizing or eliminating

🗣 GUESS WHAT?

According to www.careertest.us, the average person changes careers (not jobs) five to seven times, moving from career to career over a 20- to 40-year period of job dissatisfaction. Oftentimes when people change careers they are forced to take pay reductions and reenter the workplace at entry and lower levels. Finding a fit early in life can lead to greater personal and financial fulfillment.

any Bad Debt, the greater the effects of compounding and the faster their net worth will accumulate.

You are never too young or too rich to have a budget. Whether your income is from a weekly allowance or from a high-paying corporate position, knowing where your money goes and ensuring that income exceeds expenses is critical. Budgets can help transform people's behaviors by consciously and even subconsciously affecting their spending decisions and habits.

I cannot stress enough how beneficial a steady and diligent savings plan will be. The earlier such a policy can be implemented, the easier it becomes to buy one or more homes, automobiles, and other luxuries. A prudent long-term savings plan can lead to a comfortable retirement decades earlier than your peers. In addition, the saying that "it takes money to make money" is very true. The more money you have, the easier it becomes to make more.

3. TOO MUCH DEBT

Not only do many people lack proper savings plans, they also take on too much debt. It is too easy to borrow money and worry about repayment later. Bad habits are hard to break, but good habits can become second nature and remain with people for the long term.

As we have discussed, using affordable debt in moderation to facilitate the purchases of homes, automobiles, and other necessities can be a wise decision. But abusing debt for reckless spending is not. Having Bad Debt carried from month to month conflicts with any meaningful type of savings plan and can result in a weak and unstable financial position.

Credit cards are the easiest form of Bad Debt to obtain, particularly for young adults. But other types of lenders are more than willing to provide financing to people to buy their products. It takes discipline to refrain from excessive spending and to manage debt in conjunction with a budget and steady savings plan.

🗣 GUESS WHAT?

According to the U.S. Department of Commerce, the American savings rate declined over a 65-year period, and in some years, the national savings rate was actually negative.

According to www.crosswalk.com, the average historic interest rate on credit cards has been over 18 percent. If payments of $200 a month ($2,400 a year) were being made on a credit card balance of $10,000, assuming an 18 percent interest rate, it would take almost eight years to repay the debt. In addition, the cardholder would have paid approximately $8,600 in total interest.

---

4. EMOTIONAL INVESTING

Most people lack enough information to make sound financial decisions. In such cases, it is usually better to allow a trained financial advisor to make investment recommendations. But many financial advisors are poorly trained, and others make investment recommendations based upon the specific commissions that they receive. Therefore, even if you rely on a financial advisor, you should still have a rounded understanding of the types of investments being chosen and how they fit within your personal circumstances and overall objectives.

Studies have proven that most investors make their decisions based on emotion. Some investors sell stocks, mutual funds, and other investments during a market downturn only to see a recovery soon afterwards. Others try to time the market and sell during a downturn and buy during an upturn, which usually leads to missing the best performing periods of time. These strategies often result in "buying high and selling low" and in suboptimal investment performance.

Allowing emotions such as fear and greed to guide investment decisions has proven to be a poor strategy. In addition, following the crowd can lead to booms and ultimate busts. You cannot control the markets, but you can control your emotions. Knowledge is a powerful asset, and understanding how markets work can help. Take a long-term perspective when investing in assets having significant volatility such as stocks and real estate.

5. POOR DIVERSIFICATION AND PORTFOLIO ALLOCATION

Many portfolios are poorly diversified. I constantly see people picking individual stocks based upon personal intuition. They place a significantly large amount of money in a handful or less of stocks and watch them daily. Just like when gambling in a casino, many people find this type of investing by chance and guess to be exciting.

A study by the National Association of Securities Dealers found that 78 percent of Americans could name a character on a sitcom, but only 12 percent knew the difference between a load and a no-load mutual fund. Most Americans also responded that financial literature was too complicated and difficult to understand.

⚡ BEWARE!

According to a study performed by William N. Goetzmann and Alok Kumar, unsophisticated investors tend to hold poorly diversified portfolios. The majority of individuals within their sample study were deemed to be underdiversified. Over 25 percent of the sample portfolios included only one stock, and over 50 percent of the sample portfolios included fewer than three stocks. This indicates that from a risk versus return perspective, the majority of individual investors are underperforming the general stock market and assuming unnecessary risk.

People often think that because a company's stock price falls, that it becomes a great buy. But stock prices usually fall for a reason. For example, a decline in earnings, lower than expected sales and demand, and greater competition are all factors that will affect a company's stock price. Unless someone is reviewing the financial statements of a company and assessing competitors and industry cycles prior to purchasing its stock, they should stick to mutual funds and other diversified investments. In addition, individual stock pickers should own enough stocks in unrelated industries to produce a diversified portfolio that minimizes risk. This is a difficult task for the average investor.

Another problem with unsophisticated investors is that they do not properly allocate their money between asset classes. For example, people know that stocks tend to provide much higher returns than bonds over long periods of time. However, the values of stocks fluctuate much more widely than those of bonds, which leads to a much greater risk of losing a portion of a person's investment at a given point in time. When people become greedy and invest too much money in stocks, they expose themselves to too much risk. For example, a 65-year-old woman relying on a specific amount of income from her retirement portfolio should not have 80 percent of its value invested in stocks. Numerous people in this situation lost over 50 percent of their money during the 2008 stock market crash.

6. IGNORING THE BENEFITS OF RETIREMENT ACCOUNTS

The government encourages people to save for retirement by offering tax deductions and tax deferrals when using retirement accounts. Retirement accounts are one of the most powerful investment tools available and should not be ignored! For every dollar saved or deferred in taxes, an additional dollar can be invested and compounded over time. These benefits can result in hundreds of thousands of dollars in additional savings over time!

💬 GUESS WHAT?

According to a 2007 article by www.careerbuilder.com, 25 percent of workers reported that they do not participate in a 401K plan, IRA, or other retirement account, and 20 percent of people said they do not save at all. Another 28 percent of respondents said they save less than $100 a month, and another 16 percent said they saved less than $50 a month.

✎ BEWARE!

Over a 20-year period, if the inflation rate averages 4 percent per year, you would need $21,910 in 20 years to buy the same things that $10,000 would buy today. If you invested $10,000 in bank products earning an average annual interest rate of 2 percent, at the end of 20 years you would have about $14,860. By investing in bank products during this period, you would have lost around $7,050!

Employers often match a portion of employee 401K plan contributions. People that do not fully take advantage of this benefit are essentially giving up free money. If an employer is willing to match up to 3 percent of your 401K contributions, you should focus on contributing at least 3 percent to the plan to fully take advantage of this generosity. If you can contribute more, you should do so to maximize the tax deductions and deferrals.

7. INVESTING TOO CONSERVATIVELY

Many people are fearful of investing their money other than in products such as bank and money market accounts and certificates of deposit. Perhaps they do not trust financial advisors, or they may have experienced a loss in the past. Maybe this is what their parents taught them. Or maybe they just do not feel comfortable with the idea of using other investment products. As studies have proven, most individual investors find investing to be complicated, and they do not understand how most investments work.

But remember that in order to even start getting a return on your investment, you need to be earning more than the country's average inflation rate. If you are earning less than the inflation rate, you are actually losing money. Most bank products pay interest rates that are less than the rate of inflation. These instruments are good for holding cash for emergencies and short-term commitments, but they are not appropriate for building long-term wealth.

8. TAX RETURN ERRORS AND POOR TAX PLANNING

Tax laws are extremely complicated. Even people that spend their entire careers focused on tax matters can make mistakes. It is important that you choose a qualified tax professional for guidance and that you proactively seek advice early in the tax year and before making decisions that can have serious tax consequences.

When unqualified people prepare tax returns, they might be missing deductions that could materially lower tax bills or result in greater tax refunds.

🗣 GUESS WHAT?

Internal Revenue Service centers set up to help people prepare their tax returns gave incorrect answers or no answer at all 43 percent of the time when Treasury Department investigators posed as taxpayers (The Associated Press).

✎ BEWARE!

According to Crown Financial Ministries, whether American taxpayers complete their own tax returns or have a tax preparer do it for them, about 35 percent of all personal tax returns have at least one error that negatively affects the taxpayer, and at least 17 percent have at least one error that affects the taxpayer positively.

Conversely, tax return errors could result in significant interest and penalty costs and delays in receiving any tax refunds. Carefully consider whether you are suited to prepare your own tax returns, and be very selective when considering a tax professional.

9. THE UNINSURED

People that do not maintain proper insurance place themselves and their families and assets at great risk. Without proper personal, automotive, homeowners' or renters', and business insurance, accidents can result in huge financial losses. Too many people ignore the possibility of accident and the seriousness of the potential repercussions. Just one unfortunate event can lead to the loss or garnishment of income, forced asset sales, bankruptcy, and massive expenses and liabilities that can take many years to repay and that can ruin a person's credit history.

The more assets you accumulate, the greater the chance that someone will sue you if the opportunity arises. And it does not take much for an opportunity to present itself. In addition to proper personal and property protection, make sure that you have adequate liability insurance coverage.

🗩 GUESS WHAT?

According to a poll undertaken by Citizens Against Lawsuit Abuse (CALA) in their "Sick of Lawsuits" campaign, 79 percent of respondents "believe advertising by personal-injury lawyers encourages people to sue, even if they have not been injured" (www.inside prison.com).

✎ BEWARE!

In early 2009, the Securities and Exchange Commission (SEC) charged financier R. Allen Stanford and three of his companies with orchestrating a $9.2 billion investment and sales fraud. The SEC's complaint alleged that the fraud centered on a CD program in which Stanford International Bank promised "improbable and unsubstantiated high interest rates." Complaints allege that Mr. Sanford used investor funds to support his lavish lifestyle, including sponsoring a $20 million cricket match on the island of Antigua. In 2008, *Forbes* magazine ranked Mr. Sanford #205 in its "400 Richest Americans" article.

10. FALLING FOR A SCAM

It is easy to be duped by a professional con artist. These people are talented, skilled at deception, and they spend significant time thinking about and practicing their schemes. In addition, they make investment opportunities seem so attractive that they count on greed dominating rational thinking.

Consider the reputation, size, and track record of any company that you are planning to do business with, and ask a lot of questions when evaluating new investments. Do not feel pressured. Being rushed into a decision quickly or being told that you need to act immediately is a troubling sign. Do not be afraid to ask trained professionals such as tax advisors and attorneys for their opinions as well.

Appendix

Household Budgeting Model

ASSUMPTIONS

This model was created to assist investors in quantifying and tracking their monthly cash inflows and outflows and to help them maintain financial discipline and meet targeted savings objectives.

You must have a sufficient version of Microsoft Excel to open and use the model. To access and download the model, visit my Web site at www.Lawless Investing.com.

Once the file is open, you will see various assumptions numbered from 1 through 35. The numbers that are required to be inputted by the user of the model are shown in red. The user can only change the numbers in red and is responsible for the accuracy of each of these figures. If a specific income or expense category is not appropriate, either enter zero or leave it blank. Any number highlighted in red will factor into the model's results.

The numbers provided in the initial model are only intended to provide an example, and these figures should be changed or deleted to reflect the user's personal circumstances.

Following is a description of the assumption categories and some helpful hints.

1. *For the Month of*—This is the month for which you are preparing a budget. If you would like to create an annual budget (which I recommend because each month may have differing revenues and expenses), you can save the file 12 times (each for a different month) and track each month individually.

2–8. *Monthly Income*—These seven line items allow the user to enter any sources of monthly income. The first two lines (Assumptions 2 and 3) are labeled "Paycheck" and were created to allow the user to enter two net paycheck amounts per month. These lines can be used or ignored and made blank (or zero). Assumptions 4 through 8 allow the user to enter additional income categories to reflect other sources of monthly income and the corresponding dollar amounts. All dollar amounts for Monthly Income items should be entered in column D across from the appropriate line item.

9–34. *Monthly Expenses*—These 26 line items allow the user to enter various monthly expenses. Assumptions 9 through 24 have specific headings that are intended to represent common household expenses. Any of these lines can be used or ignored and made blank (or zero). Assumptions 25 through 34 allow the user to enter additional personalized expense categories and corresponding dollar amounts. All dollar amounts for items within the Monthly Expenses category should be entered as positive numbers (do not enter negative numbers even though they are cash outflows) in column F across from the appropriate line item.

35. *Monthly Savings*—This is the amount of money that you intend to save each month. Investors will often back into this number after they have listed and assessed all of their monthly income and expense figures. For example, when there is excess cash remaining for the month, the monthly savings number can be increased. If there is a cash shortfall for the month, the monthly savings figure must often be decreased. Sometimes investors can reduce or eliminate certain expense items in order to meet their targeted monthly savings figure.

After the user has entered all of the Monthly Income, Monthly Expenses, and Monthly Savings amounts, the figures at the bottom of the model sum the monthly cash inflows (Monthly Income) and cash outflows (Monthly Expenses and Monthly Savings) and any excess or shortfall between the two figures is shown. The Total Cash (Shortfall) or Excess column indicates whether the investor has excess cash (a positive number) or a cash shortfall (a negative number).

If the investor's Total Cash Inflows and Total Cash Outflows perfectly match, the word *BALANCED* will be shown in the Budget Status column. The words *EXCESS CASH* will be shown when the investor's Total Cash Inflows exceed Total Cash Outflows and the words *(CASH SHORTFALL)* will be seen when Total Cash Outflows exceed Total Cash Inflows.

Glossary

Active Investment Strategy: An investment approach based upon an investor or mutual fund manager or other paid professional attempting to "beat the market" by selecting specific securities to buy and sell at specific times.

Adjustable Interest Rate: A variable interest rate on a loan or security that is periodically adjusted up or down based upon the performance of a specific benchmark interest rate.

After Tax Interest Rate: The effective interest rate on a loan after considering any tax deduction benefits from the interest paid by the obligor.

Alternative Investments: Investments other than traditional stock, bond, money market, and bank products. A general definition includes assets such as financial derivatives, hedge funds, private equity funds, wine, art, and rare coins.

Amortization Schedule: The schedule of required principal payments under a loan, note, or bond agreement that specifies when a lender will be repaid.

Angel Investors: Individuals and small groups of individuals that invest money into startup companies.

Annual Percentage Rate (APR): The interest rate charged on the dollars borrowed and outstanding on a credit card stated on an annual basis.

Annuity: A fixed income investment issued by an insurance company that pays the investor a fixed or variable rate of return until the annuity expires or until the time of death of the holder(s).

Ask Price: The price that a seller or market maker is willing to accept when an investor is buying a security.

Asset-Backed Securities (ABS): Notes and bonds issued by securitization vehicles usually structured by investment banks and backed by pools of consumer product loans, credit card receivables, and other assets.

Asset Class: A general grouping of investments having common characteristics. Asset class examples include equity ownership, fixed income, real estate, and alternative investments. An asset class can be broken down much more granularly to include many different types of investment instruments with varying features and levels of risk.

Back End Load: A fee paid when an investor sells a certain type of shares in a mutual fund (usually Class B shares) before a certain date. Also known as a "deferred sales charge."

Balloon Payment: The unamortized portion of a loan, note, or bond principal balance that is due to a lender on the maturity date.

Bank Reserve Requirements: A legally required minimum amount of funds held by banks on reserve in case of unexpected cash outflows.

Bank Savings Account: A deposit account held with a financial institution that does not permit check writing.

Barclays Capital U.S. Aggregate Bond Index: A broad bond market index maintained by Barclays Capital used to represent the performance of investment grade bonds being traded in the United States.

Benchmark: A market index or interest rate used for comparative purposes when measuring investment performance and setting lending policies. Usually active investment strategies are compared to passive market index benchmarks to assess performance. Lenders also use interest rate benchmarks when setting and adjusting interest rates on loans.

Bid-Ask Spread: The difference in the bid and ask prices of a security. The bid-ask spread is normally the profit received by a market maker when facilitating a trading market for a specific security and serving as an intermediary between buyers and sellers.

Bid Price: The price that a buyer or market maker is willing to pay when an investor is selling a security.

Bond: A fixed income debt instrument issued by a government, corporation, individual, or other entity that obligates that issuer to pay the investor principal and interest on specified dates. A bond can be unsecured or secured by specific collateral, and the interest rate can be fixed or adjustable. Bonds have maturity dates of 10 years or longer.

Book Value: The per share value of a company's common stock computed by taking total common shareholder's equity on a company's balance sheet divided by the number of outstanding shares of common stock. Book value per share is essentially the value expected to be received by common stockholders if a company were to cease operations and sell all of its assets.

Boom: A period of prosperity and rapid growth for an economy, market, or industry.

Bridge/Pre-Public Stage Financing: A company's final stage of venture capital financing in which the company is preparing to go public or sell itself.

Business Plan: A written summary of how a person or company is going to carry out a particular set of initiatives in order to achieve specific goals.

Bust: A period of significant productivity and/or value declines for an economy, market, or industry.

Call Option: A financial derivative that grants the holder, in return for a premium, the option to buy an underlying security at a specified price by a certain date. The call option holder may choose to exercise the option or let it expire worthless depending upon the value of the underlying security within the option period.

Capital Gain: A profit resulting from the sale of a financial asset that has appreciated in value. The tax rates applicable to capital gains often differ from those related to ordinary income.

Central Bank: A government agency responsible for a country's financial and banking systems and for making and implementing monetary policy decisions.

Certificates of Deposit (CD): Time deposits commonly held by individual investors and issued by banks and other financial institutions. Most CDs have maturity dates ranging from one month to five years and pay a fixed rate of interest to the holder at the time of maturity.

Charge Card: A plastic card that allows the user to make purchases of goods and services. Charge cards require outstanding balances to be repaid in full each month and often have higher and sometimes unlimited spending limits when compared to credit cards.

Checking Account: An account with a financial institution that allows the holder to write checks against deposited funds. Checking accounts that pay interest are often referred to as negotiable order of withdrawal accounts (NOW).

Chicago Board of Options Exchange (CBOX): An exchange founded in 1973 that focuses on option contract trading for stock, index, and interest rate financial instruments and serves as the world's largest options market.

Closed-Ended Mutual Fund: A mutual fund having a limited number of shares outstanding. Shares are not issued or redeemed liked open-ended mutual funds. Rather, shares are usually traded between buyers and sellers on a stock exchange.

Commodity: Materials that are sold in bulk in the financial markets. Examples include gold, silver, copper, oil, natural gas, oranges, pork bellies, wheat, corn, and cocoa. Commodities are generally raw materials that are used to produce other products. Manufacturers buy commodities as needed for production. Investors also buy commodities as investments through the use of financial instruments.

Common Stock: A security issued by a corporation granting an equity ownership interest in the company and entitling the holder to a portion of the entity's profits.

Compounding of Money: The concept of generating earnings from earnings previously earned and passively watching an investment grow larger and larger.

Conforming Mortgage Loan: A home mortgage loan meeting specific criteria established by federal agencies including maximum loan size, type of underlying property, minimum borrower documentation, and debt-to-income limits.

Copyright: The legal right granted to an author, composer, playwright, publisher, or other artist granting the exclusive production and distribution rights.

Credit Card: A plastic card backed by a line of credit provided to the cardholder by the issuing credit card company. The user can borrow money from the credit card company to make payments to merchants and to receive cash advances. Balances can be carried from month to month as long as minimum required payments are being made.

Credit Rating: A published ranking of the financial strength of a security, company, or country by a recognized credit rating agency.

Credit Rating Agencies: There are three widely recognized credit rating agencies including Standard & Poor's, Moody's Investors Service, and Fitch Ratings. These agencies provide unbiased financial credit ratings on securities, companies, and countries around the globe.

Credit Score: A score rating a person's credit strength based upon credit history, debts outstanding, and payment status.

Day Order: An order to buy or sell a security that remains outstanding for the current day only. If the trade does not get executed at the specified terms by end of day, it expires.

Debit Card: A plastic card used to pay merchants and service providers that is linked to the user's bank account. Any charges are immediately subtracted or "debited" from the cardholder's bank account.

Debt-to-Income Ratio: A comparison of the income earned and the income needed to pay individual debt obligations and living expenses. Often reviewed by lenders when considering loan requests.

Depreciation: The reduction in value over time for assets such as residential and commercial buildings, automobiles, and machinery as a result of wear and tear, aging, and obsolescence. When depreciable assets are used in business and for investment purposes, periodic depreciation expense often results in favorable income tax deductions.

Discounted Value: When a fixed income security is paying an interest rate that is less than the current market interest rate for similar securities, it will sell at a price that is less than its principal balance.

Discount Rate: The interest rate charged on short-term loans to financial institutions by a central bank.

Discount Window: A lending program and monetary policy instrument that allows eligible financial institutions to borrow funds from a central bank on a short-term basis.

Diversification: Spreading invested dollars over a wide selection of investments to reduce risk and potentially increase investment profitability.

Dividend: A distribution by an entity to its owners. Most dividends are cash payments representing profit distributions to common stockholders of a corporation that are often made on a quarterly basis.

Dividend Yield: Determined by taking the amount of dividends paid to shareholders over an annual period on a share of stock and dividing this amount by the current stock value.

Dollar-Cost Averaging: The technique of buying scheduled, fixed dollar amounts of an investment so that more purchases are made at lower prices than at higher prices.

Dow Jones Industrial Average (DJIA): An index that measures the common stock performance of 30 large companies that trade on the New York Stock Exchange. Often referred to as "the Dow," the DJIA is the most closely watched stock market index in the world.

Economic Depression: A rare and extreme form of prolonged economic recession.

Economic Recession: A slowdown in economic activity often measured as being two or more quarters of negative growth in gross domestic product. Recessions are often accompanied by high unemployment, low business investment and production, reduced lender credit, and low inflation.

Economy: The economic-related activities including the production, consumption, and distribution of goods and services within a particular country or geographic region.

Entrepreneur: A person that starts and assumes responsibility for a new business venture.

Equity Investment: An ownership interest in an entity that entitles the holder to certain rights such as a percentage of profits and losses.

Equity REIT: A real estate investment trust having a primary business strategy of buying and leasing real estate properties.

Exchange Rate: A measurement tool between two currencies that indicates how much one currency is worth when compared to the other (also known as a foreign-exchange or FX rate).

Exchange Traded Fund (ETF): An investment vehicle that holds a basket of stocks or bonds and trades on a national stock exchange. Most ETFs hold the same securities as a specific index, such as the S&P 500 Index or the Dow Jones Industrial Average.

Exit Strategy: A planned event by a company to repay its investors and lenders by means such as a stock or asset sale, the sale of the company, or the acquisition of the company by another entity.

Expense Ratio: The total fees of a particular mutual fund expressed as a percentage of the fund's average assets. Comparing expense ratios among funds having similar investment strategies can identify funds having higher and lower fee structures.

Federal Funds Rate: The rate of interest charged by banks when lending funds deposited with the Federal Reserve to other banks, which is usually on an overnight basis.

Federal Open Market Committee (FOMC): A component of the Federal Reserve System in the United States that is responsible for overseeing the country's monetary policy through open market operations by buying and selling government securities and other financial instruments.

Federal Work-Study Program: A program sponsored by the United States to assist college students in paying for school through part-time jobs.

FHA Loan: A federal assisted mortgage loan insured by the Federal Housing Administration provided to aid lower income Americans in purchasing homes.

FICO Score: Created by Fair Isaac Corp., the most common type of credit score used by lenders when assessing a borrower's credit worthiness. FICO scores range from 300 to 850.

Financial Derivative: A financial instrument that derives its value from the value of an underlying asset. Examples of financial derivatives include option and futures contracts and interest rate and foreign currency swap agreements.

First Stage Financing: A financing stage in which companies begin seeking capital from outside investors to facilitate growth.

Fiscal Policy: Actions by a government intended to move the rate of growth within an economy through changes in business and consumer tax rates and the level of government spending.

Fixed Income Investments: Investment products and securities that pay a fixed or adjustable rate of interest including bills, notes, bonds, annuity contracts, certificates of deposit, and savings and money market accounts.

Fixed Interest Rate: A predetermined rate of interest for the term of a loan, note, bond, annuity, or other fixed income investment.

Focus Group: A small group of people that is representative of a larger targeted audience and used to gather market research and product feedback.

Foreclosure: The taking of collateral securing a financial obligation from a borrower by a lender. Upon foreclosure, the owner of the underlying collateral changes from the borrower to the lender.

401K Plan: A retirement investment account sponsored by an employer that allows employees to save a percentage of pretax wages that grow and compound on a tax-deferred basis. Many employers also match a portion of employee contributions as a form of additional compensation.

Front End Load: An upfront sales commission charged by a mutual fund to the investor at the time of purchase. Front end loads are usually charged on Class A mutual fund shares.

Futures Contract: A standardized financial derivative contract that trades on an exchange and allows buyers and sellers to fix the price and quantity of an underlying asset for a specified period. Futures contracts are written on individual stocks and bonds, market indexes, commodities, and other financial instruments.

Good 'Til Cancelled Order: An order to buy or sell securities that remains in effect for 30 days or until cancelled.

Grant: A form of financial aid to help students pay for college. Grants do not require repayment and are awarded by governments, colleges and universities, and many private organizations.

Gross Domestic Product (GDP): An economic measurement of the total value of goods and services produced within a country, normally measured using a one-year period.

Growth Stock: The common stock of a company that is viewed as having high growth potential. Growth stocks are often compared to value stocks, which sell at discounted prices but have less growth potential. Growth stocks typically sell at higher Price/Earnings multiples and Price/Book ratios when compared to value stocks.

Hedge Funds: Investment funds normally used by wealthy individuals and financial institutions that are allowed to employ complex strategies often unavailable to mutual funds, such as the use of short selling, financial derivatives, and leverage.

High-Yield Bonds: Fixed income debt obligations sold to investors by issuers having weaker credit strength when compared to issuers of higher-credit investment grade bonds. High-yield bonds pay higher rates of interest or "yields" due to the greater risk that the issuers will default on their obligations (also known as "junk bonds").

Home Equity: Equals the value of a home less any debt obligations secured by the home.

Home Equity Line of Credit: A revolving line of credit secured by a borrower's home equity that provides for the borrowing, repayment, and reborrowing on the line as needed. The line is secured by a second mortgage on the home and has an adjustable rate of interest.

Home Equity Loan: A loan secured by a borrower's home equity that has a fixed repayment schedule. The loan is secured by a second mortgage on the home and usually has a fixed rate of interest.

Hybrid REIT: A real estate investment trust in the business of both owning real estate for lease to tenants and lending money to real estate owners.

Identity Theft: A crime in which someone steals someone else's personal information and pretends to be that person in order to charge and borrow money at their expense.

Illiquid Asset: An asset that cannot be sold quickly without a significant price concession. Illiquid assets often include substantial transaction costs when being bought and sold.

Index: A market index used to measure the performance of a specific securities market such as a broad stock or bond market. Examples include the S&P 500 stock market index, the Barclays Capital U.S. Aggregate Bond Index, and the various Morgan Stanley Country Indexes.

Indexed Mutual Funds: Mutual funds that hold the same stocks, bonds, and other securities in the same proportions as a specific index. The use of indexed mutual funds is considered to be a passive investment strategy because the security selection process is performed by computers, and there is very little buying and selling.

Individual Retirement Account (IRA): An investment retirement savings vehicle granted under federal tax law that allows earnings to compound over time on either a tax-free or a tax-deferred basis depending upon the type of IRA chosen. The two primary types of IRAs are the Traditional IRA and the Roth IRA.

Inflation: An economic term that measures the periodic price increases for goods and services within a particular country or region.

Initial Public Offering (IPO): The first time a company publicly sells its common stock, which usually includes the listing of the company's stock on a major stock exchange.

Insurance: A risk management tool that allows individuals and businesses to transfer certain risks to insurance companies in return for a fee or "insurance premium."

Interest Only Loans: Loans that require the borrower to make interest payments for a portion or the full term of the loan. Principal repayment is deferred until some point in the future.

Internal Rate of Return (IRR): The annualized rate of return that is earned or expected to be earned from an investment or business venture. Investors often consider the projected IRR on an investment when determining whether or not to invest.

Investment Grade Rating: A formal rating issued by one or more recognized credit rating agencies generally being BBB– or higher.

Investment Scams: Illegal actions taken by con artists and other criminals intending to steal money from victims through false promises of abnormal profits and money-making opportunities.

Jumbo Mortgage Loan: A nonconforming residential mortgage loan having a principal balance above the dollar limit specified by federal agencies.

Lagging Economic Indicators: Measurements of economic activity that tend to follow behind the general economy and demonstrate how an economy has performed.

Large Cap Stock: Refers to the common stock of a large company having a market capitalization of over $5 billion.

Leading Economic Indicators: Measurements of economic activity that tend to move ahead of the general economy and serve as a predictive tool when assessing the future direction of an economy.

Leverage: The use of borrowed funds to supplement existing monies for investment purposes, which tends to magnify positive and negative investment returns.

Leveraged Buyout (LBO): When management teams and/or third-party investors purchase a controlling interest in a company from existing shareholders by borrowing a substantial amount of the money and increasing the amount of debt owed by the company upon purchase.

Like Kind Exchange: The deferral of capital gain taxes by rolling the profits from the sale of one investment property into the purchase of another investment property under the parameters of Internal Revenue Code Section 1031. Also known as a "1031 exchange."

Limit Order: An order to buy or sell a security at a specified price. The order will not be executed until the limit order price has been reached.

Liquid Asset: An asset that can be sold quickly with little if any price concession and with minimal transaction costs.

Loan Maturity Date: The date when a loan becomes fully due and payable.

Loan Origination Fees: Fees or "points" charged by lenders in return for providing loans to borrowers that are quoted as a percentage of the principal balance of each loan.

Loan-to-Value Ratio: The amount lent by a lender in proportion to the value of the underlying collateral expressed as a percentage.

London Interbank Offering Rate (LIBOR): The interest rate that banks use when lending money to one another. Different LIBORs cover different borrowing periods (i.e., 1-month, 3-month, etc.). The interest rates on many business and consumer loans are tied to LIBOR.

Long-Term Capital Gains and Losses: Profits and losses earned from the sale of financial assets when the time period between purchase and sale is greater than 12 months.

Macroeconomics: A subset of the field of economics that focuses on the study of the behaviors of an overall economy such as the effects of unemployment, inflation, and product and service imports and exports with other countries.

Managed Investment Portfolios: An investment strategy usually employed by wealthy investors that rely on one or more professional money managers to choose and manage their portfolio of investments. Portfolio holdings are often at the manager's discretion and might include stocks, bonds, real estate, and alternative investments.

Managed Mutual Funds: Mutual funds holding stocks, bonds, and/or other securities that are actively managed by professional investment managers responsible for choosing which securities to purchase and when to buy and sell these securities.

Market Capitalization: Measured as a company's total number of shares of common stock outstanding multiplied by the current share price. For example, a company having 10 million shares of common stock outstanding that are currently selling for $5 per share would have a market capitalization of $50 million.

Market Maker: A person, bank, brokerage firm, or other financial institution that is buying securities from sellers and selling securities to buyers and "making a market" for one or more securities.

Market Order: An order to buy or sell stocks and other securities immediately at the prevailing market price.

Microeconomics: A subset of the field of economics that focuses on the behaviors of sectors within an economy, including the cause and effect relationships related to supply and demand decisions made by businesses and individuals.

Mid Cap Stock: Refers to the common stock of a mid-sized company having a market capitalization of between $1 billion and $5 billion.

Monetary Policy: Actions by a government intended to alter the rate of growth within an economy through changes in the supply and cost of money.

Money Market Account: A savings account that shares some of the characteristics of both a mutual fund and a checking account. Such accounts usually provide limited check writing ability and pay higher rates of interest than traditional savings accounts.

Morgan Stanley Country Index (MSCI): A series of stock market indexes that track the performance of specific countries or regions. For example, the MSCI Europe Index measures the stock market performance of developed European countries.

Mortgage: A transfer of an interest in property to a lender that serves as the lender's security when making a loan to a property owner.

Mortgage-Backed Securities (MBS): Notes and bonds issued by securitization vehicles usually structured by investment banks and backed by pools of commercial or residential mortgage loans.

Mortgage Loan: A loan collateralized by a mortgage on real estate.

Mortgage REIT: A real estate investment trust having the primary business strategy of lending money to real estate owners.

Municipal Notes and Bonds: Fixed income debt obligations issued by state, city, and local governments ("municipalities") used to raise money for general governmental purposes and specific projects, such as roadway and school development.

Mutual Fund: A collective investment vehicle that pools investor funds to purchase stocks, bonds, money market instruments, and other securities.

Mutual Fund Share Classes: Investment alternatives within the same mutual fund that have varying fee structures based upon differing upfront sales charges, redemption, and ongoing marketing and promotional fees.

Nasdaq Composite Index: A stock market index that tracks all of the stocks listed on the Nasdaq stock exchange, most of which operate within the technology sector.

Negative Amortization: When some or all of the interest payments on a loan are deferred and added to the outstanding principal balance of the loan and scheduled to be paid at a later date.

Net Asset Value (NAV): The current value of the net assets that a mutual fund owns. Commonly shown as a per share amount that is usually calculated at the end of each trading day.

New York Mercantile Exchange (NYMEX): An exchange where a variety of metals and energy futures and option contracts are traded.

New York Stock Exchange: A stock exchange based in New York City considered to be the largest in the world.

Nonconforming Mortgage Loan: A home mortgage loan that does not meet specific guidelines established by federal agencies including maximum loan size, underlying type of property, required borrower documentation, and debt-to-income limits.

Noninvestment Grade Rating: A formal credit rating issued by one or more recognized credit rating agencies generally being below BBB–.

Note: A debt obligation of an issuer (i.e., a government, corporation, or individual) to repay an investor a specific amount of principal and interest at scheduled times. Notes have maturity dates of 10 years or less and can be unsecured or secured by specific collateral. Interest rates on notes can be fixed or adjustable.

Open-Ended Mutual Fund: A mutual fund that continually issues new shares and redeems existing shares, usually on a daily basis.

Option Contract: A financial derivative that provides the contract buyer with the right (not the obligation) to purchase or sell a certain quantity of a financial asset at a specified price within a predetermined period of time. The buyer pays a fee to the seller or "writer" of the option contract.

Opt Out: Federal law requires banks, brokerage firms, and insurance companies to provide clients with the option to "opt out" of having their personal information shared with other parties.

Ordinary Income: Income received from wages, bonuses, tips, commissions, and other forms of compensation earned from being employed. Ordinary income can also include interest and dividends received on investments, net income on rental properties, and self-employment income from business ownership. The tax rates applicable to ordinary income often differ from those related to capital gain income.

Par Value: When a fixed income security is paying an interest rate that is equal to the current market interest rate for similar securities, it will sell at a price equal to its principal balance.

Passive Investment Strategy: An investment approach based upon the assumption that attempting to time the market by actively buying and selling securities will not produce greater profits than just buying and holding a diversified portfolio over the long term. Indexed mutual funds and exchange traded funds are often used to facilitate passive investment strategies.

Patents: A government grant to an inventor or creator that secures the sole right to make, use, and sell a new idea or product for a specified period of time and prevents competitors from doing so.

Phishing: Refers to fishing for confidential information so that identity theft and credit card and bank fraud can be committed by assuming the victim's identity or accessing his or her accounts.

Portfolio Turnover Rate: Measures how many times the dollars within a particular mutual fund are being reinvested based upon the buying and selling of securities. High portfolio turnover rates often lead to greater investor tax liabilities when compared to funds having lower portfolio turnover rates.

Preferred Stock: A class of stock issued by companies that pays a specific dividend before any common stockholders are paid. Preferred stock is considered less risky than common stock because preferred stockholders are repaid their investment before common stockholders.

Premium Value: When a fixed income security is paying an interest rate that is greater than the current market interest rate for similar securities, it will sell at a price that is greater than its principal balance.

Present Value: The value of a dollar today that is expected to be received in the future assuming an expected annual return. For example, $100 scheduled to be received in one year has a value today of $95.24 assuming a 5 percent interest rate.

Price/Book Ratio: The current market price of a share of a company's common stock divided by its book value per share. High Price/Book ratios are often associated with growth stocks, while low Price/Book ratios are often associated with value stocks.

Price/Earnings (P/E) Multiple: The current market price of a share of a company's common stock divided by its annual earnings per share. High P/E multiples are often associated with growth stocks, while low P/E multiples are often associated with value stocks.

Prime Interest Rate: The interest rate offered by banks to their preferred customers. The interest rates on many business and consumer loans are tied to the prime interest rate. Also known as the "prime rate."

Private Equity Fund: An investment vehicle used by wealthy individuals and financial institutions to diversify their portfolios and to provide opportunities to earn significant profits. Private equity funds focus on venture capital financing, buyout strategies, distressed lending, and investment and real estate opportunities.

Private Mortgage Insurance (PMI): Allows home buyers to avoid the normal 20 percent down payment when buying a home by purchasing insurance. This insurance covers lenders in case home buyers default on their loans.

Private Student Loans: Loans made by banks and other lenders to students and parents to help finance the costs associated with attending college. These loans are not government guaranteed.

Prospectus: A legal document required by the Securities Act of 1933 offering securities or mutual fund shares for sale that includes information to aid investors in making well-informed decisions.

Put Option: A financial derivative that grants the holder, in return for a premium, the option to sell an underlying security at a specified price by a certain date. The put option holder may choose to exercise the option or let it expire worthless depending upon the value of the underlying security during the option period.

Real Estate Investment Trust (REIT): A company that invests in real estate–related assets, including hotels, shopping centers, apartment buildings, warehouses, marinas, golf courses, and other property types. In addition, some REITs make loans to borrowers that are secured by real estate.

Roth IRA: An individual retirement account that allows investors to deposit and invest after-tax dollars (up to specific annual limits) that can grow on a tax-free basis.

Russell Indexes: A series of stock market indexes that track the common stock performance of U.S. companies. The Russell 3000 Index tracks 3,000

U.S. stocks. The largest 1,000 stocks within the Russell 3000 Index comprise the Russell 1000 Index. The smallest 2,000 stocks within the Russell 3000 Index make up the Russell 2000 Index.

Scholarship: A form of financial aid to help students pay for college. Scholarships do not require repayment and are awarded by governments, colleges and universities, and many private organizations.

Second Mortgage: A mortgage placed on a property having an existing mortgage, such as when a borrower receives a home equity loan or line of credit in addition to a first lien mortgage loan. Under a foreclosure, the second mortgage lender does not get paid until the first mortgage holder is repaid in full.

Second Stage Financing: A venture capital financing stage for a relatively new business that is trying to gain market share and become profitable.

Securitization: A structured financing whereby notes and bonds are sold to investors backed by pools of residential and commercial mortgage loans, automobile loans, credit card receivables, and other assets.

Seed Stage Financing: A startup stage for a new business in which a new idea is being pursued. Financing is often only available at this stage from family and friends and management, but angel investors and venture capitalist firms may also invest.

Service Marks: A word, name, or symbol that is used to identify and market a service that is legally registered to limit the use and production to its owner.

Short Selling: The sale of stock that is not owned by the seller, but rather borrowed from a brokerage firm for a fee. The short seller must ultimately repurchase the stock and return it to the brokerage firm. Short sellers sell borrowed stock expecting it to decline in value at which time they can repurchase the stock at a lower price and make a profit.

Short-Term Capital Gains and Losses: Profits and losses earned from the sale of financial assets when the time period between purchase and sale is 12 months or less.

Small Cap Stock: Refers to the common stock of a small-sized company having a market capitalization of less than $1 billion. A "micro-cap stock" often refers to a company having a market capitalization of less than $250 million.

Spoofing: Criminals using fictitious e-mail addresses in order to gain passwords and personal and account information from victims in order to facilitate identity theft.

Spot Market: A market in which commodities such as gold and oil are bought and sold at current market prices for immediate delivery. Also known as the "cash market."

Standard & Poor's 500 Index: An index that measures the performance of 500 of the largest U.S. common stocks. Often referred to as the "S&P 500."

Startup Stage Financing: The next financing stage for a company after the seed stage. The startup stage implies that a new product or service is worth pursuing further and additional capital is targeted, usually from angel investors and venture capitalist firms.

Stop Loss Order: Places a trigger price on a security. Once the security price drops to or below the price specified in the stop loss order, the order immediately converts to a market order and the securities are sold at the best available price.

Student Loans: Loans provided to students or parents to help finance the costs of college. Student loans can be government subsidized or unsubsidized.

Subsidized Student Loan: A student loan in which interest is paid by the government as long as the student is enrolled on at least a half-time basis.

Surrender Fee: A fee charged on annuity contracts when funds are withdrawn early.

Surrender Value: A redeemable value of a variable annuity contract that accumulates over time and that can be withdrawn and borrowed against by the insured.

Swap Agreement: A financial derivative contract between two parties with differing investment objectives that provides for the exchange of interest rates, foreign currencies, credit risk, and other financial obligations.

Sweetheart Swindles: Investment scams whereby con artists nurture relationships with victims, usually through Internet chat rooms and dating sites, so that they can convince them to send money one or more times.

Tax-Deferral: Paying taxes in the future for income earned in the current year such as through a 410K plan or individual retirement account.

Term Life Insurance: Life insurance that covers a specified period of time in which the beneficiary is only paid the insured amount if the policy holder dies.

Third Stage Financing: A venture capital financing stage in which a business is in its expansionary phase and focused on building market share.

Time Value of Money: The concept that money today is worth more than an equal amount of money in the future due to its earnings potential.

Trademark: A distinctive mark, sign, name, or logo used by an individual or business to identify and sell a particular product or service. A trademark can be legally registered and protects the owner from replication and use by others.

Trading Commission: A fee paid to brokers and other agents in return for executing buy and sell orders for investors. The amount of each trading commission varies based upon the level of service being provided by the broker and the specific security being bought or sold.

Traditional IRA: An individual retirement account that allows investors to deposit and invest pretax dollars (up to specific annual limits) that grow on a tax-deferred basis.

Treasury Bill: A short-term debt obligation of the U.S. government having a maturity date of one year or less and issued at a discount to the amount of principal that will be received at the time of maturity.

Treasury Securities: Bills, notes, and bonds issued by the U.S. Department of the Treasury sold to investors to raise money for the federal government. Treasury securities are often used as a benchmark when pricing loans and other fixed income securities.

Triple Net Lease: A lease agreement on a property in which the tenant agrees to pay all insurance, real estate tax, and maintenance expenses in addition to any other expenses specified in the lease.

12b-1 Fee: An ongoing marketing or distribution fee on a mutual fund named after a provision in a securities law.

Unsubsidized Student Loan: A form of student loan that accrues interest expense while the student is in school, and the repayment of interest and principal is the responsibility of the student.

Value Stock: The stock of a company that is viewed as being "cheap" and selling at a bargain price. Value stocks are often compared to growth stocks, which sell at high relative prices but are expected to have significant growth potential. Value stocks typically sell at lower Price/Earnings multiples and Price/Book ratios when compared to growth stocks.

Variable Life Insurance: A form of life insurance that allows a portion of the premiums paid to be invested in securities like stock and bond mutual funds. The payment of income taxes can also be deferred on earnings generated from the invested funds until the time of withdrawal. A policy begins to have a redeemable or "surrender" value that continues to accumulate over time. Also known as "whole" or "universal" life insurance.

Venture Capital Firm: A private entity that provides financing to promising startup companies and business ventures in hopes of earning substantial profits through an ownership position.

Yield: Typically shown as the annual return that an investor can expect from an investment expressed as a percentage.

Yield Curve: The relationship between current interest rates and the maturity dates of certain securities typically shown using U.S. Treasury securities (bills, notes, and bonds). A normal yield curve is upward sloping representing higher yields for longer-dated securities.

Bibliography

http://www.livescience.com/health/070417_job_satisfaction.html

http://inflationdata.com/inflation/Inflation_Articles/Education_Inflation.asp

http://www.collegeboard.com/prod_downloads/about/news_info/cbsenior/yr2007/
ed-pays-2007.pdf

http://www.census.gov/Press-Release/www/releases/archives/education/011196.
html

http://www.collegeview.com/articles/CV/financialaid/i_cant_afford_college.html

http://ohioline.osu.edu/ss-fact/0200.html

http://www.fool.com/investing/general/2006/11/02/beat-the-pros-at-their-own-
game.aspx

http://www.destroydebt.com

http://www.bankrate.com/brm/news/Financial_Literacy/June07_credit_scores_
ABC_a1.asp?s=1&caret=36b

http://www.wifr.com/home/headlines/6780932.html

http://www.organizedaudrey.com

http://entrepreneurs.about.com/od/famousentrepreneurs/Famous_Entrepreneurs.
htm

http://www.usgovernmentspending.com/year2006_0.html

http://www.careertest.us/your_career.htm

http://www.learntosave.com/facts.htm

http://www.crosswalk.com/finances/11550138/

http://www.efmoody.com/investments/diversification.html

http://www.stevebullock.com/White_Papers/Cyber_Predators.pdf

http://www.nclnet.org/news/2008/top_ten_scams_02222008.htm

http://www.entrepreneur.comttp://www.careerbuilder.com/Article/CB-622-The-Workplace-Do-You-Live-Paycheck-To-Paycheck-Too/

http://www.abalert.com

http://www.reit.com/portals/0/PDF/REIT%20Story%202008.pdf

http://en.wikipedia.org/wiki/Hedge_fund#Industry_size

http://media.pimco-global.com/pdfs/pdf/Global%20Bond%20Approach%20Final%2012%2020%20US.pdf?WT.cg_n=PIMCO-US&WT.ti=Global+Bond+Approach+Final+12+20+US.pdf

http://netscientia.com/tax-taxes.html

http://www.taxpolicycenter.org/briefing-book/background/numbers/revenue.cfm

http://www.bpp401k.com/articles/benchmark_your_401k_plan.html

http://www.hrblock.com/taxes/tax_tips/tax_law_changes/filing_statistics.html?pgnavp=tl&pgnavc=tl_bs&pgnava=tl_bs_7

http://www.therealestatebloggers.com/2006/03/14/adjustable-rate-mortgage-confusing-homeowners/

https://realtytimes.com/rtpages/20040705_paymentshock.htm

http://www.iii.org

http://www.cbsnews.com/stories/2005/09/30/business/main892347.shtml

http://www.nchc.org

http://www.daveramsey.com

http://www.disabilityquotes.com/occupations/faq-odds.cfm

http://www.usatoday.comttp://www.crown.orghttp://www.insideprison.com/lawsuit-abuse-statistics.asp

http://www.gaebler.com/Small-Business-Failure-Rates.htm

http://entrepreneurship.mit.edu/Downloads/AngelReport.pdf

http://internationaltrade.suite101.com/article.cfm/top_global_brands

http://en.wikipedia.org/wiki/Mutual_funds

http://hotjobs.yahoo.com

http://www.investopedia.com

http://www.optioneertrading.com/

http://money.howstuffworks.com/credit-default-swap.htm/printable

http://www.benchmarkfunds.com/year2004/passive.htm#index

http://en.wikipedia.org/wiki/Foreign_exchange_market

http://www.bloomberg.com

http://www.insideprison.com/lawsuit-abuse-statistics.asp

Index

About the Author

ROBERT E. LAWLESS has held several executive level positions including managing director, senior vice president, chief financial officer, and treasurer for public and private companies owning billions of dollars of investments within the real estate, finance, and investment industries. Mr. Lawless has an MBA from Vanderbilt University and is a certified public accountant (CPA) and a chartered financial analyst (CFA). He is also the author of *Retire Richer and Faster!* and *How to Make Money in Any Real Estate Market.*